Foreign
Bodies

Foreign Bodies

Alphonso Lingis

Routledge - New York   London

Published in 1994 by
Routledge
29 West 35 Street
New York, NY 10001

Published in Great Britain in 1994 by
Routledge
11 New Fetter Lane
London EC4P 4EE

Copyright © 1994 by Routledge

Printed in the United States of America.

Library of Congress Cataloging-in-Publication Data
Lingis, Alphonso, 1933–
    Foreign Bodies / Alphonso Lingis
      p.   cm.
    Includes bibliographical references (p.   ) and index.
    ISBN 0-415-90989-9 — ISBN 0-415-90990-2
    1. Body, Human—Social aspects. 2. Body, Human—Symbolic
    aspects. 3. Body, Human (Philosophy) I. Title.
    GN298.L55 1994   93-49537
    306.4—dc20   CIP

Contents

Preface   *vii*

Part One: THE FORCE OF THE BODY

   1   The Competent Body   *3*

   2   Orchids and Muscles   *29*

   3   Bodies Our Own   *47*

Part Two: THE PLEASURE AND THE PAIN

   4   The Subjectification of the Body   *53*

   5   The Insistence on Correspondence   *77*

   6   These Alien Feelings That Are Our Own   *99*

Part Three: THE LIBIDINAL ECONOMY

   7   Hard Currency   *107*

   8   Fluid Economy   *133*

   9   Strange Lusts That Are Our Own   *161*

Part Four: IMPERATIVE BODIES

   10   Imperative Surfaces   *167*

   11   Elemental Bodies   *189*

   12   Foreign Bodies   *215*

Notes   *227*

Index   *237*

Preface

The human body is a product of natural evolution, but also of our own history. Nietzsche called for a history of culture that would be not only a history of the successive epochs of the cultivation of the planet's resources with new kinds of technological contrivances, nor only a history of the successive kinds of social, economic, and political organization of the human multiplicity—but also a history of the successive epochs of the human species's cultivation of its own mind and of its own body. Every great culture is not only an elaboration of specific kinds of ritual, costume and raiment, technology, science, and metaphysico-religious speculation—a specific kind of mind, but also an elaboration of a specific body-ideal. How diverse are the astronomic-architectural intelligence of the ancient Egyptians, the tragic vision and then the Socratic-Euclidean rationalism of the ancient Greeks, the ceremonial and sumptuous glories of the Byzantine, Inca, or Balinese spirituality, the sacralizing talents of the Brahminical and medieval-Christian ecclesiastical culture, the refinements of Gnostic, Franciscan, Sufi, or Zen mysticism, the mathematico-technological intelligence of Enlightenment Europe, the moral intelligence of rabbinical and Jansenist culture! So diverse also are the body-ideals elaborated by the Hittites, the yogis of India as ancient as Mohenjo-daro and Harrapa, the Mayas whose physical nobility is so strange to us, the samurai of feudal Japan annealed with martial arts, the skyward-leaping Maasai, the Greeks whose bodies were shaped in Olympic games and epitomized in the statues of the age of Pericles, the heroic proportions Michelangelo sacralized in the Sistine chapel, the Pygmies and Watusis in the rain forests of Africa—and by the competitive athlete, body builder, ballet dancer, bullfighter, or guerrillero today.

The studies of this book are so many soundings in this cultivation we find our bodies have elaborated on themselves. It is our own bodies, those of today, we wish to elucidate. It is the new—and divergent—ways to explore them opened by contemporary thinkers that we have chosen to pursue.

The studies of this book are organized in four cycles: The Force of the Body, The Pleasure and the Pain, The Libidinal Economy, and Imperative Bodies. In each cycle, a first chapter draws from theoretical literature—from contemporary philosophical work informed by physiology, social technology, psychoanalysis, and ethical theory. The second chapter of each cycle elucidates the practice of the body as we find it formulated in a quite different kind of language, that of plastic art (the artwork a body builder makes of himself), biography, anthropology, and literature.

It will be seen that the philosophical analyses examined in the first chapter of each cycle are retrospective. They explain how we today experience our own powers of perception, our postures, attitudes, gestures, and purposive action; how our susceptibility to pain and excitability by pleasure acquiesce in and resist the ways they are today identified and manipulated; how cultures code our sensuality with phallic and with fluid identities; and how, in facing us, others address appeals to and put demands on us. These philosophical investigations elucidate the bodies that natural evolution and cultural history have elaborated for us to inhabit today.

Through the plastic art, biography, anthropology, and literature explored, the second chapter of each cycle envisions the bodies we might become.

A third chapter in each cycle discusses some theoretical results of the confrontation of the philosophical with the non-philosophical explorations of our bodies.

Phenomenological methods, as elaborated by Maurice Merleau-Ponty, make it possible to understand the active forces of our bodies in a new way. Objective physiology had envisioned the setting in which our bodies stand, move, and undertake initiatives as a segment of the material world such as natural science represents it. Physiology represented our bodies as objects whose behavior has to be correlated with external events conceived in physico-chemical, electromagnetic, and dynamic terms.

In fact, the stances, postures, and initiatives of a living body respond to the environment as that body perceives it. The setting our bodies perceive does not consist of drifting sense-data, nor of objects as physico-chemical science represents them; our sentient bodies perceive nutrients, paths, obstacles, and objectives. The perceptual patterns stabilize and acquire the consistency and coherence of "real things" in the measure that they fit in with the consistency and coherence of other things in the field and with the outlying past and future fields consistent with the present layout.

There is a competence in our bodies to perceive things and the layout of paths in which they can be reached. The body's stances, gestures, and initiatives are not simply resultants of the external stimulations that would provoke them. Our bodies form within themselves postures and goal-oriented diagrams of movement, which address the layout of perceived obstacles and objectives. Phenomenology is the description of our perceptual and practical competence as we ourselves experience them.

Are the norms of practical competence in our bodies the norms intrinsic to their natural evolution? Have not the technical contrivances that our body's competence has invented had a feedback effect on its own evolution as an animal species? A tool, we say, is an extension of an organ of our body. Is it not also an exteriorization of that organ—a separating from our body of its own organ? Have the successive epochs of technological equipping not been a divestment of the body of its own organs for cutting, chopping, and grinding, its motor forces, its powers of surveillance, and its programming faculty? Natural evolution produced the orchid. Is our technological history making us into carnal orchids, showy sex-organs, that no longer rise on their own stems, blend their own saps, or impregnate one another?

The figure of the body builder, a condensation of force that is strangely incompetent and gratuitous (who emerges today just when massive physical strength is unnecessary in industry, now automatized, and irrelevant in war, now computerized), will be for us the image of this question.

Our bodies are not only structures of competence; they are also sensitive substances, substances that produce pain and pleasure in themselves. The second cycle of studies in this book explores the susceptibility and sensuality of our bodies in the world of today and of tomorrow.

As painful and voluptuous substances, our bodies attract and repel one another. They are identified by others, and are pained or gratified by the identities assigned them. They can deny these identities, mock them, defy them, acquiesce in them. To study the penal, medical, pedagogical, administrative, and psychiatric institutions dispersed in our social space is to map out the ways we torment and gratify one another.

Michel Foucault has given us an analysis of the effects on our bodies of the penal practices of our recent history. Foucault shows bodies emblazoned with the glory of the transcendentalized body of the sovereign in the torture of

Europe's ancien régime, and coded with the civil law in the punishment devised by the penologists of the Republic. He shows the social technology that makes our body competence disciplined in those internally gridded enclosures that have restructured modern social space—school, barracks, factory, hospital, asylum, prison.

Foucault shows that the pleasure that simmers in our bodies is also coded, inciting the discourse and power operations of others. The power operations on our bodies as sensual substances do not simply oppress and suppress them; they diversify, differentiate, and incite, they produce a multiplicity of bodies individuated sexually. They subject them to the new biopolitical strategies of the modern state, strategies contrived for the administration and management of life.

Of his own will, the Japanese writer Yukio Mishima subjected his body to a discipline and a pain that modern physiological technology, as well as ancient martial arts, made available to him; he found in this discipline the most intensive eroticization of his body. He sought through modern bio- and psycho-technology to reincarnate the ancient epic and heroic ethics of Japan and hurl them, with his body and his words, into the future. His exemplary itinerary reveals to us the combat to which the unreserved investment in the body's powers leads, an agon of power freed from the imagination that feeds on muscles and on the power couplings with others that code them. He came to see that the summit of human glory is a figure of radiant power, disconnected from mundane means and objectives, held before the black light of death.

The third cycle of studies in this book explores the inner libidinal economy of the body that participates in the economy of the body politic. How does the infantile libido, which simmers in contact gratification, a surface of excitations that spread about oral and anal couplings and that are consumed in discharges of pleasure, become significant—that is, a sign put forth to others, putting demands on others? The Freudian theory of the phallic stage, elaborated especially by Jacques Lacan, explains how a child comes to identify himself with the phallus, perceived to be lacking in the other. He thus makes himself a corporeal figure answering the demands of others, putting demands on others. With this identification, the infant enters language; his physical presence becomes, for himself and for others, a sign. And his posturings, gesticulations, and modulations of voice become signs; their intentions acquire vocative and imperative force. It is also as a phallus that the infant makes himself a value, an interchangeable term in a system of exchanges. He puts the voice and the law of the father in his own body, sets out to take the place of the father before the other—the mother—and one day fathers a child marked with the sign of the phallus who will take his place.

Foucault has pointed out that it was in recent Western history that the family, no longer the fundamental unit of the organization of economic production, no longer the primary space of the elaboration and transmission of coded knowledge—the nuclear family—was invested with the task of socializing individuals by fixing the fundamental identities and reproducing the primary authority figures. Psychoanalysis then was contrived as a specific technology with which individuals who are nonfunctional in political economy and excluded from it are returned to its language and their posts in the family. Psychoanalysis was born at a late date in European history, whose codes had ceased to be cosmic or tellurian, when the power coded as law and sacralized in the body of the monarch was giving way to the vast system of micro-couplings of power where power is coded as norms. The psychoanalytic theory of the Oedipal triangle, in which each of us first acquires an identity for himself, belongs to this transitional period of our history.

We have chosen a selection of Melanesian cultures, in the second chapter of this cycle, in which to explore another coding and another economy, primarily because of the extraordinary richness of the material very recently published on these cultures by Gilbert Herdt and his associates. In these cultures too, identity—assumed identity, attributed identity, subjective identity, and optative identity—are based on gender identity, libidinal identity. But at the core of these cultures, there is an experience of one's own body not according to its form, its morphology, but in its fluidity. For us, it is the structure of our bodies and of their organs that is the essential, a structure whose stability is for us the image of the stability of our psychic identity. The fluids in our bodies but circulate refurbishment throughout the structure; their seepings into it and evaporations or discharges from it are neither regulated by our public codes nor valued in our politico-economic discourse. For the Sambia of Papua-New Guinea, it is the fluids that are the essential. The body is perceived essentially as a conduit for fluids—for blood, milk, semen. Body fluids are drawn from without, from couplings with other bodies, from couplings with other organism-conduits in outside nature. Among the Sambia, the transmissions of fluid from one body-conduit to another are metered out as social transactions.

As the Oedipal and phallic structure invested in our bodies in the period of late capitalism is an archaic structure reinscribed by modern social technology, so the specific fluid body and fluid identity coded by Sambia culture may be detached from the ecological, economic, and political system of that culture and be inscribed in other places, other times.

The final cycle of studies in this book concern the respect that our bodies call for and require. The first chapter elaborates themes drawn from the philosophy of Immanuel Kant and of Emmanuel Levinas. When the other presents himself or herself by facing us, his or her face and body are not simply a surface upon which signs—indicative and informative signs—take form, for our interpretation. When a face faces, it calls for our attention, it appeals to us, it summons us, it puts demands on us. The eyes that look at us, the voice, disarmed and disarming, that addresses us, the hands turned open before us, the exposed skin of other bodies stop our advances, contest our initiatives, order us.

Is it only the face of another of our own species that has this power tossummon us, contest us, order our sensibility and our initiatives? We found in Michel Tournier's novel *Friday*, which retells in contemporary, libidinal terms the adventures of Robinson Crusoe—that hero of Victorian imperialism created by Daniel Defoe—a destiny we have found understood in no philosophical literature. In Tournier's narrative, Robinson sets sail from the objectives of his English world, sets sail too from paternal and reproductive sexuality, of his own will, but he finds himself carried yet further by the winds and the sea. On the island Speranza, which Robinson thinks has only accidentally saved him from the storm and the shipwreck, he finds himself led from the mire of immediate gratification, beyond the surface island subjected to cultivation and law, beyond the tellurian island in which he finds rebirth—still further, led now by Friday, to an elemental domain, that of the free winds, earth, skies, sun, that of vegetative and solar sexuality. When he elects to remain on the island and let sail on without him the ship which after thirty-five years had come to him, it is in obedience to the imperative addressed to him from the free elements and understood in his body. The exemplary destiny of Tournier's Robinson makes us understand that our bodies are not just, as existential philosophy and also as our technological society taught us to think, contrivances destined for things, that is objects-objectives, destined for implements or wealth. They are substances destined to stand with the earth and to ground, to capture the way of the light and illuminate, to breathe the wind and chant.

The last chapter of this book contemplates the transubstantiations our carnal substances undergo under the touch and in the embraces of those condensations of the free elements which are others, and brings to light the imperatives that command those transubstantiations.

Traditionally the pronoun "he" was used alone to designate individuals without sex or gender specification; "he" was taken to be a grammatically unmarked term, and "she" marked. Feminist writers have argued that rhetorically "he" is marked as male, and femaleness is elided in this usage. They have promoted grammatical and rhetorical reform, where "he" is marked male, "she" female.

But individuals are not only male and female, they are also hermaphrodites, transsexuals, Siamese twins, lacking or with nonfunctional reproductive organs. They are not only masculine or feminine, they are transgendered, multigendered, nongendered, cyborgs, werewolves, angels; they elaborate a semiotics and culture coupling their organisms and their sensuality across species, with animals, with hermaphroditic organisms, with plants and with rivers, with machines, and with spirits and death. The new usage being promoted, where "he" is to be taken as marked male and "she" marked female, grammatically and rhetorically discredits and silences all these individuals. They are left with "they."

In this book I have conformed, with bad grace, with the new usage. "He" and "she" are used as sexually marked. Where individuals do not find in their reproductive organs their core identity, "he" or "she" are used as gender marked. The reader will find, especially in the discussion of authors such as Immanuel Kant or Martin Heidegger, "he" being used alone to designate individuals without sex or gender specification. I intend to indicate that femaleness is being elided in their discourse.

The second chapter of each part of the book gives expression to sexualities and genders elided under the old usage where "he" was taken to be unmarked, and silenced even more under the new usage which takes "he" and "she" to be sexually or gender marked.

part one

The Force
of the Body

The Competent Body

The positions our bodies assume, the gestures they make, and the operations they perform are not responses to the objective representation of the material universe elaborated by scientific thought. Our sensory-motor organisms respond to the environment as they perceive it. To understand why a spider does not respond to a dead fly put in its web, but crouches and leaps when a vibrating tuning fork of a certain kind touches its web, we have to view the spider not as a material mass reacting to all the forces our physico-chemical representation of the environment identifies, but as an organism capable of activating itself in certain organized ways in response to the range and structure of its environment as its own perception presents that environment. When we sit down on a park bench or wander through the azalea plantings in bloom, our movements are not spasmodic reactions to clouds of atoms, nor to masses of sensations scintillating in our minds, but responses to the shapes in our perceptual field. The physicist who conceives material things as electromagnetic fields perceives the contours and solidity of the chair he reaches for.

Maurice Merleau-Ponty's phenomenology of perception[1] worked out a vocabulary designed to describe the structures and organization of the environment as our sentient bodies perceive it. Our bodies maintain a gait in walking and a rhythm in acting, they assume postures and initiate coordinated manipulations which shift the perceived field, alter the range and relief of the perceived forms that field contains, and respond to those forms. The phenomenology of perception requires a vocabulary proper to describe body postures and movements responding to perceived landscapes and gestures and operations responding to perceived objectives. Merleau-Ponty's work describes our bodies, not as material objects of nature agitated by stimuli, but as organisms capable of perceiving and activating themselves in organized ways—our bodies as structures of perceptual and behavioral competence.

Things

What is it that we perceive? We perceive *things*—configurations against a background. From time to time, it is true, perceptions of radiance, darkness, fog, sky, rumble, or stench get mentioned in Merleau-Ponty's text, but they are moments of instability or nonachievement, not the normal case. Merleau-Ponty finds that there is a finality in perceptual consciousness; perception is a positing of things. A dark tone marginally visible, then shifted to the focal center of the visual field, then brought out of the shadow is not simply appearances that succeed one another; there is a sense of the right lighting, the real color, and the real size and shape of something explorable. What determines the real and the true and the right is the possibility of a thing taking form and stabilizing before us. And there is a normative coherence, a consistency in the evolving zone of perception. Our perception opens, not upon one shape that replaces and effaces another, but upon a field of coexisting, compossible things. That is why, despite the fog, despite the darkness, despite the rumble, Merleau-Ponty can say that a figure against a field is the essence of, the very definition of, perception.[2] We cannot explain the apparition of things by a subject of the perception which collates or synthesizes its sensations; it is instead the thing that polarizes and focuses the various sensory surfaces and organs of the perceiving subject.

Things are wholes which involve a multiplicity of parts or aspects. *Phenomenology of Perception* argues that a perceived thing has the constitution of a gestalt. There are different sensible aspects, and each does something in its own place and moment to contribute to the composition of the thing. But they do not exist outside of the whole—which partitions them, gives them their role, and makes them function. The soap molecule we conceptually identify does not exert a force of cohesion in the directions it does to occupy its present place when it is outside of the soap bubble. And the perceived red of the brick is the red it is only when involved with this solid texture, this light, this expanse of more red or of other colors. We cannot say what this red is, or see it, outside of this complex of the colors that intensify it, contrast with it, reverberate with it, the textures that modulate it, and the form that molds it, condenses it, or fragments it.

What holds the different sensible elements of a thing together is neither simple extrinsic relations of juxtaposition, nor some universal factor also intuited along with them, nor some ideal factor to which they would be predicated. Their unity is not intuited, conceived, or posited apart from them; it is sensible and perceived with them and in them. It is, then, not an essence in the sense of an invariant nucleus of traits. It is also not an order or a system or a law that is instantiated in them, but of itself is universal. Merleau-Ponty introduces the concept of a "sensible essence."[3] It designates the way each element in a perceived thing leads to, involves, implicates, reflects, and is in its own register equivalent to, the next.

When we see an *apple*, this identity is not something conceived at once like a concept; it is not an invariant found in all the various aspects; it is not a law or principle like triangularity found in all triangles. We see it by looking, by looking at the way this shiny red and dense white involves—makes visible—a certain sense of pulpiness, a certain juiciness, even a certain clear and homogeneous taste. What we see does not have that tomato look, that pear granularness, that peach feel. Each quality or aspect occupies its own spot and moment with its own schema, its own way of filling, condensing or rarefying its space and its moment. And there is an equivalence between a certain whiteness and a certain pulpiness; each reflects something of the schema of the other. The white is the white it is because it is condensed in this pulp, makes visible this contained liquidity, emanates this clear and tangy savor. The apple-sense is in that red and that white, in that pulpiness felt or chewed, in that taste and acrid smell. That "sense" is not an identity, an invariant, or a principle instantiated in different registers of sensoriality; it is a "style," that is, the generality of a schema which is recognized by seeing that each phase is a variant of both the previous and the next one.[4] The apple in the color, the pulp, and the savor is the style, like the personality is a style—a sensibly perceived schema that makes all the conversations of a person recognizably his or her own, even though one can isolate in them neither identical elements nor identical arrangements of elements that recur.

The sensible essence, the schema, the style, is given from the start; our perception does not first see the black color of the ball-point pen, but goes straight to the substance, the somber power condensing there, occupying a site, of which the black color, the dense matter, the hard solidity are registers that our analysis—first perceptual, then linguistic—then isolates. The thing itself is the materializing style.

The Transcendence of Things

This explication of the things that we perceive already makes it impossible for us to suppose that there is in them something given—"sense-data," which are simples—and something we add to make things out of the data—the organization, the relations among them. For, on the one hand, without their cohesion, without their involvement in one another, the isolated sensible aspects can no longer be said to be anything. And, on the other hand, their cohesion or coherence is not a kind of unit, that of a meaning or a universal, which we grasp at once, intuitively; it is sketched out, open-ended, caught on to progressively, as we go further. Perhaps we see enough to attach a name to it from the start, but what a winesap apple or the calvados distilled from apples really is and means is something that we understand in touching, smelling, chewing, savoring, without ever ending at something like the definitive key to it—in the sense that, one day, having acquired the formula, we possess all there is to understand about a triangle.

The sensible elements themselves are not really particulars. They should not be defined as items that are what they are, when and where they are. Not one of them is just a here-and-now particular, contingent and unfounded such that it can only be recorded or not recorded.[5] Each of them goes beyond simple location; there is not one that is instantaneous, that does not prolong itself in duration. And there is not one that is simply here: a point of red reduced to itself is not visible and is not red; it needs to be reinforced, prolonged by other spots, to be red. It is not simply red within its own borders since it can be the red it is only if the background is the color or colors it is. And this red looks tangible, is a tangible red.

Existential philosophy defined the new concepts of ecstasy or of transcendence to fix a distinct kind of being that is by casting itself out of its own given place and time, without dissipating, because at each moment it projects itself—or, more exactly, a variant of itself—into another place and time. Such a being is not ideality, defined as intuitable or reconstitutable anywhere and at any moment. Ex-istence, understood etymologically, is not so much a state or a stance as a movement, which is by conceiving a divergence from itself or a potentiality of itself and casting itself into that divergence with all that it is. This bizarre concept of an ecstatic or self-transcending existence was formulated so as to define the inner constitution of subjectivity and to distinguish it decisively from the way objective reality, the facts, are—which have to be located where and when they are because for them being is being at a point p and a time t. Now we find that it is this very concept of transcendence—on which the whole twentieth-century existential philosophy of subjectivity was built—that Merleau-Ponty's phenomenological existentialism calls upon in order to describe the irreducible givens, the sensory phenomena.

The increasingly elaborated conviction that the sensible givens have to be described, ontologically, as self-transcending existents commands the new descriptions of the sensible field we find in Merleau-Ponty's later writings and in the posthumously published *The Visible and the Invisible*. The sensible field is a realm of being where all points become pivots, all lines become levels, all surfaces become planes, all colors become atmospheres, all tones become— as in dodecaphonic music—keys. There are not particulars and universals in the sensible field; what there are are particulars generalizing themselves, a whole landscape concretizing momentarily in this red, a whole love given in condensation in a vase of flowers, a whole adventure or fatality sounded in the five little notes heard in *Swann's Way*. Each given is the spot and moment in which a schema of being is being elaborated. Artists have a precise knowledge of this; their knowledge consists in knowing what a color does to a field, to another color, to a zone of space; in knowing what a line does to the zone it molds, to the space it bunches up, bulges out, or flattens, to the color, to the field of tensions; and in knowing what shapes move, creep, crawl, leap, set up movement in a whole field.[6] This knowledge is not conceptual; it is not a possession of laws or principles. Artists know how, with a few lines, a few strokes of color, to make *things* visible.

The Hold on Things

What, now, is the sensing of things? Classical epistemology, distinguishing in the thing perceived between the de facto multiplicity of sense-data and their relationships, whether additive or synthetic, distinguished also between a passive and an active side involved in the perceiving of things. There would be a passive receptivity for the sense-data, and an active collating or synthesizing of them. The sensing properly so-called would be a passive being-impressed by sensory qualia, psychic conversions of physiological stimuli. In Husserl's phenomenology, intentionality intervenes to take these sense impressions to mean something, and thus to identify them, synthetically taking them as signs of one and the same signification. The intentionality makes impressions into sensations, that is, givens of sense, of meaning.

Merleau-Ponty takes the sensing to be active from the start; he conceives the receptivity for the sensuous element to be a prehension, a *prise*, a "hold." The conception is Heideggerian; Merleau-Ponty envisions looking—palpating with the eyes[7]—tasting, smelling, and even hearing as variants of handling. The tactile datum is not given to a passive surface; the smooth and the rough, the sleek and the sticky, the hard and the vaporous are given to movements of the hand that applies itself to them with a certain pressure, pacing, periodicity, across a certain extension, and they are patterned ways in which movement is modulated. "The hard and the soft, the grainy and the sleek, moonlight and sunlight in memory give themselves not as sensorial contents but as a certain type of symbiosis, a certain way the outside has of invading us, a certain way we have to welcome it."[8] The striking experiments of Goldstein and Rosenthal[9] enable us to extend this insight to visual data: the emergence of blue induces a sliding up-and-down movement across the body schema; the emergence of orange, an increased tension and extension of the body. Since a blue obtained by contrast is apprehended with the same sliding up-and-down movement, the movement cannot be understood as a motor reaction to a sensory impression defined by a certain wavelength and intensity; the sensitivity is motile from the start and it is in and by the modulation of the motility of the gaze, and of the whole body that steers and supports the eye movements, that the blue or the yellow is sensed, that is, taken up, communicated with.

The moist, the oily, the sleek, the restful green, and the aggressive orange are palpated by the hand or the look, which takes up in its own positioning and pace something which in it is an induced program for its own motility, and which, in the thing, is the sensible essence, the essence of oiliness or of green. This essence has to be conceived verbally (like "insistence," "dissidence"); it is a specific way of occupying its space and time actively, of condensing or rarefying its space and moment, of bulging it out or hollowing it out, a specific way of polarizing, sustaining, spreading its tension across a certain field. The inner sense of the green is also realized in its own way in the register of the tangible, in the pulp of the cucumber, and in the register of flavor and odor. Already the whole palpable and edible cucumber is captured by the movement of the eyes.

A gesture captures the sense of something. The hand that rises to respond to a gesture hailing us in the crowd is not preceded and made possible by a representation first formed of the identity of the one recognized. It is the hand that recognizes the friend who is there, not as a named form represented, but as a movement and a cordiality that solicits—soliciting not a cognitive and representational operation from us, but a greeting, an interaction. The hand itself in the range of its gesture signals our presence and our welcome, measures the distance between us, and effects the recognition. How do we recognize the brash and garish colors of the Snopes suburbs, the bluegreen waters of the coral seas, the lines of the giant sequoias rising on the landscape? They too are recognized in the movements with which we face them.

The sizes and shapes of things are also captured actively; it is in dilating the scope of my look or my grip, eventually filling out the whole field—that is, approaching the limit of what my look or my hearing can hold together before me—that the bigness of the visual object or the full-bodiedness of a sound comes to be and becomes manifest. In the equilibrium of my gaze traveling about the rim of the plate the circular is sensed and comes to be before me. In experiencing the length of the wall becoming less clearly articulated for me I feel that end of it pulling away from the hold I have on it, and thus oriented away from me, receding into distance. It is my maximal hold on it—when its form and grain are clear and distinct for me, when I feel myself centered on it—that determines the normal, true, or right appearance of a thing from its variants, from shapes turned to the side, from round or rectangular planes set askew, from things of comparable size staggered out over a distance, from white sheets of paper scattered in the dim light of the hall.

Things have their own orientation. Things are recognized to be right-side-up, front-side-facing when we sense ourselves positioned before them in ways that can explore and handle them efficaciously. The sense, the recognizability, of a thing is in its right-side-up, front-side-facing orientation (in French "sens" means both "meaning" and "direction"), which lends itself to the habitual ways our gaze moves across them and our hands handle them. The upside-down lamp or umbrella stand, in being set upright again, visually reorganize to manifest their lost identity.

From the first, not a patch of color or a pressure but some thing touched the sensibility; from the first, both eyes respond to converge on it, the fingers close upon it as one organ, the body shifts to center its sensitive surfaces on it. As the whole sensibility converges, the presence and apparition of something appears normal, right and true, and the spatial axes—the sense of what is up and what is down, what is close and what is far, what is left and what is right—stabilize. The relationship of the sensory-motor body with its surroundings tends to an optimum state when the body in all its powers is geared into the setting, centered on something, when there is an inner sense of equilibrium and efficacious adjustment. The body takes hold of the levels and axes of the field on which things materialize.

The body, in centering on things, does not tend to a state of rest; it maintains levels of tension available for efficacious operations. The normative state—which perceives real things beyond their phantom and their medium- and perspective-distorted appearances, real things in their upright positions and therefore recognizability—is the state in which the body can operate in its field, deal with those things in the most centered, dexterous, and forceful ways. Clinical psychologist G. M. Stratton rights the reversed retinal images by special eyeglasses and thereby sets the visual field askew in relationship with the field of the other senses. In the days that follow, the visual appearances of the things which he effectively handles rejoin their tangible surfaces at the end of his hands, drift back to an upright orientation, and rotate planes of the visual background with themselves, so that the subject realigns the up-down axis of his vision. He has not realigned the visual field in terms of the objective space of geometers or astronomers—where an up-down axis has no meaning—nor has he realigned the visual field in terms of his body's de facto position. The up-down axis in the visual field is maintained correlative with the body's upright position, not as statistically the most frequent position (true vertical is not the statistically most frequent alignment of the head), but as the most efficacious. The body's verticality is that of an inner diagram of competence become habitual. When we install ourselves in our compartment in a train, involved in our book, our lunch, our conversation, then it is the adjacent train that slides across the window even when it is ours that is leaving the station. The sensory and practical installation maintains our compartment level on the hillside, and it is the trees on the landscape that tilt as they slide by. Perceiving real things with their own characteristics is being-in-the-world in the strong sense of inhabiting the world, that is, having a field of operations within reach, being efficaciously at grips with it.

The sensible stratum does not consist of colors, sounds, lights, shapes, and shadows, opaque qualia that confront a passive intuition. The colors are crystallizing or vaporizing, contrasting and veering into depth; the points are pivoting; the lines are damming up space, vibrating it; the tones are echoing across the silent regions of color, luminosity and shadow, pliancy, liquidity and vapor, and materializing into reality drums, shattering glass, cascading water, panicked birds, frightened infants. The sensitive and motile body is exposing itself to these patternings, capturing them with its own movements, centering and integrating its forces upon them. It is positioning a figure before itself, an intersensorial thing it can deal with; it is measuring a field for its occupations and preoccupations, a habitat for its adjustments and initiatives.

The Transcendent Essence of Things

The essence, according to Husserl's phenomenological and logical definition, is the universal. The essence of the brandy is in its specific kind of visible surface cohesion and in its visible depths, which precipitate and tincture the light, and in all its tangible, olfactory, and gustatory aspects—and it is in all glasses of brandy. It is in all the glasses of brandy of my periodically festive history and also in all the glasses of brandy that figured in the hospitality of others; it is what we share out of the particularities of our—each time individual—sensory conviviality. Classical epistemology conceived the essence as an ideality, something selfsame that transcends, or recurs the same in, any moment and any place. There would have to be something the same in all of us, an impersonal or interpersonal transcendental ego, to account for the possibility of the thing's essence being the same for me as for anyone. How is this universal character of the essence conceived in Merleau-Ponty's phenomenology?

The sensuous essence of a perceived thing recurs in all its visual, tangible, resonant, and gustatory aspects, but not in the way that one same ingredient recurs in different compounds nor in the way that a law or principle recurs in each of its instantiations. It recurs in the way that a musical theme is one in all its variations, or in the way that one style is found in all the novels of an author who speaks with his or her own voice, or in the way that one gait is visible in the varying steps made over uneven ground. This red is not only at work here, on these lips or in the petals of this rose that multiply themselves into profiles resurfacing in different moments and in different perspectives; it is a node in the field of the visible, a punctuation in the discursivity of color. There are colors it is reinforcing or contrasting with. All the other reds, those of the tiles of rooftops, the flags of road-construction workers or of revolutionaries, those of hills near Aix or in Madagascar, those of the robes of bishops and of the skirts of the gypsies who danced, twenty-five years ago, in an inn of the Champs-Elysées, are iridescing in it. It is not just that there are to be seen elsewhere things that resemble it. The visual field is one connective tissue and each of its concrescences precipitates the tensions of the surrounding region and sends its own intensities across that region.

I who see this red do not do so by contriving a particular organization for what is a drifting mass of sense-particulars. I focus in on this red and explore it with movements of my look which take form as variants of an oscillating, sliding, or staccato rhythm of visual movements of a certain focus and range and periodicity. The seeing that captures this red forms as a variant of the seeing that was captured by the rooftops, the hills, the lips of women, the scarves and skirts of the gypsy dancers. This red gives itself as a variant of a schema of being picked up in other places at other moments.

The seeing of this place and moment picks up the schema it varies and actualizes from the seeing of another place and another moment. The sentient flesh is an element in which every particular position schematizes itself, maintaining itself as the theme of further variations. The seeing of this place and moment also picks up the schema it varies and actualizes from the seeing of others. As we sit or walk together, our looks view more or less the same range of things and more or less in the same way. I see from a position, for a time, with a focus which I have picked up from others, and I pass on to others, not the sensory qualia imprinted on my surfaces, but the motor diagram and orientation with which I see what there is to be seen. What I see is what others have seen, what anyone can see—the visible in itself. In the continual contagion of schemas of posture and movement, corporeality becomes one, common; each of us is for himself or herself and for the others a variant on sentient corporeality.

The Levels

When I open my eyes I see the light—a depth not set at a distance, a medium visible through its chromatic tone. My gaze enters the light and lets itself be led by the light to the surfaces and the contours of gleaming, glowing, or somber things. As I approach the cafe in the evening, I see a volume of amber-colored light in which the tables and clients are steeped. When I sit down and begin to look at the menu and at my friends, the amber of the space and of their faces neutralizes and their normal colors surface. I cease to see the light as a medium of a particular color; I see with it and according to it; my look situates itself at this level to see illuminated surfaces and incandescent substances as gradations of divergence from this level. When I enter a room where a party is taking place, at first I hear the hubbub of the room; it seems to me impossible that anyone could be following the words of another in this mix. But then I station myself before someone and set out to listen to what she is saying, and my ears are able to take the ambient sonority, not as sounds of a particular pitch and volume, but as a level at which the hearing is buoyed up, and I begin to discriminate particular patterns as crests and troughs distending from that level. When my hand sets out to feel something in the density of the tangible medium, it gives itself the pacing and pressure that pick out the particular pattern from the level of tangibility; I discern the relief of the letters in Braille from the grain of the paper. When I set out to apprize the size and shape of a thing, I set my look and my touch at a certain viewing distance taken as normal, and my eyes or touch record the extent and the contours with which the particular thing occupies and distends that plane. As I station myself before my tasks, shifting my head and torso this way and that, I take a certain orientation as the up-down axis and look at particular things, and feel myself to be upright or tilted in terms of that level. The up-down axis is not seen—I do not align everything in terms of any particular stable thing nor in terms of any particular position of my own body; it is maintained virtual, unperceived for itself but implicated in the stability and tensions of the variations of my stand. The real world is a matrix of sensible levels.

Each actual vision arises, not as a spontaneous invention, but as a variant of a schema of looking which our body has contracted. I find the focus and pacing and periodicity with which to see this green of the lichens by varying the staccato or sliding pace with which my look travels across the density and hue of the woodland floor. And as soon as this focus and pacing are found they engender variants of themselves; my look, now maintained at the level of the green of the lichens, discerns beads of dew and small colored insects. The gaze captures the color level of the field and the vibrancy of the light in the range and periodicity of its movements. I do not look at the light and at the tonality of the field, but look with them and according to them. In the motile schemas my sensibility contracts, it maintains itself adjusted to the general levels of visibility along which things form and phosphoresce, to the general murmur of nature and rumble of the city, and to the levels by which each field upon which perception opens connects by continuous transition to further fields of the sensible, even when interrupted by that withdrawal from every field of tasks and solicitations that is sleep. Our bodies are embedded in the axes of the world; the world is that with which we perceive.

Comprehension and Postural Schema

The body does one thing at a time, gestalt physiologist Kurt Goldstein wrote;[10] it also perceives one thing at a time, one figure against the ground of the rest. The sensibility is positioned—is postured—on things as on objectives. To understand the integration of the sensibility—its comprehensive hold on things and its comprehending grasp of their contexts—we have to, Merleau-Ponty argues, not postulate mental operations, but elucidate the nature of the postural schema. The postural schema has to be conceived as a dynamic gestalt that maintains and varies itself. The body's stance at any moment is not simply the resultant of the positions of the parts, each determined by the force of gravity and the outside pressures and internal tensions; the orienting axis of force of the whole positions each of the parts. The body does not tend to a state of rest, but maintains a state of tension, expressed in its typical thresholds of excitability, a state of motility available for its typical tasks in each specific kind of environment. The internal vectors of its functional intergration of its parts and powers are oriented so as to apply its force to a specific objective. This internal diagram of oriented force maintains itself in the systematic variation and redistribution of parts and powers. It is not elaborated at a central synthesizer or will. Each energized part determines the force and orientation of the other powers: the hand that reaches for the book on the shelf above the desk induces a tilt in the axis of the torso and stabilizing displacements of the other arm and the legs. The present diagram of the hand's move contains in itself the schema for a series of functionally equivalent moves, and contains also the schema for the corresponding moves of the supporting trunk and limbs. A new gesture or move does not arise as a spontaneous invention, but as an actualization of one of the variants contained in the typical diagrams of organization the body has contracted. The motile body, Merleau-Ponty writes in *The Visible and the Invisible*,[11] exists neither as a particular nor as a universal, but as an *element*, a medium where every particular position in a space and a time generalizes itself into a schema engendering a specific range of variations.

The apprehension of an exterior objective, as something soliciting the synergic hold of the sensibility, dynamically orients the postural schema. Conversely, it is the posture that centers the sensibility and perceives a transcendent and intersensorial—that is, real—thing. The sense of the lemon taken up by the look is inscribed on the whole sensibility; what is prehended is not a colored shape only, but something synesthetic from the start. The level of excitability of the whole sensibility, its fatigue, its distraction, or its disintegration, affects the functioning of sight; the contours and color intensity of the lemon become more visible in the measure that it becomes for the awakened hand more palpable and for smell and taste more distinctively pungent. There is in the body an immanent knowledge of how to center, how to position itself, how to take hold of things such that they are given and manifest in their intersensorial essence. There is in the body a knowledge of a lemon—a competency, a praktognosis, a knowledge of how to deal with such a thing, how to station itself before it, how to apply itself to it—such that the sensible essence of the lemon, its way of being, is communicated to the body's own visible, tangible, sonorous reality. This knowledge is not a priori; it is not a possession of the formula for the lemon, of the principle or the law for the assemblage of the disparate sensory patterns so as to make them instantiations of the diverse implications of one meaning-unit. It is a knowledge, progressively instituted in the postural schema, of how a sensitive body is to position itself before this detachable fruit, how it is to move its organs and surfaces so as to pick up the style and organizing schema of a lemon materializing on the planes and levels of the sensible.

To see a visible thing in real space is to feel how to get to it and how to handle it. Monocular images float over reality, on the margin of the visual field, out of reach, and are infra-things or phantoms that dissipate as one approaches the real thing; real things are seen by a motor intentionality mobilizing both eyes as one organ and are situated in a space where we can see how to approach them. The moon as it rises over the planes and paths of the landscape in which I circulate loses its determinate color and size; the mountain which I never address with a body-intention of climbing floats as a phantom over reality. These are, Henri Wallon says, ultra-things.

Conversely, to contract a motor diagram in my postural schema is already to visualize things.

> When I awoke like this, and my mind struggled in an unsuccessful attempt to discover where I was, everything would be moving round me through the darkness: things, places, years. My body, still too heavy with sleep to move, would endeavour to construe from the pattern of its tiredness the position of its various limbs, in order to deduce therefrom the direction of the wall, the location of the furniture, to piece together and give a name to the house in which it lay. Its memory, the composite memory of its ribs, its knees, its shoulder-blades, offered it a whole series of rooms in which it had at one time or another slept; while the unseen walls, shifting and adapting themselves to the shape of each successive room that it remembered, whirled around it in the dark.... My body, the side upon which I was lying, faithful guardians of a past which my mind should never have forgotten, brought back before my eyes the glimmering flame of the night-light in its urn-shaped bowl of Bohemian glass that hung by chains from the ceiling, and the chimney-piece of Siena marble in my bedroom at Combray, in my grandparents' house, in those far distant days which at this moment I imagined to be in the present without being able to picture them exactly.[12]

The sensitive body is the locus of inscription of inner postural axes on external visibility and of external visibility on its inner postural diagram. To perceive is not for a transcendental agency to extract itself from a drifting mass of sensations; it is to belong to the world one works oneself into.

The Posture and Its Image

What psychologists have improperly named the "body-image" is not posited by an act of imagination when we detach our perception from things; it emanates from the mobilized posture and extends across it. As I sit at my desk I have a sense of the visible shape with which I fill out a volume in the room; as I stretch my legs under the table I have a sense of how their position looks. When the psychologist projects a videotape of people in silhouette walking across the landscape, we find we can pick out ourselves from among them by the gait. As we walk we cannot look at our gait, even in a mirror, for the observing eye interferes with our natural gait and alters it. Since we can recognize it on the screen, we have had while walking an immanent sense of the way our gait looks from the outside. The hand that touches a solid or elastic mass and that is a vector of force and feeling spreads about itself a latent sense of its pulp tangible from the outside. The body is the locus of a primary reflexive circuit, doubling up into inner motor diagram and externally observable thing, each inscribing itself in the other. In looking at the contours of my hand, I sense the inner lines of force that mobilize it; in extending my leg under the table I extend it across the map of the visible. When one hand touches the other the sense of a tangible mass hovers about the agile vector of sensibility of the touching hand, and in the felt mass of the touched hand, a vector of feeling stirs. When I look at myself in a mirror I feel the cigarette burning against the mirrored image of my fingers.

In mobilizing into a posture, the body situates the levels where other viewing positions lie and emanates an "image" of itself as something visible, tangible, audible in that space. The "body-image" is the outer aspect, quasi-visible to oneself, of one's body as it would be seen by someone viewing it from a distance sufficient to see the whole posture, the tangible aspect of one's body as it would be felt by someone within range to feel it freely, the sonority of one's utterances as they would be heard from the outside.

This primary correspondence between postural schema and body-image in oneself extends to take in others. As the outer aspect of the other takes form before us, the postural diagram corresponding to it takes form within us, and with it a sense of his "body-image." The infant that, at fifteen days, smiles at the sight of his mother's smile, has not yet seen what his own face looks like and will never see the benevolence in the mind of the mother. He then does not set up in his mind an explicit relationship between the arc he sees in visual space, the muscular configuration in the body schema of the mother, and the sentiment of benevolence produced in the mother's mind—and then between a sentiment of benevolence he produces in himself, a muscular enervation, and the resultant arc on his face as a visible surface. Instead, from the first the corporeal *element* doubles into motor schema and outward aspect, and the infant and his mother are superimposed in this reflexive circuit. The visible figure that the dance partner's limbs and parts extend before me is not observed and then interpreted in reverse projection. In perceiving the outer forms of the others, we capture in our postural schema the corresponding inner lines of their postures and movements. And in contracting inner motor diagrams we quasi-perceive the corresponding visible, tangible, and audible outer form of ourselves turned to the distance where others stand.

The perception of external things forms the wider arc of this primary reflection by which the postural schema inscribes the "image" of its outer form upon itself. In perceiving the outer forms of things, we capture in our postural schema the inner lines of their tensions and orientations. And in contracting inner motor diagrams, we quasi-perceive the visible, tangible, and audible form of ourselves turned to them. When I look at the sequoias I do not focus on them by circumscribing their outlines; the width of their towering trunks and the shapes of their sparse leaves drifting in the fog appear as the surfacing into visibility of an inner channel of upward thrust. I sense its force and measure its rise with the movement of my eyes and the upright axis of my body. I comprehend this uprightness of their life, not with a concept-generating faculty of my mind, but with the uprighting aspiration in my own vertebrate organism. This postural axis emanates about itself a body-image which is shaped not as the visual form my body would turn to a fellow human standing at normal human viewing distance, but as my body looks to the sequoia. To see the weight of the rocks is to feel the diagram of a grip forming in my postural schema, and the weightless force in my arms now emanates about itself an immanent sense of the weight of my limbs which the rock would feel as it struggled with my force. To see the magnesium flash fires on the wind-caressed lake in the summer is to dance my eyes over it, and the look that cannot turn back to see itself emanates about itself a quasi-visual form of itself as seen by the vast eye of the lake. To listen to another is already to know how to pronounce what she says; the audible patterns she presents before me I capture on motor diagrams for my own speaking, and when I activate them in turn, the shaping and resonating of my breath through vocal chords and mouth emanates about itself an immanent sense of how my vocalizations sound to the other. As we hum while strolling across the fields and shout to the cliffs, we hear how we sound to the murmuring meadows and to the great ear of the canyon.

The Reality of the World

If a momentary pattern in the road is not confirmed by more visibility, I doubt that I was really seeing. If a brief cry heard in the night is not followed by another sound or something visible, I doubt that there was anything and that I had heard. If, observing her more, I doubt that this woman has anything really engaging or seductive about her, I doubt the reality of my love. If, among the colors and sizes and shapes of things, my perception discerns the real properties from the colors, sizes, and shapes distorted by the medium, the distance, or the perspective, if I see the sheets of paper scattered on the floor under the desk as white even though they reflect light waves objectively measurable as gray, if I see the snow in the troughs as white seen through blue shadow—it is because my perception is destined for coherent and consistent things that maintain their properties as they endure.

The double monocular images dissipate as my eyes advance to the sight of a real thing; the visual form of a furry animal disappears and is not reworked and integrated into the form of the porous rock which materializes as I get closer. Seeing is not gathering signs of an inferred reality, nor composing reality out of appearances; seeing is seeing in the real and believing. The visible form of a furry animal gave itself out as a pattern in the world and in the real, but not as the final reality grasped in its truth. It was provisional, attendant upon confirmation through more seeing. The apparition of the real is not composed out of such appearances, for when I step closer it dissipates to give place to the more dense apparition of the porous rock. Yet real or true being is not something apart from these always presumptive appearances, since what motivates the dissociation of the furry animal from the real world is not an apprehension of the logic and necessities of the field, but the subsequent apparition in its place of the rock. The "belief" in the reality of the first appearance is "revoked" only by being transferred to the next. More exactly, there are not successive acts of judgment; we take as real the appearance that is maintained and consolidated on the sensible levels of the world. The things have to not exhibit all their sides and qualities, have to compress them behind the faces they turn to us, have to tilt back their sides in depth and not occupy all the field with their relative bigness, because they have to coexist in a field with one another and that field has to coexist with the fields of the other possible things.

Some sensory patterns disconnect from the map of reality and float like phantoms before it, because they do not fit into the coherence and consistency of the world. But the coherence and compossibility of the levels of the world is not that of dimensions given in a perception nor of principles of arrangement given in a conceptual representation. It is the consistency and solidity of the thing we perceive that anchor the order which extends further things to perceive about it. The coherence and compossibility of the fields of our various senses and the perceptual fields of others are known only in the continuous transitions by which each field opens upon the next. We recognize the coherence and consistency of the world whose fields evolve about us *by the style*. As we awaken it is not by recognizing things seen before but by recognizing the style of the visible that we know we are no longer dreaming. We separate the ringing of our own ears, the aftereffects and shivers of our own fears, from the audible and the tangible by the style. The term "style" here designates a coherence and consistency we do not comprehend but take up and are caught up in.

The reality of the sensible field supplying things coherently and consistently is not effectively doubtable, since every doubt we can have and every disillusioning we can experience concerns only particular configurations within it, and we doubt the reality of any appearance only by believing more in another perceptible configuration. Any more intelligible or more coherent representation we could have of the universe, including that of the universe of fully determinate objectivity which we posit as the ideal term of all our scientific investigations, could not be more certain or more real than the field we perceive, for every such representation is a re-presentation—in the linguistic formulations and calculus of our reason—of the field of our perception, and has to verify its calculations of what is real by controlled observations of the perceivable.

The World-Imperative

Kant argued that the consistency and coherence of the phenomenal field derives from the ordering activity of thought. He takes the objective thought that represents things as objects and that represents the sensible field as nature, that is, a totality governed by laws, to be a re-presentation of the thought already involved in the perception of things in the sensible field. For he saw in the perception of things sensations identified with the requisite general concepts that make them recognizable, and he saw in the perception of the world-order a layout of things related in rationally recognized universal and necessary relationships. The thought that organizes its perceptions into a representation of objective nature, like the thought that first organizes sensations into a perception of things, is commanded by an imperative for the universal and the necessary that it finds not a posteriori in the world but a priori in itself.

The imperative to which thought finds itself subject is a fact. It is the first fact. Kant argued that it is the imperative laid on thought to think according to the universal and the necessary that makes the empirical facts recognizable as facts. The ultimate imperative is ungroundable and unrepresentable. Every principle from which we might try to derive it and every argument with which we might try to demonstrate it already presuppose a thought subjected to the imperative to formulate principles with correct concepts and to reason rightly.

For Merleau-Ponty, thought finds itself commanded to think the consistent and the coherent because it is destined to think of real things and the real world. Thought, which to actualize itself as thought has to think content, conceptualizes and reasons about what is perceived. But perception has to perceive things, and can actualize itself as perception only by being receptive to the levels and ordering axes of the world which lead it to things as to objectives. Things are the objectives of perception because perception is subjected to the coherence and consistency of the field, that is, the world-order. The imperative is first in the world, to which the sensory-motor body finds itself ordered, prior to any formation of dream images, appearances that are not appearances of things, desiderata, implement-structures, or cultural signals. The world in which every field and every real thing is set is not given but is there as an imperative: the imperative to perceive the coherence and the consistency by going further. The world *is* as an imperative. What makes things the objectives of perception is the imperative force of the world.

The Imperative Competence

The perception of intersensorial things is done by the postural schema which integrates the body's powers and converges its sensory surfaces. It is the postural schema that makes the body's mass into force and power. The postural schema that advances unto things and takes hold of them is not a momentary invention, but a dynamic diagram for operations which maintains itself and varies itself. The postural schema is the locus of perceptual competence. A movement perceives an object, aims at an objective. Perceptual competence is motor competence.

For Merleau-Ponty, the world-imperative is received, not on our understanding in conflict with our sensuality, but on our postural schema which integrates our sensibility and mobilizes our motor forces. The world-imperative commands our sensibility first to realize itself, as a praktognosis oriented to things. It commands our sensitive-sensible body to inhabit a world of things with the most centered, integral, and efficacious hold, from which every subsequent kind of comprehension will be derived. It orders our competence.

The ordering force of any particular objective derives from the imperative character of the world in which it emerges; no thing can materialize, no objective take form, save on the levels of the world. As the reality of any thing is conditional upon confirmation by the further exploration of the world, but the reality of the world is not conditional, so the imperative character of every particular objective is hypothetical, but the imperative character of the world of objectives, the practicable levels of reality, is categorical. For every particular competence one can adduce a reason in another objective—comfort, production, nourishment, survival, reproduction of the species. But survival—whether of oneself or of one's kind—in the world does not explain the evolution and constitution of the human organism as a competent body, for every explanation of things in the world owes its validity to the fact that our life is in its perception, its motility, and its understanding subjected to the world—which *is* as the fact from which all reasons are derived and *is* as a practicable field and *is* as an imperative. That the body contract competence is imperative categorically.

Practicable and Unpracticable Spaces

We can see without necessarily seeing things and without necessarily seeing a world. We can see monocular images and not binocular visions of things; our eyes can get caught up in phantasms and pre-things, in the caricatural doubles and mirages which the sensible levels and planes also engender. Our look can record only the contours and patinas that our desires and our obsessions, our loves and our hatreds have put on the crests and hollows of sensible reality; our eyes and our hands can touch only the shapings culture and industry have left on the levels of the natural world. We can take refuge from the planes of sensible reality in a dream-space; we can drag fragments of things into a delirious space without levels and consistent dimensions; we can, as in advanced states of melancholia, settle in the realm of death.

What of the disengagement from things, and from the levels and planes which engender things, toward those refuges from the space of the world where the phantom doubles of monocular vision, perceptual illusions, mere appearances, refract off the surfaces of things? What of the dream-scene, the private theaters of delirious apparitions, that realm of death in which the melancholic takes up his abode? What of the possibility of releasing our hold on the levels, drifting into a sensible apeiron without levels, into that nocturnal oneirotic, erotic, mythogenic second space that shows through the interstices of the daylight world of praktognostic competence?

For Merleau-Ponty the practicable field alone is imperative; it is reality, and not the ideal or the phantasmal nor the layers of the purely sensory, that is imperative. Merleau-Ponty's main argument is that the unpracticable spaces are inconsistent and incoherent and made only of fragments of the real and the practicable. The screen of the purely visual disengaged from the substance of things, the enchanting field of colors in which the gaze of the visionary moves, is made of the properties of dispossessed things.[13] The musical space in which tones resound and interact is lifted off the reverberant strings and metal tubes and stretched leather of the instruments. The marvelous apparitions of dreams are nothing but fetishized shreds torn from the bodies of perceived and functioning things. If indeed they polarize our movements, capture, enchant, and obsess, it is still the world that holds us in these fragments. It is in holding us by fragmentary evidences of its levels and directives that the world is, not given, but precisely imperative.

The situation and movement of the body between the real world and its objectives and the unpracticable spaces—those of monocular phantasms, mirages, and depths of floating color and shadow, tonalities and scents, erotic obsessions, nocturnal phantasms, mythogenic and magical realms—is constitutive of its competence. The disengagement is only the opening of the zone of commencement, initiative, and obedience to the imperative.

> The relation between the things and my body is decidedly singular; it is what makes me sometimes remain in appearances, and it is also what sometimes brings me to the things themselves; it is what produces the buzzing of appearances, it is also what silences them and casts me fully into the world. Everything comes to pass as though my power to reach the world and my power to entrench myself in phantasms only came one with the other; even more: as though the access to the world were but the other face of a withdrawal and this retreat to the margin of the world a servitude and another expression of my natural power to enter into it.[14]

The body that advances down and retreats from the levels at which things are found is the competent body, which can have objectives because the futures and possibilities of things are open-ended and the imperative that makes each thing an objective is relativized by the next thing, and because the levels do not hold one unless one takes hold of them. There are reflections, mirages, will-o'-the-wisps that arise in the interstices of the practicable world of perception because the things are open-ended and have to be in order to be objectives. There are deviant unpracticable paths and snares in which we get caught in a space that leads nowhere, and there are zones of enchantment where apparitions answer every velleity and distances and intermediaries have no resistance, because the levels of the practicable reality are levels by being given as predetermined.

Thus for Merleau-Ponty, the unpracticable spaces enter into the imperative force of the practicable and real world. The retreat into the margins of the world has a necessary relationship with the power to advance into practicable reality and take hold of real things. The incompetent, phantasmal body, the infantile body or idol or fetish, has an intrinsic relationship with that competent body.

Should we not go further? We do not find convincing Merleau-Ponty's argument that the unpracticable spaces are made of fragments of the perceived world, broken and drifting now, without coherence and consistency and without imperative force. Beethoven and Mahler do not find that they have let go of the order where things are imperative and contrive out of tones cut free from the resounding world willful constructions; they discover rigorous neces-sities and find the worlds of music imperative. Painters find hidden laws in the colors of the manipulatable things of the world, and obey visions they find more imperative than the carpentry of practicable reality. They know they must follow what enchants and obey what obsesses though it lead to impasses in the world. The space of dreams is not a private space made of fragments velleities have pulled from the world; it is a domain into which we are led when we have to let go of the world and its tasks. The uncharted regions into which we are led by erotic obsessions reveals its imperious imperatives. In the desolate regions of grief withdrawn from the world one knows one has to grieve.

If we can identify the apparitions that form in the unpracticable spaces as fragments of the practicable world of perception, these spaces are not frag-mented zones of its space; they extend outside of it. We would argue that the world in Merleau-Ponty's sense—the light that forms a level along which color-contrasts phosphoresce, the key about which the melody rises and falls, the murmur of nature from which a cry rises, the rumble of the city beneath which a moan of despair descends—these levels themselves form in a medium without dimensions or directions: the luminosity more vast than any panorama that the light outlines in it, the vibrancy that prolongs itself outside the city and beyond the murmur of nature, the darkness more abysmal than the night from which the day dawns and into which it entrusts itself. We propose that the world itself, in Merleau-Ponty's sense, is set in depths, in uncharted abysses, where there are vortices in which the body that lets loose its hold on the levels of the world, the dreaming, the visionary, the hallucinating, the las-civious body, gets drawn. Vortices marked by those appearances without anything appearing, those phantoms, caricatures, and doubles that even in the high noon of the world float and scintillate over the contours of things and the planes of the world. Vortices in which it finds not fragments broken from the carpentry of things, but apparitions made of light, voices of the abyss, enigmas made of darkness.

If the sensibility is drawn into these vortices beyond the nexus of levels where the world offers things, it is drawn imperatively. Does not the visionary eye that is not led to the lambent things which the light of the world illumi-nates obey another imperative in the light, the imperative to shine? Does not the vertigo that gives itself over to the abyss that descends and descends with-out end obey not the imperative of the depth to maintain surfaces, but another imperative that depth promotes and is: to deepen? Does not the hearing that hears, not the particular songs, cries, and noises of the world, but the vibran-cy beyond the corridors of the world, obey the imperative of hearing that it become vibrant?

And what of the imperative not to hold onto things and maintain the world, but to release every hold and to lose the world, an imperative which everyone who has to die knows? In Merleau-Ponty's *Phenomenology of Perception* there is no word of this; there is only the imperative figure of an agent that holds on to things that are objectives and that maintains himself in the world. Heidegger recognized the having to die with all our own forces to be our very nature, but he equated it, dialectically—and to us, incomprehensibly—with the resolute and caring hold on things and on the world. We wonder if the one that dies to the things and to the world does not know the imperative, not of becoming nothing, but of becoming elemental, following the light beyond every direction, following the depth that deepens without end, following the reverberation of the vibrancy beyond one's situation and every situation in the world?

The body in turning its competence to the practicable world materializes as a visible, palpable, sonorous thing. In mobilizing to envision objectives it takes on for itself the form of something visible in the view of the factory or of the sequoias; as it rows across the waters it becomes for itself something seen by the lake and the distant shore; as it grapples with the rocks it takes on mass and weight. In handling implements and advancing toward objectives, it rises as a power addressed by and answering to the manifest reality of the practicable world.

But in letting loose its hold on things, letting its gaze get caught up in the monocular images, reflections, refractions, mirages, will-o'-the-wisps, our body dematerializes itself and metamorphoses into the drifting shape of a Chinese lantern among them. In slackening its hold on the levels and the layout of objectives, wandering among the obsessive presences and haunting absences of erotic space, it materializes for itself as a dissolute and lustful substance. In letting go of its hold on things and tasks, in delivering itself over to sleep, in indulging in the nocturnal phantasms of a dream theater—where objectives appear without distances and means, where apparitions realize whatever velleities may form—the magical competence of the body takes on the aspect of something infantile and phantasmal itself. In withdrawing from the monotonous layout of daily tasks and demands into the desolate landscapes of melancholia, the bored, depressed, and catatonic body materializes in the form of an unquiet corpse in a landscape of tombs. In rising unballasted into the zones of the mythogenic space where words and gestures have their effects across distances and without intermediaries, it materializes as an idol or fetish. In the substance of our competence other bodies emerge, ethereal and phantasmal—bodies that materialize forces and powers that are other than those of praktognostic competence.

We can begin to see them when we look at those who set out to build up the motor power of the body by building musculature. For the bodies that the body builders build are without relevance for the practicable objectives of the world. They belong to another history, that of the enigmatic imperatives obeyed by the slow-creeping triton conch designing another coil of arabesques on its shell, the swallow-tailed moth fluttering forth from its cocoon that cannot feed itself and dies in a few days, the quetzal bird shimmering its filmy plumes fit for Aztec gods.

Orchids and Muscles

The Body Builders

Body building is a cult, certainly, not an enterprise—that of *mens sana in corpore sano*—that culture can know and integrate. It has its clandestine repairs, its passwords, its initiations, its legends, its rituals, its undeciphered codes. The alerted eye can spot the body builders in the crowds, not, like punks, by the tribal garb and arcane jewelry, but by the way neither work nor leisure garb fit their bodies, by the strained fabrics, the pulled seams. Sportswear and beachwear, designer conceived for voyeurist eroticism, are pulled tight over their loins like chastity belts. If they wear jewelry, they most often wear it not as embellishments or citations but as amulets. In the bus stations and sidewalks, in the midst of the streams of the busy and the preoccupied, space warps and strains about them as though lacking the gravity these sprung arms and plowshare thighs are made to furrow. The civilized head that looks at them is deviated; it wonders not where they are going but where you can get with them. The erotic eye, that which scouts the erotogenic terrain in the body of another—not the rolling surfaces of taut cutaneous membrane, but the spongy zone of susceptibility just beneath and the mucous membrane of the orifices—is disconcerted to run into packed thongs of drawn muscle. Not muscle that answers to the ungendered resistance of tools and implements, but specifically male and specifically female muscle alignments. One cannot resist feeling the very hardness of these muscles to be the badgering of the glands of lust—whole anatomies pumped like priapic erections, contracting poses and shifting with held violence from one pose to the next with the vaginal contractions of labor pains. They flaunt in the nose of an antiseptic consumer public leathery rutting odors; they gleam with oils that deviate the hold the inspecting eye fixes on these bodies into the sliding suctions of octopus eros.

Their codes are undeciphered; one does not understand the programming or the decision process that assigns them their hours in cellars full of iron millstones and rudimentary machines. The process that elaborates, selects, and distributes the programming is not in the control rooms of culture nor even in the science of coaches and trainers; it is rigged up in their own taciturn and superstitious skulls. The unguarded, unwary eyes with which they walk in the frenetic halls of stock exchanges or in the night of urban jungles do not seem practiced in the predatory uses of the sense organs perfected by the millennia of hunters whose genes we inherit and, unlike the surveillance a miller maintains on the ox or the waterwheel that turns the millstone, their eyes unfocused on their unrotating wheels of iron seem instead to watch the inward spread of monotonous fatigue and seeping pain. Their arms that handle but poles without fulcrum and wheels that grind nothing are uneconomic, detaching or transforming nothing from the raw or recycled materials of nature and industry. In their handshake we feel no understanding; we feel an indexterous hand that is not held to the equipment of our culture. Like kundalini yogis forcing the semen flow back upstream and upward, they detach the few implements they use from the instrumental complex of civilization, detaching themselves from these very implements even as they fit themselves into them, forcing the power and the mass back upstream, from clenched fist toward drummed vortex of the solar plexus.

The Civilizing of the Body
‒ ‒ ‒ ‒ ‒ ‒ ‒ ‒ ‒ ‒ ‒ ‒ ‒ ‒ ‒ ‒ ‒ ‒ ‒

Natural evolution elaborated the neurological and physiological potentials in the human primate that made culture—implements, language, social institutions—possible. But Homo sapiens is a domesticated species; his nature is civilized. What has civilization done to the biological nature of this primate? Paleoanthropologist André Leroi-Gourhan[1] distinguishes four stages in the technological history of our species that have decisively evolved our biological nature.

The first stage is that of the use of tools—cutters, choppers, and grinders. The baboons, as all earthbound mammals, advance into the world snout first; it is with their teeth that they maneuver their way. The human primate puts chipped stones in his front legs to cut, to chop, and to grind. He exteriorizes the functions of his teeth and powers them with what have now become hands. He transforms himself biologically into an upright animal feeling his way with his hands, lifting his eyes to survey the distances. At the same time the senses of his nose and the power of his teeth begin their atrophy. The exteriorized teeth, the chipped stones, still have to be maneuvered with muscle power.

The next species-decisive stage is the harnessing of exterior motor power— that of animals, water, and wind—to drive his implements for him. The primacy of the sense of the vision that surveys is definitively enhanced—even in his sexuality, which now, Freud hypothesized, becomes unseasonal, for primarily excited not by menstrual odors but by the visually exposed genitals of the upright ape. At the same time his hide thins into skin and his muscles begin their atrophy.

But the wind, water, and draft animals that operate his implements in place of his own hands still require his surveillance. The next species-decisive stage is the invention of machines—contrivances that start and stop, control, and, more and more, correct their operations. This stage begins with the invention of the mechanical clock. Its new virtue, by comparison with the sundial and the clepsydra, is that it recycles itself and can trigger other movements. The first clockmakers of Europe immediately set out to construct clocks which filled towers and, as they struck the hour, opened doors from which the three kings and the four horsemen of the apocalypse advanced and gesticulated, while the cathedral clarion tolled above without a bell ringer. Mechanisms now liberate humans from their surveillance—and the attention span of machine-age humans begins its atrophy. Television-viewers, their fingers on channel-change knobs, today look with incomprehension at Guatemalan Indians whose attention may be held on the patterns of a loom for hours on end.

Still, the surveillance mechanisms have to be programmed by the neurological circuitry of the human brain. Today our technological civilization has entered into an information-processing revolution—which is also a new state of our biological evolution. Computers henceforth assemble and evaluate the data, and make the decisions. The faculties of memory, reason, and decision— evolved in our nature through the history of our civilization—now begin their atrophy. The film *The Terminator* is set a generation from now, when the master-computers deciding the racing of the military-industrial complex determine the use of all resources and of the human species. A band of guerrilla resistors, led by John O'Connor, is waging operations of sabotage against the cybernetic police. The master-computers select the Terminator (Arnold Schwarzenegger) to be time-projected back into the twentieth century with a mission to terminate the life of Sarah O'Connor, John O'Connor's mother, and thus ensure that the guerrilla leader will never be born. The human species has, with the next evolution of its technological civilization, undergone regression back into manpower, and the film plots its retrogressive abortion as a biological species endowed with initiative. This film is in fact no science-fiction fantasy; today the stockpiling of weapons of extinction is the most important sector of our industry, and its exponential advance is already programmed by internal feedback circuitry. This forty-year-old industry has already stockpiled nuclear weapons enough to detonate a Hiroshima-size thermonuclear bomb over a city of our civilization every day for the next three thousand five hundred years. The equivalent of the annual production of the poorest fifth of toiling humankind is now devoted to weapons—the total productive energy of one human being employed to fabricate weapons to exterminate the other four. Certainly it is not our fellow citizens, and not their political leaders either, who are in control of the military industry. Our secretary of defense awaits the data, electronically satellite-espionaged from the other military powers, to be processed by the Pentagon computers, and they will make the decisions as to what new weapons our technology must manufacture. The executive offices of the other powers are only relaying the decisions of their computers.

We have already evolved into pure spectators, the Mouse Folk Kafka imagined,[2] with huge eyes feeding into massive brains, floating in the air, with minuscule atrophied limbs dangling. Or, Leroi-Gourhan says, into orchids. Orchids are plants with atrophied trunks and limbs, parasitically clinging to the rising trunks that shut out the sun, flowering their huge showy sex organs, awaiting the bees for their orgasmic unions. With our sight disconnected from any decision or motor functions, its content determined by the image-industry programming, our bulbous and succulent organisms, hoisted into the space of visibility on the massive trunks of cybernetic forests, are biologically evolving into mammalian orchids.

Is not the glorification of our primary and secondary sexual splendors—the orchid-woman flowering against the hood of the Mercedes, the orchid-man flowering under the skydiver parachute—also destined to lose its biological relevance and to atrophy, in the measure that it will be the flickering computer chips of biological engineering, and not our physiological ostentations, that decide which genes will be reproduced?

Every great epoch of culture, Nietzsche wrote, is not only an epoch in humankind's cultivating of nature—transforming of nature's resources in accordance with its own idea—it is also an epoch in the history of humankind's cultivation of its own nature—transforming its own nature in accordance with its ideal. Every great culture, marked by distinctive intellectual, artistic, and moral productions, has also set up a distinctive icon of bodily perfection. The physical ideal of the yogi, of the lion-maned moran of the African savannah, of the serpent-plumed Mayas, of the Olympians of the age of Pericles, of the samurai, of the baris knights of Bali—each great center of culture has set up the corrals, perfected the breeding and training methods, ordered the subjugations and testings for its own body-ideal. In the new institutions specific to modern Western society—barracks, factories, public schools, prisons, hospitals, asylums—Foucault[3] identified the specifically modern ideal of the *disciplined body*.

All these ideal bodies have now become obsolete. Yukio Mishima remarked on the anomaly of the cult of body building; it appeared in Japan only after the defeat of the Second World War, that last samurai fantasy—that is, in a Japan where massive musculature is without employ in high-tech industry and pointless in a nation whose constitution forbids remilitarization.[4] It is, indeed, irrelevant across our planet without such constitutions, where the next war will be won or lost (will be conjointly lost) by fingers pushing buttons, and where in the hour it will last there will be no occasion for ingenious strategic plans, skillful tactics, heroic feats of endurance, or nonparticipation.

The Cause, the Adventure, the Corrida

There is a pervasive resentment of the exhibitionism of body builders. It is not a resentment of physical exhibitionism; human nature in our epoch is cultivated especially by means of the glorification of athletes, female nudity, and feats of physical bravado.

A cause wins with the athlete—the school, the French nationalized automotive industry, the nation-state, the free-market world. In the team instincts of football players, the tailgaters read the name of a brand of beer that is on their own gregarious chests too; in the personal engineering of mountain climbers, the telespectators read the name of a multinational corporation in which they are programmed stockholders; in the single-mindedness of boxers they read the ruling finality of one of those multi-corporation consortiums with a world market in view that are called nations. The bodies of athletes are causes. They are also feedback loops in the marketing industry. Achievement comes from the computer-revealed genetic potential, individually computerized diet and training, drugs, and publicity and marketing. The purely abstract, formal, numerical causes of their competitions feed into the causes of the rising and falling stocks of multinational corporations.

At Penn State, which I found myself honored to belong to by readers of newspapers in London, Tokyo, Singapore, and Managua for its number one football team, a body building meet is held at the local high school. Not even the high-school kids were there, only the body builders, their siblings, and their spouses. The amateurs have no patrons and train and go to exhibitions at their own expense, which the trophy the top one of the class will receive will not reimburse; even the world-class professionals can earn extra dividends as ad layout models only for barbell companies and vitamin-supplement products bought by other body builders. One encounters the amateurs pumping and oiling themselves in the dilapidated movie theaters of small towns, in locker rooms covered with graffiti, and in classrooms whose blackboards are covered with musical scales and high-school geometry formulas. Indeed the public imagination depicts them as fixated adolescents in high-school locker rooms after hours. In the absence of a public cause before them and before us, the public mind can only rummage around for psychological causes producing these cases—distorted father-figure, antisocial underworld instincts sublimated by fear of the police, fixated libidinal compulsions. One sees them narcissistically pumping themselves into ostentatious sex symbols—but symbols the sexually liberated public recognizes as the obsolete figure of virile protector, who was also a phallocrat and wifebeater. When the mind finds itself seduced to look where there is no cause written, it turns away in resentment.

What is she trying to prove, that woman who has gotten herself hung up on a centimeter here a centimeter there on her calves and neck? The image-industry of our time instead glorifies the exhibitionism of the unathletic female—but not male—body. The nudity of the male athlete is a locker room nudity before or after the competition, just the time to buy or sell a Marlboro. The nudity of the male non-athlete is that justified baring of the arms to operate machinery, baring of the legs for speed, stripping for underwater welding. The precision-tooling gives the male body seriousness and seemliness; the axis of bravery can give it nobility. Without the gearing-into the tool—or without a vision of bravery at grips with death—the unathletic male nudity is ridiculous. The female anatomy verges on the ridiculous too, as our advertizing, our high art, and our pornography know; it has to be relayed with stage props— be they reduced to the minimum, as in Nô theater, to high-heeled shoes, a garter, atmosphere spread with vaseline on the camera lens, or, as Marilyn Monroe said, perfume. With the props, the female anatomy is exhibited in a theater—where acts, even that of lying there indolent and fatuous, have consequences and weave a plot. The theater of adventure is a space maintained alongside the politico-economic fields of our enterprises. Maleness is exhibited in an enterprise, where the causes that produce results are also the causes of our industrious and mercantile zones; femaleness is denuded in a theater, where the causes are aleatory and the chain of consequences an adventure. Secretively, clouded with gauzy sunlight, or brazenly, in front of a cast-off nurse's uniform, the female nudity is a cause in the plot of an adventure that justifies it. The voyeur, crouched behind his telescope lined up with the windows of the building opposite, or sprawled before his videoscreen, thinks not of blueprints, data, and willpower, but dreams of luck and white magic, believes the chemistry of alchemical legends, the chance encounters by which an ineluctable destiny in the time of horoscopes is deciphered. He fiercely resents those women who, rebuilding their bodies out of muscle, are ruining the anatomy of the central character required for the theater of adventure.

What about the corrida? No woman spread-eagled in a strip show is as brazenly exhibited as the matador in the corrida. His body and his blood are exalted in a monstrance of scarlet velvets, spun-silver lace, and jewels over against the black fury of the bull. Insolence flaunts his torso, contempt splays his thighs, flash fires of foolhardy intelligence crackle across his tensed and derisive posturings, his testicles and penis jeweled in the codpiece and provocatively exposed to the lust of the crowds.

It is, Hemingway says,[5] not gladiatorial spectacle, but tragic theater. It also became this only in our time. Only a century ago did the corrida change from being an activity of aristocrats for the sake of killing bulls into a theater for the glorification of the torero, whose splendor blazes not in the ecstatic love of killing (the love of, and consequently the gift for, killing is, Hemingway reports, all but obsolete in the legendary matadors of our time), but in the sovereign power to lead the raging horns of the doomed bull to his own brandished torso and to a torrent of blood and death at his feet.

Hemingway misleads us to think of it not as Roman gladiatorial spectacle, but as Greek tragic theater. Greek tragic theater is a theater not for the exhibition of deeds, but for the ineluctable revelation of a concealed truth. The death of the hero is decided by a destiny that the spectators are induced to grasp with a higher intelligence, which the insertion of the individual into a cosmic order or providence or political cause makes possible. In the corrida it is not the death of the torero but that of the bull that is plotted, in the third act, within fifteen minutes of the opening of the gates. The facts are that all the toreros do get gored, but most die of syphilis or tuberculosis. The death present in this Black Mass is not a sacrificial death; it is not the Orphic death of a god by which his power will pass into the cosmic order; it is not the intelligible exposition of death in nature where the dying of an organism is its redistribution into others; it is not a cultural death where a dynasty, an age, a revolution triumphs through or perishes with the death of the tragic hero. Here there is not a solitary life that confronts its place in a kingdom of God, the cosmic order, or a revolution; there is an animality in which nothing is visible but a condensation of the ferocity of nature, a single-minded and brave, unretreating rage that drives the bull to his death, but which has made of the organization of life in him the most powerful in nature. The corrida then is not a theater with a plot of interactions to be intelligibly grasped, nor a truth to be deduced from events, nor a confused spectacle to be understood in narrative order, with beginning, middle, and end; it is a ritual of atavistic nature, in the time of repetition, the time of "in the beginning." What is true is that the inner force that calls forth death is here revealed as what the male body is made of. This force is the dark blood of nobility that swells the phallic anatomy. All the minor arts of costume and jewelry, of choreographed mannerisms and manicuring, all the flattering cultivation of patronage and the priming of critics with gifts, which would make an athlete fall to the ridiculous, do not tarnish but set off the dark light of nobility in his exposed carnality. The ritual of the torero is made of precise and complex and instantaneously discharged intelligence, to be sure, and neurological precision, and the impeccable taste breeding and not training can produce, and the unwavering force of valor. All this visibly is inscribed on, is sustained by or produces an epiphany of arrogant and fateful phallic sexuality. It is virility erected in splendor at the brink of raging death.

What our culture's mind can understand is a *virile body*, a body where virility is virtu, the primary virtue of courage. Socrates at his trial, where the virtue or aberrancy of his pedagogical enterprise was to be defended, instead spoke of his courage in battle, which all his fellow citizens knew. Aristotle was to explain further, when in the *Nicomachean Ethics* he put courage first in the list of virtues, that courage is the transcendental virtue, the condition for the possibility of all the others; without courage neither honesty nor magnanimity nor service nor even wit in conversation are possible. All courage, the courage to endure physical pain as well as the courage required to make decisions, is but the ramification of courage in the face of death. It is from the power to hold one's own posture as the ground gives way beneath one that every other power to take a stand is derived. Is it not the dim sense that all the causes and works of civilization are so many ideals or idols set up to defy death—that the virtues of laborers and of athletes, inasmuch as they are ways of holding firm when pain assaults and when the support of others gives way, are derivative of the power to withstand the confrontation with death—that saves us from seeing a ridiculous anatomy under the glory we flood on their bodies? Is not the corrida a ritual in which this dim intuition is maintained in the midst of our laborious culture which only produces comfort and security?

There is then perhaps in our resentment of them a dim sense that the cult of the body builders desecrates the ritual structure with which we maintain dignity in and conjure ridicule from our physical nature. The public does not

see in body builders ferocious and destructive brutes which offend its sacral-
ization of civilization—they are known to use their massive power as guardians
of bourgeois property, taking jobs, typically, as night watchmen and bouncers
in night clubs where the rich idle, and are suspected of being steroid-pumped
eunuchs from whom the debutantes have nothing to fear. The resentment
senses in them a virility insulated from death. Years of training that led to no
corrida, only to the footlights of a high-school stage. Not a brave contest with
death, but a sentimental fantasy of immortality on glossy photographs,
fetishized into the metal figures of trophies. The duelling scars obligatory on
German university students of the last century confirmed the nobility of their
caste; the steel of the body builders' equipment is nothing but inertia, exor-
cised of the death that forged the saber. There is a feeling at large that the
musculature gained in work and in rule-governed contests, the bodies of construction workers, deep-sea divers, and boxers, is virile and virtuous; the musculature built in the rituals of the body builder's cult, grotesque.

The hands of the body builders do not contend with the inertia of implements or weapons, but rise to unfold in the sunlight or fold to frame their
great swollen bosoms; beneath their wasp waists their legs pirouette; Arnold
Schwarzenegger studied in a ballet studio how to walk with the grace of a
prima donna. The discomfort so voiced today before the new breed of women
body builders makes rise to the surface the vision of the hermaphrodite that
one meant when one called the excessive anatomy of the male body builders
grotesque. Psychoanalyst Julia Kristeva, after viewing the film *Commando*,
spoke of how explicit this has now become: Arnold Schwarzenegger in happy
domesticity, tender, caring, feeding his child—no mention of a woman that
would have given birth to this child or of what had become of her. The body
builder does not only stand in phallic hardness; he or she also moves rhyth-
mically with the tensed violence of labor pains.

Is it not true that this body is not ennobled with the contention of power
with death within it because it is oriented in the other direction—toward the
fatality of genetic potential it is grappling with, toward birth? Bringing the
dead weight of the steel within hermaphrodite muscles, the body builder
brings him-herself ever closer to that limit determined by birth. Our genes
harbor another death, an inner death; as soon as we are born we are old
enough to die, says an ancient wisdom. In pushing back to the genetic coding
of the genus, one pushes one's way to the death sentence written in the individual by the immortality of the genetic formula. The living organism, Freud
taught, discharges its forces to ward off the death exterior to it only in order to
seek its own death, its own advance to the death that is its own. The courage
that forces us into this internal death, this death that is for each his or her

own, is the very courage with which we are born. Freud was only thinking that every living organism has a life span that is indistinguishable from its definition as a species, even though its life forces are so many resistances to the death-dealing blows that fall upon it from without. The sequoias are not killed by the lightning that strikes them every year and burns out their cores; the seed was programmed to live for two thousand years, and then to die. But the body builder tears down, muscle system by muscle system, all the strength in his-her fibers and cells against the death of the steel, and he-she knows that the hard will that takes him-her all the way to the limits of his-her exhaustion is the very movement by which power, and new, greater, power is born. His-her work, his-her feats, are nothing but labor-pains; and he-she knows what is genetically coded to be born in him-her only in knowing the time and the effort it takes to leave all his-her force on the dead inertia of the steel. There is then in the force with which the body builder assumes all that is and could have been born in him-her also a courage and a splendor. Even if, viewed from the outside, it appears as the monstrous excrescence of maternity in the virile figure of power.

Triton Conch, Swallow-tailed Moth, Quetzal Bird

This monstrous, that is, anomalous, gigantic, and ostentatious, figure would be the way the cult overcomes the ridiculous view of the human anatomy reduced to nature. Is not the conviction that our anatomy, ridiculous by nature, has to serve as the material for art coextensive with all civilization?

The civilization our species has launched and pursued to relay its evolution appears in nature as the exteriorization not only of the powers but also of the splendors in our organs. Leroi-Gourhan[6] demonstrates that the first art is the most inward—an artistry done on one's visceral core in the yoga of Mohenjo-daro and Harappa four thousand years ago, an artistry that condensed song into a mantra that is sounded only inwardly, that interiorized the dancing motility of the body into the scanned rhythms of the circulations of air and blood and semen. The compulsion for ordering the circulation of men and goods in outer, public space—which Freud found contemporary with the first beginnings of technological civilization, and which he attributed to the compulsion of the principle of economy—we would see to be an exteriorization of the sense of inner rhythm and circulation which were the materials for the first artistry our species worked on its own nature. The first artists worked, Nietzsche wrote, with the noblest clay and oil, the artist's own flesh and blood.

The epochs of the splendors of civilization appear to Leroi-Gourhan to be epochs of the progressive exteriorization of this inwardly working artist compulsion. Thus the art of body movement and vocalization, dance and song, would issue from the older visceral artistry of the yogis. Glorification of the body surfaces exposed to view comes out of the distant epochs where dance and song were the media for our species's self-glorification; making of the body surfaces a collage of bird-of-paradise plumes and boar's tusks, or a cuneiform tablet of tattooings and scarifications is an artistry that arises in a culture of festivity and chant. A subsequent stage of exteriorization is that of the architectonic splendors of Babylonian, Athenian, Mayan, Ottoman, and Gothic culture, which honored as major artists those who framed the construction and urban layout that houses human movements. The art exteriorized on surface effects—in the age when those who are preeminently called artists are painters—the "humanist" art of the European Renaissance and subsequent modern period of painting, was an artistry worked on the exterior spectacle as blocked off and framed into a perspective by the human eye. Now the buildings that man's earlier artistry had surrounded him with serve as the points of departure for an artistic eye that orders into splendor the views from the balconies and the towers. Our contemporary art now extends itself beyond the perspective spread out before the human sense organs to the spaces reached for by the mind and by its electronic relays—to microcosmic and macrocosmic exteriority. Contemporary art is conceptual, framing the designs of microchemistry and astronomy; contemporary music captures the songs of the whales and those of the earth's magnetic field.

The meaning and the origin of the drive productive of splendor seemed to Freud as enigmatic as it seemed certainly coextensive with the defensive and utilitarian drives that transform nature and transform our nature. Living things are not only equipped with organs to perceive what is exterior; they are also equipped with organs destined to be perceived. Splendor—if created by the chance coincidence of random events in a canyon in a desert, in a sunset over equatorial waters—is also an organic production of living things. This was the thesis of Adolph Portman,[7] who argued that the patterns of animal body surfaces have their own intelligibility. The morphology of the inner, functional body, the form and the arrangement of the skeleton, of the respiratory, circulatory, digestive, and reproductive organs, and of the prehensile and locomotive organs, does not make intelligible the always regular and often intricate and ostentatious patterns of the body surfaces and extremities. These have to be understood, he argues, as organs-to-be-seen, whose designs and colors become intelligible only when we correlate them with the specific powers of the witness-organs for which they are contrived. The inwardly coiling horns of the mountain sheep and the hairless, protuberant buttocks of the baboons are, he says, organs as closely fitted to the eyes and lips of the spectator as the jaws and hoofs are fitted to the terrain and the specific foods of the species.

In the human primate, a distinctive reflexive circuit was set up with the evolution of the hand. The human species began by putting the cutter, chopper, and grinder functions of the jaws into its hands. The front legs no longer serve to drive the jaws to make contact with the world; they rise from the ground and conduct samplings of the world to the head. The human animal now acquires a face. Its muscular configurations no longer react immediately to the front line of contact with external nature, but turn to its own hands. A smile and an apprehensive grimace now become possible—movements that are *expressive*, that is, that address a sample, a representative of the independent exterior held in the hand and, soon, held with a mental grasp before an inner eye. An animal that faces considers representations it has apprehended. Its manual musculature becomes not prehensile only but also expressive; the hands position their take for an appraising eye. They address themselves also to the eyes of another animal that has acquired a face; they speak. Little by little our whole musculature has learned to speak. The throat muscles designed for devouring and for expelling substances and the body's own biles and rages now learn from the hands how to shape the samples and representatives of the outside, how to exteriorize the comprehensive expressions the hands first learned to make. The whole torso becomes organs-to-be-seen, the abdomen struts and cowers, the legs and thighs acquire humility and pride, the shoulders and back, turned from the face-to-face circuit, sway with resentment and defiance.

Unlike the birds-of-paradise and the mountain sheep and the baboons, the human species did not develop distinctive organs-to-be-apprehended in addition to its organs-for-apprehending. Its hair, become functionally obsolete, is in an advanced state of disappearance; it has not deviated into a patterned pelt. Its teeth, whose functions were exteriorized onto tools, are in an advanced state of atrophy, and have not deviated into coiling tusks to make impressive the face. With the upright posture, the primate genitals are permanently exhibited to the frontal view of another, and, Freud assumed, this has led to the primacy of the eyes over the smell as the chief organs for sexual stimulation, and to the end of a rutting season, the unseasonableness of human libido. But the human genitals remain organs fitted for contact, and have not become expressive organs. To be sure, the human species has contrived snares for the eye—penis sheaths, cache-sexes, pendants hung over the breasts—but these are exterior to its own genitalia, which remain glandular, orifices of the inner, functional body.

But the human muscular system has taken on the second, expressive, role for which the other animals have evolved distinctive organs-to-be-seen. The human muscular system is not only the scaffolding that positions and turns the sense organs, the organs-for-apprehending; the vectors and surges of motor energy illuminate the muscular network itself and make its mesh and mounds snares for the eye. On human bodies muscle frettings are their peacock tails, curls worked on the lips their crests, biceps and pectorals their coiled horns, finger waverings their lustrous pelt.

Civilization—in that epoch when the hunter-gatherers mutated into self-domesticated animals—altered the human muscular system. As it exteriorized motor efficacy from the human muscles to the animal, wind, water, and steam power that relayed them, it exteriorized the ostensive functioning of muscles into masks, talismans, and costumes.

To be sure, this exteriorization is not yet complete and definitive; there still floats in civilization an imagination that feeds on muscles. Indeed the imagination, that unpenetrating, superficial vision, vision of surfaces without depth, is a faculty of the muscles. Mishima[8] spoke of the displacement of his sense of himself when, an intellectual, he committed himself to body building; there is a specific sense of one's identity that rises out of the visceral or cerebral depths to find itself henceforth in the contours one's substance spreads out to the sun. This self, spread in the tensions of the musculature, doubles them up with an imagination fascinated with forms, patterns, and surfaces, which dwells on one's own surfaces. And muscles are not exposed without doubling up their surfaces before the imagination of another. It is the first effect of their reality; their contours excite the imagination before they displace resistances. That the visceral system does not have such an effect can seem puzzling. The awareness of the contents of fluids in us of the saline and mineral composition of ocean water, the inner gulf streams, currents, and tides, the coral reefs, the channels lined with tentacled anemones, and the floating plankton within does not double up our sense of ourselves with a vision of the oceans from which—tide pools now enclosed in a porous sack of skin—our muscles have carried us. In fact the imagination is not divinatory and does not penetrate the deep; it is a surface sense, its mirages mirroring superficial mappings of the terrain, excited by the contours of muscles. And our muscles, becoming more and more obsolete in mechanized industry and automated war, become the more designed for the faculty of imagination.

In the obsolescence of an epic imagination does there not spread now only a tropical erotic imagination? The Marlboro man, a torso hardened, according to the legend, by riding the range, is perhaps a torso riding the range in order to be hardened into a Marlboro model. The editorial writers of *Playboy* and *Playgirl* declare that the anatomies they exhibit have been fashioned by Olympic nautical training and ocean sailing, but swimming, sailing, bicycling (on stationary machines before mirrors), and workouts on universal gyms are perhaps designed to produce the play musculature. Is the human muscle sheath, strapped to machines, monitored by cardiovascular and fat-ratio dials, turning into the showy carnal corollas and petals of human orchids?

This evolutionary destiny is unclear; the future is complicated by the existence of the cults. In them the body-substance is turned into muscle everywhere, the glands of the abdomen and its coiled membranes into muscles that can parry the blows of a fist, the atrophied mammary glands of males into matrices of trust and power, the cords of the neck are not neglected, nor the bands aligning the finger joints. They use the most elementary bars and weights; to this day no world-class body builder has trained on the Nautilus machinery scientific intelligence has designed for them. These are atavistic bodies, halted before the age of the self-domestication of the hunter-gatherers. We found no real difference between the scene in Gold's Gym and on the banks of the Ganges, where the origins of every method to divinize the mind with every possible cosmological system, but also where every method to divinize the body with sublunary power can be traced back to, and where we saw, in 1980, young men making the prostrations before the idols of the Aryan ape-god Hanuman which we term push-ups and calisthenics, and, while intoning mantras, lifting before him rocks and pairs of millstones fixed on poles. Cults where we see not body-mechanisms made on machines, but primogenitor bodies made of *the elemental*—the weight of the terrestrial, and rivers, and sun.

The body builder's implements do not relay the passage of the body's force outward. The body builder confronts the steel, the opaque, inert mineralization of death, with all the body's animate power in what is no contest but a process of symbiosis or synthanatosis. He-she tears down the hermaphrodite muscles on steel, exhausting all their force on it, and when muscle failure has been reached, receives from the metal its properties. His-her biceps become tempered flails, his pectorals, that is, his mammaries, his femaleness, become gearing, the membrane of his-her abdomen a sheet of corrugated steel, his-her knuckles themselves brass. The luster of the muscle-contours acquire for the eye the opaque impenetrability of metal. At the same time in the repetitions, the contractions and flexions, the body builder internalizes into channels of surging power the fluidity of the sweat and the oils, the vaporous currents of steam, showers, surf, and sunlight. The power that holds the body builder upright is no longer that of a post before equipment civilization has erected. Tide pools of the maternal ocean enclosed in a porous sack of skin carried up to dry land by developing muscles, the muscled body stands erect now with the form that a fountain maintains by the incessant upsurge and fall of streams of power.

The body builder senses his-her identity on the bronzed, metalized luster of the beams of musculature exposed to the sun; it is on the sweat-sheets across this hard skin and the surface gleam of the sun, and on the surfaces of mirrors displaying the oiled definition that he-she now seeks him-herself. Existence, for the self, no longer means inwardness, visceral or cerebral involution, but exposure. This self is a movement to extend itself across contours and forms, and not to maintain a point of view, a repair in space. As the ego surfaces, distends, and exposes itself, it depersonalizes. The steel does not only transfer its properties into the living tissue that has exhausted its own force on the steel; the homogeneity of the steel drives out the principle of individuality in the bodies that devote themselves to it. It does away with the eccentricities—the dry and irritable skin, the concave faint-hearted chest, the indolent stomach, the furtive hand, the shifting eye—by which movements of retreat set up the as-for-me of individuality and leave their marks on the body. On his-her contours the body builder watches emerging not the eccentricities his or her tastes and vices leave in his or her carnal substance, but the lines of force of the generic *human animal*.

How little the rest of us see of our bodies! Our genitals we conceal, even from ourselves, judging them, with Leonardo da Vinci, of an irremediable unsightliness; our visceral and glandular depths, the inner coral reefs and pulsating channels of antennas and gyrating polyps, our very imagination blinds itself to. Our musculature we attend to with a clinician's or mechanic's inspection. The drive to visibility, to high noon exposure, is so alien to us that it has to be driven into our substance by the steel. The body builders have watchmaker eyes for the individual components. They do not, like the rest of us, see a charm or a brutality; their eye is specialized for details, trained in instant measurings, intolerant of dissymmetries. As they wait in the wings for the decisions of the judges, the contestants line up in almost exactly the order the judges will have placed them. As though it is not the individual eye permanently fixed in a point of view and a perspective that sees, but the impersonal eye of a species in evolution appraising its organs and limbs for an advance whose duration and direction are unknown. Body builders look at one another, and each at him-herself, also with an alchemist's eye full of chemical formulas, protein supplements, quack remedies inspired by analogies, and drugs made in biochemical laboratories. They know their muscle substance with a cellular and not general and conceptually formulated knowledge, with a knowledge that thinks in the pain of cells being stretched and elongated, being torn down, a knowledge that does not preside over, but yet somehow accompanies the invisible movements of the millions of antibodies within that are the real cause of and reality of the separateness of our bodies.

One does not know what role evolution will find for these prodigies of musculature—or what evolution their artistry is contriving for the species. No one, Nietzsche wrote, is more readily corrupted than artists. Their souls, their taste, can be bought by venal priests of pagan religions, by the big investors in the image-industry, by the master-computers of the racing military-industrial complex, and by their own followers and flatterers. Today the names of the body builders whose names are known are the names of so many industries, auxiliary epicycles in the wheels of the planetary machinery.

The imagination that feeds on muscles imagines something else—imagines that the deviation their cult makes from the path of civilization might be carried further. Civilization destined the self-driving power of human bodies to be transferred into tools, and then to be transferred out of human muscles into draft animals, wind, water, steam, atomic fission. The body builders at this late date reverse the movement, disconnect from the tools, having interiorized their elemental properties, and make of musculature a splendor. Civilization destined the powers of surveillance in human sense organs to be directed toward the motor force now exteriorized in draft animals, windmills and waterwheels, electric and atomic-fission generators, and then to be transferred out of human sense organs into automatic and feedback mechanisms. Can we imagine at some future date the eyes, the touch, the heart disconnecting from the machinery that feeds in the images and the information, and glowing with their own resplendence? Civilization evolved the faculty of memory, reason, and decision, and destined it to program the electronic sensors and feedback mechanisms that make the human sense organs obsolete. Can we imagine at some future date the faculty of memory, reason, and decision disconnecting from the computers which it now serves, ceasing to be but an organ-for-apprehending, and, swollen with its own wonders, becoming an organ-to-be-apprehended, an orchid rising from the visceral and cerebral depths of the cybernetic forest with its own power, rising into the sun?

Bodies Our Own

Objective biology, physiology, and psychology elaborate a "body in the third person," a body constructed out of the data of external observation and measuring instruments. This representation of our bodies is correlated with a representation of the environment constructed out of data collected with measuring instruments and formulated in the terminology of objective physics and chemistry.

But the behavior of a sentient body has to be understood in terms of the environment as that body itself perceives it. A phenomenological language is needed to describe the nutrients, paths, obstacles, objectives, and horizons of the zone of reality our bodies perceive and deal with. Then, a phenomenological language is needed to describe the postures, gestures, and operations which constitute our perceptual and practical competence. This language describes our postural schemas and "body-images" as we ourselves experience them—it describes a "body in the first person."

Language, which can construct models and mappings, can also designate what is perceived and perceivable. Speech is made not only with the mind, but with the voice and kinesics that is supported by the whole body posture. Speech acts are themselves movements, centerings, gestures.[1] The distinctive terminology phenomenology elaborates—"thing," "Gestalt," "sensible essence," "level," "postural schema," "body-image," "gesture"—is designed to disengage the phenomenological report from the reconstruction of the body's competence in terms of the current paradigms of objective research.

Merleau-Ponty's phenomenology takes the objects of our competence to be things, praktognostic tasks, and the world to be a practicable field of levels leading to things. But the body whose eyes have to see through the night and the radiance of the light to envision illuminated things, the body that has to rouse from its indistinctness in repose and sleep and mobilize a stand to confront a layout of tasks, the sentient agility that has to dissipate monocular images to focus on consistent things, that has to separate illusions, perspectival deformations, reflections and auras due to the medium to apprehend the orientations and identities of things, is a body whose competence relapses and which is capable of perceiving flux, transience, the twilight of things, the dissolution of the world of paths and tasks, the oncoming of the elemental.

The power of the body builders is not a practical competence. It is a power that lies in the force, not to manipulate objectives, but to compact its postures with muscular substance. To say that is to describe the bodies in which they live in the first person. Their built bodies rebuild about themselves a posttechnological world which harkens back to an age prior to the biotechnological epoch that exteriorized muscle power onto domesticated forces, leaving the animals, winds, and rivers to move in their own paths.

The one who speaks of his own body taking into account what the others can observe of it and who speaks of the bodies of others as lived in the first person invokes a power to displace himself into the perceived environments of others and into the sentient and intentional postures of others. This power is in the body lived in the first person; my body displaces itself not only into the positions extended by the material layout of nature, but into the positions perceived and explored by others; it exchanges places with others in all its moves. To be sure, it makes the place that another vacated its own; it perceives what the other perceived with its own competence.

The one who, actually or virtually, puts himself in the place of another, corrects his account of the environment his body now perceives and of the body-intentions engaged there with the linguistic reports the other formulates. The language with which we communicate and translate one another's reports is a power to discriminate reports of what one has seen with one's bodily competence and what one translates from the reports others make of what they have seen. The movements, centerings, and gestures of speech discriminate between the acts which designate what is perceived and perceivable and the models and mappings language itself constructs.[2] The anthropologist who reports on the worlds of non-Western and premodern peoples and of subcultures outside academia appeals to his own ability to inhabit many environments and appeals to his own first-person lived body to capture within itself the postures, gestures, and operations of their bodies. If he translates into his academic language what his informants tell him of their environment as they explore it with their perceptual and practical competence, he can do so because the field in which he does his field work is not only the field he surveys with the air-reconnaissance methods of the cartographer and the instruments of the geologist, but the field he has inhabited with them.[3] To be sure, because the report which a speaking and writing body makes of its own relevant environment and its own postures, centerings, movements, and gestures is a report addressed to others, its terminology, selected from the common language and shaped by its paradigms, will never be fixed in its own meaning. It will always be in the listening in to what others say that we comprehend their relevant environment and our own, their competence and our own, in our difference.

part two

The Pleasure
and the Pain

The Subjectification of the Body

Our bodies are sensory-motor systems that generate the excess force which makes them able to move themselves, systems that move toward objectives they perceive, that thus code their own movements. Our bodies are also substances that can be moved and that can be coded. Subjected to regulated operations of force, our bodies become subjects of capacities, skills, and inclinations; they can be made use of. In and through operations of force, the bodies of speakers become identified, coded, and significant. Discourse is elaborated about them. Language is itself power; the determination of what is said, in what codes, to whom, and in what circumstances organizes a power structure about interlocutors.

In a series of historical studies[1] Michel Foucault elucidated some of the structures of power in contemporary Western society that have our bodies as their object—the institutions of confinement set up for lepers, the unsocialized, and the insane; clinics set up for the sick; penal institutions; schools, factories, and barracks; and the institutions of medicine, pedagogy, social work, and psychiatry. In these institutions, different kinds of techniques are used on bodies. These power structures give rise to new bodies of discourse—the multiplying disciplines of the social sciences and of social technology. These bodies of discourse are themselves power mechanisms that have real and forcible effects on our bodies, which they subjugate as they objectify, program as they decode.

Foucault's history is a materialist history, a history of inventions that mark discontinuities, for which, once put forth in the public space, different uses are found, about them different couplings of power are set up, different elaborations of discourse become possible. Inventions invest those who seize hold of them with new powers, technological as well as social powers, powers over others; they produce new forms of identity and new forms of competence. The inventions spread laterally; new uses for them are found in different sectors of social space. The resultant of multiple centers of power functioning in different directions becomes visible, not as the finality conceived by the inventors, but as a movement that functions in certain directions, toward certain ends, producing certain effects, which were perhaps not the efficacious intention of anyone. Bodies that are forcibly subjected produce power in their turn, devise their evasions, resistances, snares, ambushes, ruses, and mockeries; they signal, feint, and delude.

It is as a sensitive substance, a substance that produces pain and pleasures in itself, that a body is a subject of and subjected to power and discourse. Pain and pleasure are not just ineffable states of transitive impotence; they incite the power operations and discourse of others, they afflict the susceptible bodies of others. It is as a painful and voluptuous substance that a body attracts forces and gets inserted into the organized channels in which capacities are imprinted on it. With these capacities it not only manipulates material things, but inflicts pleasure and pain on others. It is not just inasmuch as its musculature and nervous circuitry can materialize a gesture, a perceptible signifier, that a body makes itself a subject that issues statements and has actions ascribed to it. The body that speaks is not a tabula rasa upon which its own gestures draw signs. In speaking its substance is relieved and wounded, is gratified and excites pleasure, troubles and torments. It is as a painful and voluptuous substance that its muscular and nervous circuitry attracts forces and get coded with blazons, signs, functional identities, and gets inserted into the grammar and rhetoric of kinship relations, the distribution of resources, and the communication of directives.

The cartography[2] that maps out the distances and directions across which we identify and constrain one another maps out the ways we torment and gratify one another.

The Pain of Identity

A body as a substance susceptible to pain can be tortured, can be punished, can be disciplined, can be made delinquent. These operations characterize distinctive periods of modern Western socialization, and make the corporeal substance significant and functional in quite different ways.

The Blazon of the Tortured Body.

The ancien régime in Europe made bodies substances subject to torture and correlatively made bodies sacred. Coronation, the ceremonies of subjection and obeisance, and the royal iconography were operations of power and of discourse by which the body of the ruler was doubled up with the very substance of the body politic. And the sacred rites which consecrated his body made it the terrestrial double of the King of Heavens, the body of Jesus doubled up with eternal godhead.[3]

It was in the name of the sovereign that the body of the malefactor was subjected to torture,[4] and it was tortured for an attack on the person or the personage of the king—that is, on the sovereign double of the ruler's body. The malefactor was denounced as an insurgent, a regicide; every criminal tortured was tortured for lese majesty. Torture was a raid during the time of political armistice, an operation of the king wreaking vengeance on the enemies of his sacralized body.

Here truth was determined, not by empirical assemblage of disparate data and critical evaluation of them, but by the torture that produced confession. The truth of the crime was concealed in the entrails and by the body of the accused; it had to be made manifest on his body.[5] The tongues of avowed blasphemers were pierced, the throats of conspirators seared with acid, the hands of armed aggressors cut off with their own weapons, the bodies of arsonists burnt with their own torches. The scaffold was a public theater of royal power; torture, a liturgy. Raised before the gates and under the eyes of the heavens, the flames of its fury rising from infernal depths, the scaffold situated the regicide body of the captive and the sovereign body of the ruler on cosmic axes. In the mutilation, castration, and quartering of the body of the captive, the spectators were shown the absolute character of the outrage done to the body of the king. The body of the captive was reduced to a substance that produces nothing but pain, a pain that was branded not with ciphers and messages but with horror and infamy.

The scaffold was a theater, the victim was also an actor. On his or her flesh being scorched the crowd saw the flames of eternal damnation rising to envelop him—but this same agony may also make visible the pain that redeems and that consumes the guilt. As the torture produced the confession, it delivered from guilt and delivered to glory—or it produced the oaths, outcries, and blasphemies with which the victim cursed irrevocably his judges, the king, and his God, and turned the theater of sovereignty into a saturnalia in which the transcendental order was inverted and criminals transformed into heroes and legends.

The eventuality of such a denouement, provoking fear in the minds of monarchs—and not some contagion of compassion arising out of recognition of common corporeality—was what led to a decreasing incidence of torture, in the measure that absolute monarchy found itself the more threatened.

Punishment and the Body of Signs.
The theorists who drew up a program of punishment for modern Republican Europe were concerned to deliver the criminal from the hands of the crowd that had massed about the king's scaffold, spectators of the royal action and depositories of the insurrectional legends, into the hands of a citizenry actively united by social contract and subjected to the non-arbitrary decrees of rational law. Torture is spectacular, it is a theater of glory, whether for the monarch or for his enemy. The punishment they planned was a program of calculated and limited operations on members of the body politic, pedagogical rather than dramatic and terrorizing—essentially inglorious.

As the extremities to which torture went resulted from the transcendent nature of the sovereign's body that was being shown forth and not from the rage of the ruler, so the differentiations, degrees, and limits of intensity in punishment they argued for did not result from compassion in the hearts of the Republican penologists. The torture of the ancien régime was an operation on the body of a subject unlimited in intensity but limited to transgressions perceived as lese majesty; the punishment of the Republican regime is limited and graded in intensity in order to be virtually unlimited in extension.

The development of production, the amassing of wealth, the rapid increase in property holdings—which characterized the epoch—motivated the will to extend penalization into zones where, previously, the identification of offense as offense against the body of the sovereign had left certain activities unlegislated or had tolerated certain illegalities. Privately capitalized industries and commercial holdings became too extensive for the owner himself to maintain his domination throughout them; the previously tolerated zones of production unregulated by guilds and corporations, or of production of new and illegal substances, or of smuggling had become too extensive, regional protectionism and extortions too consolidated not to attract the legislating and penalizing will of the citizens' Republic. Soon the industrial slums and proletarian and subproletarian family housing, health, and property transfers would also attract this will.

The punishment must become differentiated and graded because it is conceived, not as an act of branding on the body as a substance of pain, but as a mechanical operation on representations—the representations of advantage that activate the body's powers. The penologists must draw up an ideally complete table of transgressions, and conceive for each an injury contrived to invert the specific advantage the transgressor represents himself or herself as gaining from the transgression. The policed Republic will be one in which those who abuse public liberty are deprived of their own, those who abuse the privilege of public office are stripped of their civil rights, speculators and usurers are subjected to fines, thieves have their assets confiscated, murderers are executed. The complete table of punishments, each conformed to the nature of the offense, will make the law appear to be in the nature of things.

The punishment will come to an end when the reform of the representational faculty is brought about and this reform verified. The sentence meted out is thus to fit not only the nature of the specific transgression, but the attitude of the criminal, his past, his way of life, his nature, his rate of transformation. The masses, whose functional identities in the agrarian, manufacturing, military, and ecclesiastical hierarchies were dissolved in the collapse of the feudal order, have a new kind of identity produced for them in the penal practices which the Republican order set out to extend throughout society.

Through punishment the body-mechanics of the offender is being made into a place where the representations it produces for itself are inverted, by outside intervention, and also where they are exteriorized, where *signs* are being produced. These signs will designate to others the identity of the ordinance violated, and associate the specific transgression with a representation of disadvantage. Punishment will turn the social space into a pedagogical tableau in which the public which judges and sentences also reads the logic of the civil code in the mortified figures of its transgressors. In quarries being worked, along roads being repaired and bridges being built, in workshops and mines open to the public, everyone will see the civil code being inscribed on the bodies of citizens.

Discipline: The Body Individuated as a Value

The industrial, mercantile, and colonialist bourgeoisie who had enlisted the masses, produced by the dissolution of the feudal order, in the struggle to overthrow the monarchies, had no intention of giving power to "the people." The new juridical order—representative government—was soon to show itself to be a coalition of the most powerful special-interest groups. The ideology of government by law, devised as a weapon in the conflict against the monarchies, would henceforth serve to mask new structures of power. For this period was not only a period of inventions of industrial and military technology, but also of social technology. The invention of those distinctively modern apparatuses of subjection, which were the barracks, the factory, the public school, the hospital, and the asylum, was to completely restructure modern social space. These structures were the decisive means by which the unleashed forces of the masses were not simply segregated, neutralized, and controlled, but made productive. Foucault identifies with the term "discipline" the new social technologies devised in them.

Barracks, factories, and public schools are spaces enclosed, and then partitioned. The bodies to be disciplined are distributed in the gridded space as interchangeable elements in a table of ranked subordinations.

Each maneuver to be performed in the assigned site is broken down analytically. The limbs of the body are separately assigned positions and directions; the position and movement of each limb or organ are fixed in relationship with the assigned overall position of the body. Each position and movement is then correlated with an object—a weapon, a tool, a machine, a notebook, a medication. The duration of the movements is calculated and timed. The timetable will make possible an exhaustive usage of each segment of time.

The multiple activities of a factory, a barracks, or a school are broken down into specific operations. They are not performed as organic and reciprocally coordinated aspects of a common team project, but are executed as preprogrammed and timed exercises. This new methodology of power is, Foucault suggests,[6] the source of the new concept of a linear and progressive kind of time which now begins to dominate in modern society. In the enclosures of disciplinary society time figures, no longer as a field which is punctuated by events and feats, but as the linear dimension of the continuous execution of successive and parallel operations.

The exercises, each determined as a performance in an assigned place and taking a determined time, distributed in gridded space and in linear time, are combined so as to produce composite results, calculable in advance. The composite operation will not be simply the additive sum of massed agents nor the synthetic momentum of a reciprocally coordinating team. The instance that commands these docile bodies is then not, as in slavery or servitude, the individual will of the master, the individuality, charisma, or caprice of the power that wills, but the tactical calculus of the headmaster, the foreman, the coach, the lieutenant, or the administrator.

Disciplining is a technical operation designed to form and to fix aptitudes in a body, thus augmenting the body's powers, increasing its functional efficacy. It also dissociates those aptitudes from the power of the body in which they are seated; they are powers in the body over which that body does not exert power.[7] The capacities that are developed in the individual body do not result in its acceding to dominion over segments of the social field; the new aptitudes are loci of subjection in the body. Disciplining makes bodies docile—adapted to instrumental layouts and productive, and also tractable. It makes bodies function as elements that can be programmed and maneuvered.

Confinement first appeared in Europe in the setting up of leper colonies. Walls of exclusion were devised for lepers; when leprosy subsided in Europe, the walls remained and the spaces they excluded were filled with beggars, vagabonds, sociopaths, and madmen.

When, in the wake of leprosy, the plague spread across Europe, the social space outside the walls of exclusion came to be partitioned, internally gridded, for the ordered distribution of bodies and movements. The advance of the plague called up not the thaumaturgic powers of medical authorities, which proved in fact impotent, but the segregating methods of the civic authorities. They acted to halt behind multiple barriers the movements of the disease whose contagion spread in the commingling of bodies, but also in order to halt the spread of the moral evil of plague times—the frenzy of lifetimes cut short, the consorting of bodies without respect for civic status and identity, the indifference to laws and prohibitions. The institution of a power that assigns to each individual his place and fixes each individual in the capacities and malady of his body, first appeared in Europe in the methods of force the public authorities marshaled to deal with the plague.

In the eighteenth century the masses threatened the cities from within; they were confined in barracks, factories, schools, penal colonies, hospitals, and psychiatric asylums, where the walls of exclusion were compounded with internal partitioning. Individuals were distributed, each at his post, in a social space become a disciplinary archipelago. The social technology of disciplining is the use of procedures of individualization to mark the confined: disciplining post-feudal mass society consisted, Foucault says, in treating lepers as plague victims.[8]

Surveillance registers the transgression as soon as it is initiated, indeed observes every possibility of transgression and every temptation to transgress, and neutralizes them in advance. It differentiates individuals, makes comparison possible between the levels, abilities, and performances of different individuals, and between the different stages in the evolution of an individual. The individual is constituted as a describable, analyzable object through a set of procedures for identification, codification, narration, and induction. Examination procedures maintain the individual exposed and visible. The disciplined body is individual in his or her school record, examination results, aptitude tests, military record, employment record, prison record, and medical file.

Surveillance and examinations make possible the establishing, for each individual, of a minimum to maintain and an optimum to strive for, and counteract deviations from this optimum. Norms are produced by the comparison surveillance makes possible between the levels, abilities, and performances of different individuals. Individuality is the zone of intersection of several such extensive classes. The abnormalities with which the individual is individuated define a fixed range of other individuals with which he or she is equivalent and interchangeable.

The individuality of the individual then does not consist in the autonomy of a singular set of powers and a singular sensibility within him or her. Nor does it consist in signifying a transcendental referent—an ideal category to which he or she would belong, or an ideal individual that his or her own individuality would reflect, in the measure that he or she participates through his or her own function in the scope of power of that ideal individual. For him or her to identify himself or herself is not to declare that he or she is a priest of a great God or a knight or servant of a great lord.

Fernand de Saussure differentiated between the *meaning* and the *value* of a term in a semiotic system. Inasmuch as a term in language has a meaning, it designates a referent. Inasmuch as a term in language has a value, it is defined and delimited by the set of other terms with which it can be exchanged, and those with which it contrasts. In the disciplinary regime, the individuality of the individual is marked by a degree of approximation to the norm, but the norm itself is nothing but the measure of the mean range of variations. In de Saussure's terminology we could say that the individuality of the individual has no meaning. Maintained visible in its post, comparable with the constellation of other individuals with which it can be substituted, the individuated disciplined body has, or is, a value.[9]

The Uses of the Delinquent Body.
The penology conceived by the theorists of Republican Europe was short-lived. Almost at once the concept of the prison was adopted, and incarceration replaced the table of fines, confiscations, sequesterings, divestment of civil rights, and the forced labor in public works that penologists had elaborated, to become the uniform chastisement for all offenses.

The prisons built were not a simple return of the dungeons of the ancien régime; its dungeons were for interrogation and for the neutralization of political prisoners, rather than themselves the penalty. The prison, as conceived by the theorists of the Walnut Street Prison and the Ghent Workhouse,[10] was the architecture of a project aimed at the nature of the felon. His transgression was perceived to issue, not simply from a representation, but from an antisocial nature. He was to be born again through a technological reconstruction of his physical nature. The Quaker theorists of the Walnut Street Prison and the Enlightenment theorists of the Ghent Workhouse conceived the prison as a model institution of the Christian utopia of the reborn or as a model of the Rousseauist city of citizens whose eyes are open only to the whole. But what they assembled within prison walls were the new methods of human engineering contrived to produce disciplined bodies.

The prison individuates—isolates the convict from the exterior world, from what motivates the offenses of which he was charged, from other prisoners. It subjects his past, his proclivities, his aptitudes, his habits, and his speech to incessant surveillance, and builds up for him an individual prison file. It imposes labor not for production, but in order to bend bodies to regular movements, to exclude agitation and distraction, and to subject them to hierarchy and to imperatives. It regulates the form and the duration of the sentence to effect a technical transformation of the body of the convict.

The inventors of the prison heralded it as an apparatus to effect reform, the reconstruction of the nature of the bodies isolated from the social space— and thus as the most effective protection of society. Within twenty years after it was instituted in Republican France, a parliamentary commission set up to report on its functioning already reported[11] what subsequent investigations of the penitentiary system to our day have continued to report: penitentiary procedures produce different effects on the inmates they mark and individuate. For, Norman Mailer writes, "it is that not only the worst of the young are sent to prison, but the best—that is, the proudest, the bravest, the most daring, the most enterprising, and the most undefeated of the poor,...those who are drawn to crime as a positive experience—because it is more exciting, more meaningful, more mysterious, more transcendental, more religious than any other experience they have known...."[12] Studies of the results of the prison system show that one part of the prison material will be made functional in other disciplinary apparatuses—factories, military barracks. One part will be marked and individuated to the point that they will be unable to function outside prison; these are the punks that will get themselves rounded up again as soon as they are released. Another part—the statistically largest part—will be made into delinquents, offenders schooled in the methods of crime within the prison and who, when released, enter into careers in illegal activities. Finally, one part will make careers of being convicts within the prison, "annealed until they are harder than the steel that encloses them"[13] and, if released, make themselves outlaws, pursuing not the efficacy of rebel commandants but the glory of bandits.

In the United States at this writing there are 628,000 convicted criminals in prisons, a number double that of ten years ago; 150,000 await trial in jails. There are, in addition, six million jail admissions of arrested people each year; a million are on parole. Nearly two-thirds of all convicts are rearrested within three years of their release. Federal penitentiaries (for non-white-collar offenders) house secret societies of convicts, bandits and killers; they are, in Jack Abbott's words, schools for gladiators. Yet legislators, penal officials, and public agree to build more prisons.

It is then that these factories producing delinquents and these schools for gladiators are judged better than the alternative: treaties negotiated among urban and rural zones held by undisciplined masses,[14] or street war against urban guerrillas;[15] an ecology maintaining zones outside the disciplinary archipelago for those who are drawn to crime as a positive experience—because it is more exciting, more meaningful, more mysterious, more transcendental, more religious than any other experience they have known[16]—or campaigns to exterminate them.[17]

The forty-five-year-old alcoholic imprisoned for robbery has, when released, the range of alternatives drastically reduced. The eighteen-year-old Black adolescent who is released on parole in the ghetto with a prison record has few alternatives to theft and drug dealing. The range of alternatives is reduced already with each truancy from school being recorded, each defective report card. In multiple penitentiary enclosures—foster homes, public assistance institutions, social workers with their disciplining of space, public schools, residential apprenticeships, juvenile homes, disciplinary regiments in the army and the marines, prisons, hospitals, asylums—delinquents are being progressively manufactured.[18] Delinquents are not outlaws, nomads prowling about the confines of the docile and frightened citizenry; delinquency is not constituted through successive exclusions from the social order, but through successive inclusions under ever more insistent surveillance.

In fact delinquents do not constitute a multitude of individuals upon whom the technology of the disciplinary archipelago has proven ineffective, and who are at large conducting a guerrilla war on its institutions. They are an identified, documented group, maintained under surveillance outside and used by the forces of order to maintain under surveillance the whole network of their contacts and their milieux. They are recruited and put to use. It is not the prostitute who lives off renting her body for pay who threatens the disciplinary structure of society, but the possibility of women generally going to singles bars for casual adventure and occasional supplementary income. The prostitutes are quickly identified by the police for whom they are needed as available forced informers; they are used by the molders of public opinion to justify the power and discourse that maintains the disciplinary structure of the family and the posts in the coded social space.

The prison precipitates the organization of a delinquent population, closed in upon itself, in relations of hostility and mutual suspicion with the strata of society from which the delinquents come. It extends its surveillance and supervision to delinquents when they are released and to the milieux into which they are released, making possible the recruiting of informers and stool pigeons. Through prohibitions on residence, probation control, and unemployment, delinquents are induced to carry out the tasks of infiltrating, rendering disreputable, and provoking into adventurism other segments of the population involved in unrest, dissidence, or illegalities. Delinquents are not only the objects of the policing of society, but its accomplices and double agents.

What about the proud and brave who are convicts, those of whom Mailer wrote that prison can only anneal them until they are harder than the steel that encloses them? It was because the monarchy that tortures shares the exhilaration of torturing with the public it assembles, as, today, the legislature that decrees capital punishment shares the pleasure of exterminating with readers of newspapers and spectators of television,[19] that it makes itself accepted.

Prisons are both the failure of the disciplinary archipelago and its loci of concentration. Today the prisons, ever multiplying, are not enough. Torture is being reinvented everywhere, and in republican societies (the incarceration of drug addicts is torture; high-tech maximum security federal prisons such as Marion are listed by Amnesty International as loci of torture). The methods advocated by 18th-century penologists—sequestrations, seizures of all personal property, forced denunciations and entrapment—are being added to incarceration.

Suffering is not simply debilitation; there rises up, in the substance of the body that suffers, a power of endurance, which can generate powers to devise mockeries, evasions, ruses, and even posthumous subversions. The suffering of the torture victim delivered him or her from guilt and delivered him or her to glory, or produced the strength to blaspheme and curse his or her judges, king, and God. In quarries and mines being dynamited, along roads being repaired and bridges being built worked with forced labor, bodies which were sentenced to write large the civil code in social space are inscribing another deposition. The travail of the schooled, barracked, proletarianized, hospitalized, and institutionalized can make intractability a pleasure and give rise to disciplined sedition. Prisons can anneal the bodies of convicts until they are harder than the steel that encloses them.

Endurance is not simply the passivity of a material organism; it slowly generates a skill or an art of endurance. When it functions as a skill in subversion of the disciplinary archipelago, it also confirms and reinforces that disciplinary archipelago: delinquents are its accomplices and double agents. Can it become an art of creating a space outside the disciplinary archipelago? Who is there to teach such an art?

The Voluptuous Subjection

Our bodies, substances of pain which can be marked and utilized, are also substances of pleasures. Mechanisms of power are contrived and fastened onto these voluptuous substances, mechanisms that produce power and knowledge. The voluptuous emotion that simmers in these substances is itself a power, a power exercised on those substances themselves as well as on other such substances.

Sexualized Natures.

Foucault finds that, at the end of the eighteenth century, four new strategic areas were isolated and specific power-knowledge apparatuses were contrived on them.[20]

The bodies of women were qualified, and disqualified, as substances wholly saturated with hysteric sexuality. Wholly *hysterike*, that is, a womb (*hystera*)—and hysterical, that is, subject to dislocations and shiftings of the womb, for the womb from Hippocratic times was taken to be a mobile organ whose displacements in the space of the female abdomen were taken to be the cause of female psychoneurological excitability and of disturbances of the sensory, vasomotor, and visceral functions. In conception, clothing, and practice, while the expanses, nipples, orifices of the virile body were desensitized, anaesthetized, and male orgasmicity was wholly located in the erected penis, all the expanses and pulp of the female body about the womb were saturated with sexual excitability. Female nature became unsettled, irresolute, neurasthenic, pathogenic. The instability and corruptibility of female nature made its forces without force, reliable for nothing but generation; its materiality was maternity. It was set under the family alliance as a material substrate of a set of power relationships.

The pharmacist and the surgeon were displaced by the family doctor, set up as the ultimate instance of decision about maternity and childbearing, and about the specifically maternal weaknesses and liabilities. By her susceptibility to vapors, fevers, miasmas, her fainting spells, her long bouts of bedriddenness, her enigmatic female ailments, the spouse withdrew from her subjection to her husband to subject her body to the knowledge and powers of the doctor. As such she was individuated in her nature; medicine was set up scientifically at the end of the eighteenth century as the first science of the individual. The agitations that the diagnostic eye scrutinized in this maternal substance were the individuating signs—more exactly, the *indexes*—about which this science elaborated its theoretical generalizations and its individuating praxes.

A second strategic area was the onanistic body of children. Childhood was subjected now to perpetual surveillance, not as the time of emergence of manual, intellectual, and economic powers and responsibilities, but as the age of masturbatory discharges. The infantile body was constituted as a substance that is a constant temptation for itself, a volume of pleasures ever on hand but in which vigor and future are being undermined. The masturbating child was taken to be wasting his substance and permanently prejudicing his physical growth, his nervous stability, his future sexual competence and potency, his mental alertness, his moral will. In the name of these dangers, the child was delivered over to the authority and power of governesses, pastors, headmasters, and educators. The pedagogical institutions which confined the child and subjected him to surveillance, also owed their authority and their power to this substance constituted as masturbatory. The pedagogical powers adjusted upon the body of the child functioned to intensify the sensations of onanism, and to invest the child with knowledge and counter-powers that locked into the adult powers set up over his so portentous compulsions.[21]

A third strategic area was the procreative performance of the couple. For a mercantilist directorate, population was wealth; for an imperialist politics, population was arms. Specific agencies for investigation, for planning, for financing, for verification, and for control were set up about projects to regulate the birthrate, the contraceptive practices, abortions, public housing, paternity responsibilities and childcare payments. They were set up not only to incite fertility, but also to administer the methods and devices that would sterilize bad blood, criminal inheritance, precocious and devitalized, senile, reproductive organs, and degenerate genes. The reproductive organs were isolated, subjected to examination, surveillance, and to economic, racist, imperialist finalities.

As geneticists conceived of the organism, not as a system endowed with, as one of its peculiarities, a reproductive capacity, but instead as the sustaining hull, itself perishable, about the genetic code for which it exists, so for the new complexes of power-knowledge agencies the reproductive organs and the genetic code of the couple were the ultimate substrate and interpretand beneath all the codes of kinship alliance, domesticity, romance, and leisure.

Finally, the whole field of sexual practices that had fallen outside of the codes and mechanisms that regulated the family structure became in the eighteenth and nineteenth centuries the concern of new mechanisms of power.[22] The prostitute, an amasser of wealth in a time when economic upheavals and imperialist adventures populated cities and ports with men far from their families, became, with her or his clients, the focus of power operations on the part of innkeepers, procurers, police, blackmailers, and protectors in high places; in addition, as a woman who refused maternity, an unnatural woman, the female prostitute and, as a man that gives himself over to the desires of others, the male prostitute were subjected to the new scrutiny and authority of the psychiatrist.

Psychiatry separated itself from general medicine by postulating a specific pathology of the sexual instinct. Debauchery, a phenomenon of excess or of libertinage, was reformulated as perversion. Wantonness was now changed from an act into a nature. Debauchery, in the Renaissance understanding, was done out of libertinage; it was an act of domination and a pleasure that one gave oneself once one had willfully determined to disobey the law for the sake of disobeying the law and to posit oneself as sovereign. For Sade, sodomy was the supreme libertine act, for he interpreted it biblically, as the use of the erected male organ not for pleasure bonding nor for the reproduction of the race, but to gore and disembowel one's partner and release the germ of the race only in its excrement. It was an act directed, then, against the human genus as such, the ultimate substrate for all the generality of discourse and of norms; it was the act by which one posited oneself in sovereign singularity. If sodomy became a mania for the libertine, the same act continually reiterated without modification or development, this was not the sign that it issued blindly from a bound instinct; it was repeated out of lucid and free decision, out of a willed asceticism of apathy, in order to free one's acts from the inconstant suggestions of pleasure.[23] The psychiatry of the nineteenth century substantized this act of transgression into a nature; there were homosexuals—the species was named in 1870—who rarely or never perform an act of sodomy, but who had a distinctive past, childhood, history, way of life, character, also a specific anatomy and nervous system which was manifested in the style of movements, tics, and gestures, in intonations of voice, in taste in colors and in artistic styles, and in certain kinds of ideas. The famous sexologists of the nineteenth century, Havelock Ellis, Krafft-Ebbing, and Rohleder, identified as many species of pervert as there are nonreproductive libidinal acts—mixoscopophiles, presbytophiles, necrophiliacs, copraphagists, zoophiles, and so on. Psychiatry gave itself importance by tracking down these strange breeds in schools, in monasteries, in isolated farms, in the clubs and mansions of the aristocrats, in ships at sea, in prisons, and in the undergrounds of cities. It drew up methods to identify them, procedures to entrap them—methods and procedures used by a vice police in blackmailing them and the espionage services in using them. Psychiatric literature also gave them a notoriety which would be profitable to owners of cabarets and publishers of illustrated magazines, and finally to themselves.

The agencies constructed about the arena of pleasures and practices outside of the family constituted a new archipelago of power that succeeded the power system set up to regulate marriage as alliance. But the new agencies of sexuality—the family doctor, the pedagogues, the social workers, and the psychiatrist—were called upon to resolve problems within marriage; the result was a sexual individuation of figures in the husband-wife, parents-children axes of the family. There now appeared the unsatisfiable wife, the frigid spouse, the indifferent mother or the mother with murderous obsessions, the impotent, sadistic, perverted husband, the hysterical or neurasthenic daughter, the precocious and already exhausted child, the homosexual who refuses marriage or neglects his wife. The axes of the family were henceforth not only relationships of economic and political commitment and nutritive and protective support; the personages of the family institution became individuated through sexual practices and pleasures identified and culpabilized. The family space became an arena where sexually individuating pleasures and practices were implanted in its members by experts, but subjected to the laws of alliance; the family became incestuous.[24]

Aristocratic Blood, Bourgeois Semen.
The place of this newly circumscribed domain of sexual identities, open to the power and delineated by the discourse of doctors, pedagogues, social workers, and psychiatrists, was the bourgeois family; it was itself that the bourgeoisie first organized with these agencies and these discourses. The feudal aristocracy had looked back to its ancestry, its bloodlines, for the authentification of its power; the bourgeoisie, a class with a future, looked instead to its descendence. The scientifico-technological preoccupation with sexualities, coded medically, was, positively, a concern for progeny. The thrust of power was not, negatively, on the repression of gratuitous pleasures, but, positively, on maximizing wholesome reproductive vigor.

The aristocracy had affirmed the specificity of their bodies; nobility is first a vital, corporeal, characteristic. Blood took on distinctive value in a society where power was monopolized power to put to death, to shed blood; where sovereignty was transmitted through bloodlines; where the orders of society are hereditary castes; and where famine, epidemics, and wars were the principal concerns of power.[25] For the bourgeoisie the distinctive value of sex will replace that of blood. The bourgeois affirmed the political value of their bodies in ensuring the health and vigor of their sexual practices. They set forth longevity and auspicious progeny as the authentification of their right to rule. Wholesome sexuality in a body became the publicness or sociality of the corporeal substance, not as a meaning, a telos, or a sign, but as a certification, a seal.

Disciplinary Biopolitics.

Disciplinary apparatuses—schools, barracks, factories, prisons, hospitals—in which our bodies are inserted, which technologically increase the utility of our individuated bodies and increase knowledge—proliferate; the bourgeois family as the matrix of truth and power continually depreciates. The individuating technologies of the disparate agencies of sexuality are relayed by those of the diverse sectors of the disciplinary archipelago. Inserted into disciplinary spaces, women, children, couples, and deviants can be made into tractable substances of pain-pleasure susceptibility. Their individuated powers and discourses can enter into the strategic policies of biological management. The twentieth century has seen the micro-agencies set up for the management of population, race, and the species integrated into the overall policies of the contemporary state.

The circuits of state power connect the large number of mechanisms that have been devised to inquire into—to subject to observation and regulation—the birth rate and the childbearing age, birth prevention and abortions, the genetic coding of progeny; to subject to documentation and control the migrations of populations; to supervise health and aging. This biopolitics is being formulated in the archaic terminology of rights—the right to life, to health, to the management of one's body, to happiness, to the satisfaction of needs. But in reality its campaigns are conducted in view of the appropriation of the positive forces of life by power and by knowledge, conducted in view of the incitement, reinforcement, surveillance, and management of forces, the increase of potentialities and of results.

A Confessional Science of Sex.

Discourse proliferates about the four kinds of sexually individuated bodies that got identified, compounded, and fixed at the end of the eighteenth century. This discourse is not that of an *ars erotica* such as that which great civilizations in India, in China, in Persia, produced: a magisterial and initiatory teaching of the varieties, specific kinds, durations, and reverberations of pleasure, a teaching designed to extend and intensify the realm of pleasures and thereby to produce absolute mastery of the body, unique enjoyment, an oblivion of time and its threats.

The truth of sex in the West in modern times was produced, not in sexual pedagogy, which was virtually nonexistent, nor in initiation, usually silent or accompanied with laughter and derision, but in the formulations of confessional literature. The first specifically Western form of discourse about sexuality was confession—first, sacramental confession, then a desacralized and commercial literature of confession.[26] In its monastic usage confession meant an explicit report of one's acts, impulses, thoughts, desires, and feelings. In medieval civil society the term "confession" had meant a testification of status, identity, value, a certification of one's family, allegiance, and protection, which was made to authenticate what one said. It meant in the torture of the ancien régime the forcing out into the open of one's inner insurgent and regicide nature. The production of truth by confession, which ceased to be the fundamental method to produce truth in penal institutions during the age of the Republican reformers, found a whole new region in which to invest, that of the practices and pleasures of sexualized individuals. The doctor assigned to the mother, the pedagogue to the child, the social worker to the couple, and the psychiatrist to the pervert subject these individuals to interrogations, confrontations, hypnosis, and free-association sessions.

The West also produced forms of public discourse about sexual practices. It produced economic and political discussions about population, a rational and technical discourse designed for the administration of sexual practices by specific public agencies. It produced a silent discourse about sexual pleasures in the architecture of school buildings, hospitals, and prisons and the layout of desks, recreational spaces, and dormitories. It produced medical, psychiatric, and penal discourses about the kinds of sexually individuated bodies. Interrogations, questionnaires, interviews, biographies, and surveys supplied the data which these various kinds of public discourse organized, coded in rational and calculative vocabularies and grammar, recast in the pseudo-scientific form of medicine, and worked into legislative decrees.

The secret of sex that is confessed has to be interpreted by another. Sexual practices will be interpreted no longer in the register of fault and sin, excess or transgression, but according to the axes of the normal and the pathological. The hermeneutics of sexual data will delineate a pathology of instincts behind unhealthy tendencies, images, pleasures, and practices—abnormal and pathogenic, in turn, of physical and psychic maladies.

The truth confessed produces power effects. The pastoral practice of confession was designed to produce specific effects on the desire that is formulated in discourse—mastery of and detachment from desire, spiritual conversion toward God; it was designed to intensify the identifying signs of temptation and of the solicitations of grace. In the laicized forms of confession, the specific effects of confession are therapeutic, not only in that the conclusions gleaned prescribe medical treatments, but in that the truth itself produced confessionally is now taken to *heal*.

But the effects of the truth produced by confession are multiple. The confessional subjugation intensifies the depths of sexual inclinations and obsessions in the one confessing, electrifies the surfaces of contact and of sexual inscription, and dramatizes the troubled moments and the phantasms. And the powers that subjugate in these apparatuses give themselves a dividend of pleasure—the pleasures of subjecting to interrogation, of pursuit, of espionage, of maintaining surveillance, the pleasures of surprising and exasperating and provoking betrayal. And these pleasures of knowledge and power induce new pleasures in those subjected to them—pleasures of defying, of scandalizing, of parodying, of shamming, pleasures of captivating and seducing in turn. The power maneuvers between parents and children, adults and adolescents, educators and students, doctors and patients, psychiatrists and perverts, social workers and parents turn in reinforcing spirals of pleasure.

Confession is a procedure of truth-production; it is also a procedure of individuation. The injunction to confess, issuing from multiple mechanisms of power, postulates lines of consequences to be tracked down, a clandestine causality of the sexual drive. Sexual conduct is sought out as the cause of bad behavior in children, phthisis in adults, apoplexy in the aged, nervous illness, the degeneration of the racial stock. The confessional imperative identifies a general and concealed sexual causality as the principle of individual significations, values, and tastes in the subject of attribution. In the end nothing will be more individual than our sexual tastes and our sexual penchants, and our discourse, our interests, our conducts, and our commitments, with which we figure as moments of the common discourse of a society and as supports of common projects and undertakings, are singularized inasmuch as they also refer to, and are interpretable as symptoms of, our sexual tastes and appetites.

Conspiratorial Strategies of Dismemberment.
The sexual liberation movements of recent times have taken the form of a struggle of the representatives of sexuality to emancipate themselves from the law of alliance. Women assert their sexual identity and struggle to liberate themselves from the patriarchical law. Children and adolescents finance cults to youth folk heroes who sing the pleasures of premarital sexual gratification. Couples claim the right to birth control practices and the legitimacy of a couple that aborts its offspring. "Perverts" set up their own clubs, places of

encounter and dens of pleasure, and fight the police, the courts, and public opinion for the protection of their combat zones.

The sexual liberation advanced is that of hystericized women, narcissistic adolescents, sterile couples, and proud perverts struggling to assert their identities, to valorize them by founding and protecting institutions, spaces, and organs of power and of knowledge for themselves. They take themselves to be repressed, subjugated to the laws of the family, the laws of the sovereign patriarch, reinforced by a patriarchical state apparatus. But in reality, today the enclosed spaces of disciplining, the panoptical surveillance, and the individuation by disciplinary examinations and norms transmogrify our bodies as the old laws of alliance no longer do. The school system is far more effective than the family in its capillary application of power; it succeeds in making public accountants and junior executives—whose body parts are distributed in cellularized space, whose body movements are meticulously regulated by timetables, whose bodies are permeable to the impersonal surveillance of corporate bodies, and whose operations are responsive to the signals of programs—of those that the family apparatus proved impotent to transform into responsible fathers, faithful wives, or respectful children. The army and the transnational corporation are far more effective mechanisms to render bodies compliant and efficacious at a time when the family demonstrates its impotence to make women mothers, adolescents self-controlled, couples fertile and home-oriented, and perverts straight.

These individuated figures of sexuality are not natural species which a monolithic culture represses and a politico-economic authority oppresses. It is the medicalization of the body of the woman and the elevation of the figure of the doctor into the authority, power, and wealth he manipulates today that has made the woman know herself as a sexually saturated substance. The incarceration of infancy in the power systems of pedagogy has constituted the child's body as vulnerable and an object of power operations by reason of a narcissist and onanist sensuality diffused throughout it. The network of social-work programs, fiscal systems, and population management has made the heterosexual couple into responsible or delinquent biopolitical agents. The sado-masochist, pederast, gerontophile, homosexual, fetishist, etc. are made by the psychiatrists and by their accomplices—the pastors, the pedagogues, the police—just as the delinquent is produced by the penitentiary archipelago and pursues a career within it which feeds its knowledge and serves its power. The psychiatrists, along with the priests, the pedagogues, the police, the advertisers, and the stockholders constitute, produce, and regulate the pervert, and organize and augment his forces for the production of their power and their riches, as well as of their forms of cognition and their pleasures.

The sexual revolution is proclaimed in the name of "sex." What is this new concept now taken to be fundamental, the source, the cause, and the secret, the generating source of each one's nature and the principle of his or her intelligibility? It is, Foucault says, an artificial compound of anatomical elements, biological functions, behaviors, sensations, and pleasures set up as a causal principle.[27] It is set up as the formula that gives us access to an understanding of our identity, our behavior, the totality of our bodies. In reality this "sex" is a construct formed in the practice and the discourse that sexualizes bodies—as hystericized mother, masturbating child, Malthusian couple, and pervert; it is reified as the causal and intelligible principle of which hysteria, onanism, coitus interruptus, and fetishism are taken to be the symptoms.

Will these personages—the hystericized woman, the narcissist child, the Malthusian couple, and the pervert—succeed in emancipating themselves from the codes and power mechanisms of the patriarchical family? Will they emerge as the dominant forms in which we are subjects of sexuality and subjected to sexuality? Will they in turn be subjected to the multiplying mechanisms of discipline, and the global strategies of biopolitics?

Foucault does invoke a possible counter-strategy, in the name of bodies and pleasures and knowledges, in their multiplicity and in their disparate possibilities of resistance. "Mastery and awareness of one's own body can be acquired only through the effect of an investment of power in the body: gymnastics, exercises, muscle-building, nudism, glorification of the body beautiful." Insistent, persistent, meticulous work of power on bodies leads to desiring one's own body. "But once power produces this effect, there inevitably emerge the responding claims and affirmations, those of one's own body against power, of health against the economic system, of pleasure against the moral norms of sexuality, marriage, decency. Suddenly, what had made power strong becomes used to attack it. Power, after investing itself in the body, finds itself exposed to a counter-attack in that same body."[28]

In the first volume of *The History of Sexuality*, Foucault wrote of an *ars erotica*, like that which other civilizations—China, India, Persia—produced, a magisterial art and teaching of pleasures and of their powers. In different interviews during the last years of his life, he spoke of the artist-ideal—not only of the art of knowing how to multiply and intensify pleasures and powers, but also of an art that would make of those pleasures and powers an artwork. "What strikes me is the fact that in our society, art has become something which is related only to objects and not to individuals, or to life. That art is something which is specialized or which is done by experts who are artists. But couldn't everyone's life become a work of art? Why could the lamp or the house be an art object, but not our life?"[29] An *ars erotica*, then, which would teach, not only skills in obtaining pleasures and acceding to their powers, but an aesthetics of bodies and of pleasures and of their powers.

What could such an art be, in an age of biopolitical administration? Can an *ars erotica* be an epic or heroic art? Would it be but a minor art—flower arranging of tropical orchids, after the swords have been melted into the transistor circuitry that is programming the final epidemic and the unending nuclear winter? Where is there the master that could tell?

The Insistence on Correspondence

Kamitake Hiraoka was a child when the disciplinary archipelago of militarized Japan ended in the thermonuclear apocalypse. From the ashes of the defeat, the disciplinary archipelago of the economic high-growth Japan would be built. But wandering in the ashes, the child Kamitake Hiraoka sensed an immemorial cosmic doom, the emptiness in the passage of the sensory world about us, the void in the Heraclitean flux of time.

> My first—unconscious—encounter [with the sun] was in the summer of the defeat, in the year 1945. A relentless sun blazed down on the lush grass of that summer that lay on the borderline between the war and the postwar period—a borderline, in fact, that was nothing more than a line of barbed wire entanglements, half broken down, half buried in the summer weeds, tilting in all directions. I walked in the sun's rays, but had no clear understanding of the meaning they held for me.
>
> Finespun and impartial, the summer sunlight poured down prodigally on all creation alike. The war ended, yet the deep green weeds were lit exactly as before by the merciless light of noon, a clearly perceived hallucination stirring in a slight breeze; brushing the tips of the leaves with my fingers, I was astonished that they did not vanish at my touch.
>
> That same sun, as the days turned to months and the months to years, had become associated with a pervasive corruption and destruction. In part, it was the way it gleamed so encouragingly on the wings of planes

leaving on missions, on forests of bayonets, on the badges of military banners; but still more, far more, it was the way it glistened on the blood flowing ceaselessly from the flesh, and on the silver bodies of flies clustering on wounds. Holding sway over corruption, leading youth in droves to its death in tropical seas and countrysides, the sun lorded it over that vast rusty-red ruin that stretched away to the distant horizon.[1]

Kamitake Hiraoka fled the sun into the nocturnal existence of the intellectual. He devoted himself to words, and in them found another sun that reduces the ashes themselves to void.

The Words

Kamitake Hiraoka was a master of words at a prodigiously young age.[2] There is mastery in words themselves. Words fix as objectives, as objects, termini, the reliefs on the foaming surf of time before which we stand—or rather, the foaming surf of time in which we are being swept away. "By marking off each moment, they ceaselessly chop up life's sense of continuity, they act in a way that seems at least to translate the void into substance of a kind."[3]

> Through the accumulation of these "endings," through the moment-to-moment rupture of life's sense of continuity, words acquire a certain power. At the very least they diminish to some degree the overwhelming terror of the vast white walls in the waiting room where we await the arrival of the physician, the absolute.[4]

But Kamitake Hiraoka found that to master words is to master a medium that reduces reality to its inner skeletons. "Any art that relies on words makes use of their ability to eat away—of their corrosive function—just as etching depends on the corrosive power of nitric acid...."[5]

The words themselves die away at the forms they etch out. In doing so they have the ability to eat away at, disintegrate, time. "It might be more appropriate, in fact, to liken their action to that of excess stomach fluids that digest and gradually eat away the stomach itself."[6]

Fleeing the sun that lorded it over that vast rusty-red ruin of the world, Kamitake Hiraoka sought himself in the night in which he mastered words. He found himself in words, consumed by words. "If only one can direct the eye of self-awareness so intently towards the interior and the self that self-awareness forgets the outer forms of existence, then one can 'exist' as surely as the 'I' in Amiel's *Diary*. But this existence is of an odd kind, like a transparent apple, whose core is fully visible from the outside; and the only endorsement of such existence lies in words."[7] Self-consciousness is, metaphorically, described as an immanent intuition, a ray of sight turned inward, or as a reflection, a mirror surface on which the movements of one's life can be watched. What the eye can then see, in the transparency of the core, are words inscribing themselves on one's inner agitations, one's appetites, one's hungers. To be conscious of one's states and acts is to accompany them with a commentary: I am breathing, I am hungry, I am looking for... I am doubting, I am thinking of... I am.

The words, which, like nitric acid, eat away at the outer surfaces of things to etch out their essences, eat through the surface contours with which one's own skin, that vital borderline which divides our exterior from our interior, endorses our separateness and our form.[8] Etching out hollows on our surfaces, the words eat away at the inner plenum of the body.

That which gets articulated in words on the surface of self-consciousness— the skeletal forms of intentions, wants, and needs—is, Nietzsche says, "the most superficial and worst part."[9] Superficial, because wants, needs, and intentions are negativities only possible in a material organism which is at bottom plenitude, a body which fully, forcefully, excessively occupies a physical space,[10] an occupancy that can engender the surplus force required for an initiative, even when it is needy. In the voids opened by needs and wants—these moribund spaces—the imagination plays—the morbidity of imagination.

That which gets articulated on the surface of self-consciousness is, Nietzsche said, "the worst part" because wants and needs are addressed to others, and formulate life as dependency. They interest the will to subjugate in others. The life that formulates itself in self-consciousness makes itself servile. "The sphere of which we can become conscious is only a surface- and sign-sphere, a sphere that is made common and meaner; whatever becomes conscious *becomes* by the same token shallow, thin, relatively stupid, general, sign, herd signal; all becoming conscious involves a great and thorough corruption, falsification, reduction to superficialities, and generalization."[11]

Kamitake Hiraoka knew the fevered darkness of night in which words work, eating away at the skins with which realities surface in the sun, the vital borderlines that endorse their separateness. He knew the dry, lusterless skins and sagging stomachs of men who indulged in nocturnal thought, inscribing words over their visceral sensations. The acid of those words eats away at the stomach itself, doubling up visceral needs with needs for others.

The words added to one's visceral cravings make them the more empty. The inner artistry of a life that endorses itself with words makes movements that terminate as they fix their designs. They chop up the continuity of the existence in the plenum of the body.

The Taciturn Body

Self-consciousness seeks through all the words it utters and that flow back into it a substance in the physical space one occupies. It calls for the body as the ideal opposite of the skeletons etched out by its words. This ideal body is counterposited to, and by, the negativity of words as "existence." It can be summed up, Kamitake Hiraoka says, in taciturnity and beauty of form.

The words fade out as soon as they are proffered or imagined, washed away by the cold waters of time, leaving the mind waiting for the Yuzen fabric to appear mute and splendid. The visceral sensations die away, the words fixed on them fade out in the inner night, and one waits for the body occupying its physical space with the *formositas*, the beauty, of its form.

The corrosive words that invoke this body must not touch it; they must be kept at the distance of their longing for it. Kamitake Hiraoka resolved to keep this acid far from the existents. He used the words of self-consciousness to construct fictitious personages, confessions of the masks that covered over and protected the physical space he occupied. The name "Yukio Mishima" is the mask Kamitake Hiraoka gave himself when, at the age of sixteen, he published "A Forest in Full Flower." The autobiography he published he entitled *Confessions of a Mask*.[12]

The body maintained as an ideal district at an absolute distance from words gave its telos to the only possible positive usage of words: the ideal in the verbal arts must lie solely in the imitation of the formal beauty of the taciturn and statuesque body. It is what made Mishima's writing that of a classicist. He will write plays for Nô theater, words uttered by the formal beauty of masks worn by *onnagatas*, transvestites.

The Physical Clairvoyance

There were days when gongs were heard in the street, and Mishima would run to his window to look for what he had once seen in his early childhood: young Japanese men with eyes turned to the sun.

They were bearing that day an old and heavy shrine on their shoulders. Bodies gleaming with sweat, they struggled under its weight, which seemed to compress power into them—they crashed through the gates of the Hiraoka home and trampled the courtyard to ruins.

> They were intoxicated with their task, and their expressions were of an indescribable abandon, their faces averted; some of them even rested the backs of their necks against the shafts of the shrine they shouldered, so

that their eyes gazed up at the heavens. And my mind was much troubled by the riddle of what it was that those eyes reflected.

As to the nature of the intoxicating vision that I detected in all this violent physical stress, my imagination provided no clue. For many a month, therefore, the enigma continued to occupy my mind; it was only much later, after I had begun to learn the language of the flesh, that I undertook to help in shouldering a portable shrine, and was at last able to solve the puzzle that had plagued me since infancy. They were simply looking at the sky. In their eyes there was no vision: only the reflection of the blue and absolute skies of early autumn. Those blue skies, though, were unusual skies such as I might never see again in my life: one moment strung up high aloft, the next plunged to the depths; constantly shifting, a strange compound of lucidity and madness.[13]

The eyes of the shrine-bearers were not opened to the thaumaturgic force of a religious icon or a participationist myth. What lifted their eyes was not an idea, from the old religions, that would have its own consistency, maintained through verbal constructions, and that would justify itself and justify the world it comprehends into itself. Are there any words that could refract the light of the sun from the blood flowing ceaselessly from the flesh and the silver bodies of flies clustering on wounds?

Ideas are foreign to the body. Ideas can take possession of the mind unbidden, with the suddenness of a stroke of fate. Their fatality can invade the determinism of the automatic, uncontrollable functions of the organism and leave it spread-eagled and bleeding with their stigmata. The body of Christ, a body crucified not by the will of his enemies but by the Word of which it was wholly the enfleshment, is an icon of the fatality of ideas and their fatal effect on the body.

What spoke to Kamitake Hiraoka so eloquently was the massed bodies of the shrine-bearers. It is an eloquence one believes—one does not believe the intoxication of feeble or debauched bodies; what they say one consigns to pathology and private compensations. One believes the eloquence of health and power. The body insists on correspondence and fittingness—strength in the body is this insistence.

Mishima's mind, his verbal virtuosity or his imagination, was not able to join the ecstatic vision that illuminated the shrine-bearers. It was only when his body had become powerful enough to correspond with and fit in with theirs that he discovered that what they saw was the "swaying blue sky that, like a fierce bird of prey with wings outstretched, alternatively swept down and soared upwards to infinity,"[14] making surge in its shadow the substantiality of the world in phosphorescent impermanence. "Glory was surely a name given to just such a light—inorganic, superhuman, naked, full of perilous cosmic rays."[15]

The Eloquence of the Body

Mishima went to find the body that insists on correspondence and fittingness with bared existence in the tempering of his organism by steel—"heavy, forbidding, as though the essence of the night had in [it] been still further condensed."[16] He fitted his arms, legs, torso to the inertia, opaque weight, mineral death of the steel. In the coupling of organism with steel, the vital substance with the extreme condensation of night and death, there was not competent intentional force shaping inert substance into implements, but a transference of properties. The properties that came to compose the excess musculature came from the steel and were its own properties. In the contact with the substance of steel, Mishima found a body become ferric substance.

This is not the gearing into the world of implements, which Merleau-Ponty's phenomenology declared to be reality; it is not the resolution to inhabit one's body as an intentionally conducted functional system, which existence philosophy declares to be the primary form of comprehension and the fundamental form of selfhood. The body that takes hold of the instrumentality of things—their utility, the sense of their existence—identifies its own existence with its competence. But in this seeking of the sense of existence in the sense of some object, Mishima says, we "can only live in the false world of relativity."[17]

How strange to seek in the death and night of steel the body that could open to the sun and skies! If what one is seeking is the open skies and the universal light that illuminates all reality, all impermanence, is not this ascent to the universal necessarily through words, all generic, all universals? Is it not language that Being inhabits, the Being that through its meaning determines what is and what is not, determines that earth and skies are, that mortals are, and that immortals are? Does not, as all Western ontology has understood, the body exist as a particular, a hic et nunc; do not its appetites bind to it only the particular? Is it not what has to be transcended in order to accede to the universal?

Mishima found that the mastery of words—the appropriation of things and of oneself effected in words—consists of using words in singular, deviant ways. Words too exist in the present progressive tense; their force exists in dying away. Every verbal construction once found illuminating fades away in being repeated. New verbal formulations jolt the mind that passes along the grooves of discourse; this moment of surprise, this jump, is the leap of the spirit. It is produced, Cioran wrote,[18] through an inappropriate conjunction of adjective with noun, a distortion of grammar. With these stratagems, intellectual work combining words produces moments of astonishment that induce the mind to stop and gape at reality. The illumination that words produce is in this astonishment—the staring at things that had been passed over as familiar. The insight that apparently captures the universal essence is the moment when the mind is jolted and perplexed through the effect of a word that names this hammer in one's hands "form," "substance," "reality," "objectivity," or "being." The mind, Cioran said, is one with *preciousness* in style. It is maintained by producing astonishment with oneself, devising new words—"spirit," "soul," "consciousness," "subjectivity," "free will," "individuality," "ego," etc.—to provoke wonder over oneself. The artistry of words, Mishima understood, consists in a subtle arrangement of words, which excites the reader's imagination to an extreme degree, thus making words the medium for a contagion of the individual's singularity. "Author and reader become accomplices in a crime of the imagination."[19]

There once existed, to be sure, essentially impersonal and monumental words with which epic art was composed. But the conditions for their functioning are lost to us today, and Mishima comes gradually to divine the reasons why.

It is in the density and night of matter that Mishima makes contact with the universal. The opaque weight of the steel makes the muscular body tempered by it *generic*. It drives out idiosyncratic psychic penchants that had particularized the body—indolence incarnated in a slovenly posture, sensuality or impressionability materialized in dry, lusterless skin and flaccid abdomen. The night and death of steel brought out, empowered, affirmed, the generic, the animal type, in the individual body. As a generic individual, the body would be the receptacle for the universal; its strength, which is its inner insistence on correspondence and fittingness, would also, as in the essentially epic and not eccentric vision of the shrine-bearers, be the medium of communication.

This body is no longer the taciturn and resplendent ideality of form, which words designate in a remoteness beyond contact; the night of the steel transferred into its musculature becomes lambent force. There is not a unitary and univocally oriented intentional arc mobilizing and activating a postural or motor diagram, as in the body that operates equipment; the muscular masses were multiple seats of power each energizing itself. "Muscles, I found, were strength as well as form, and each complex of muscles was subtly responsible for the direction in which its own strength was exerted, much as though they were rays of light given the form of flesh."[20]

This body as a muscular complex radiating light in all directions abstracts itself from mundane dependence—and, one day, from the steel itself—to figure as an absolute.

> Away from the steel...my muscles seemed to lapse into absolute isola-
> tion, their bulging shapes no more than cogs created to mesh with the
> steel. The cool breeze passed, the sweat evaporated—and with them the
> existence of the muscles vanished into thin air. And yet, it was then
> that the muscles played their most essential function, grinding up with
> their sturdy, invisible teeth that ambiguous, relative sense of existence
> and substituting for it an unqualified sense of transparent, peerless
> power that required no object at all. Even the muscles themselves no
> longer existed. I was enveloped in a sense of power as transparent as
> light.[21]

This absolute seeks an absolute of exposure.

The Self Exposed

Fleeing the sun in horror, the summer of the defeat, Mishima had retreated into the intellectual's cave, that dark, amorphous, warm, visceral inwardness. Now the steel had routed the self from this retreat, displaced its locus onto the surfaces. He does not feel the ridges and reliefs of his musculature from within, out of his visceral ego, but contemplates them on the surfaces of mir-rors and feels them in the cool breeze on their glistening sweat. The self had become a surface self, a self no longer in inwardness but in distension, expo-sure, and exhibition.

It is a self whose sense of the world exposed to the sun is a surface thought. For this self, thought no longer means identifying the inwardness beneath the dispersion, the substrates beneath the phenomena, the principles behind the appearances.

> Yet why must it be that men always seek out the depths, the abyss?
> Why must thought, like the plumb line, concern itself exclusively with
> vertical descent? Why was it not feasible for thought to change direc-
> tion and climb vertically up, ever up, towards the surface? Why should
> the area of the skin, which guarantees a human being's existence in
> space, be most despised and left to the tender mercies of the senses?
> I could not understand the laws governing the motion of thought—the
> way it was liable to get stuck in unseen chasms whenever it set out
> to go deep; or, whenever it aimed at the heights, to soar away into
> boundless and equally invisible heavens, leaving the corporeal form

undeservedly neglected.

If the law of thought is that it should search out profundity, whether it extends upwards or downwards, then it seemed excessively illogical to me that men should not discover depths of a kind in the "surface," that vital borderline that endorses our separateness and our form, dividing our exterior from our interior. Why should they not be attracted by the profundity of the surface itself?

The sun was enticing, almost dragging, my thoughts away from their night of visceral sensations, away to the swelling of muscles encased in sunlit skin. And it was commanding me to construct a new and sturdy dwelling in which my mind, as it rose little by little to the surface, could live in security. That dwelling was a tanned, lustrous skin and powerful, sensitively rippling muscles. I came to feel that it was precisely because such an abode was required that the average intellectual failed to feel at home with thought that concerned itself with forms and surfaces.[22]

The discovery of the body formed in strength as an artwork—formed into splendor not by virtue of the mute proportions it fixed but by its distribution of rays of power—was to counterpoise itself to the words, to replace Mishima's first classical writing with a muscular style. Mishima's first classicism was animated by a constant and vigilant sense of the corrosive effect of words, maintained at a distance from reality— the distance of death, in which the voluptuous imagination that elaborates its fictions abandons itself. The eloquent and surface body Mishima has now acquired seeks words—impersonal and monumental words that disindividualize and conduct one to the contours and the reliefs, the crests that form and deform in the impermanence, in the fields of death illuminated by the perilous rays of the sun.

The Imagination That Feeds on Muscles

We might think that the world, its trees, mountains, and clouds are arrayed for our look without guile or clandestineness. In fact, the surface that we view in the world, and which does not return our scrutiny, is the presumptive outcome of a series of profiles already passed by. There is time for the word that names the object, and about that word, like barnacles on the hulk of a sunken ship, images accumulate. The surface thought must dissipate the images to make contact with the vital borderlines of things that endorse their separateness and their forms.

With the people with which we have commerce in civilized sociality, there are always contractual rules that govern every exchange of smiles, words, gestures, goods, and pleasures; we transmit coded signals down the wires of the rules, on which the scum of the imagination collects. With time, we find that our own face which we confront in the morning light is covered with makeup we can no longer remove.

Above all, the eloquence of the surface body ignites the imagination. A departicularized, generic, transparent, peerless power that requires no object at all, radiating light in all directions, the muscled body is exposed to every eccentric penchant; every phantasm spawned in the inner darkness of singularity is projected in its light. With time, the self that dwells in tanned, lustrous skin and powerful, sensitively rippling muscles sees their contours through the bombast of the imagination.

Mishima sought an existence, an exposedness that dissipated all imagination, whether of the self or of others.

The Victorious Artistry

This existence is pure action. Combat pushes existence entirely into the medium of the seen, that of exposedness. Mishima trained in karate and kendo. "It was natural that my rephrasing of the pure sense of strength should turn in the direction of the flash of the fist and the stroke of the bamboo sword, for that which lay at the end of the flashing fist, and beyond the blow of the bamboo sword, was precisely what constituted the most certain proof of that invisible light given off by the muscles."[23] Wherever one looks one is seen, and what one sees is the other's power galvanized into a look fixed on one's self wholly surfaced.

In combat one knows the mass, position, momentum, rhythms, nerves, insightfulness, and foresightfulness of the opponent with the eloquence of one's musculature. The blows of the other break through the wires across which coded signals, gestures, intentions are transmitted; they hurl through the distance of time in which the flotsam and jetsam of the imagination drift.

The "abstract quality" of muscles—their work of eating up the particularities, the eccentricities, of one's body features individuated by psychic penchants that germinated in the inner visceral darkness—now becomes a medium of communication. The disindividuated surface self shimmering across the surfaces of the musculature receives into itself the forms and forces of the other. The eloquence is that of the force of each creating form in the other.

Victory does not consist in assaulting the opponent with the superior quantity of one's force and momentum; one does not combat with those weaker than oneself. Through combat one becomes the equal of ever more powerful opponents, transferring, as in the struggle of muscles with steel, their properties onto oneself.

One's blow creates a kind of hollow in space in which the fatal blow it provokes on the part of the opponent fits perfectly. In the instant that the force of the other has taken shape, "it must already be snugly ensconced in that hollow in space that one has marked out and created."[24] The victorious blow does not crash against the ineptness of the opponent, but captures his very mastery with one's own. The power of the other has been taken possession of the instant it thunders against one's surfaces of exposure.

Victory arises as a summit of eloquence.

> At the height of the fray, I found, the tardy process of creating muscle, whereby strength creates form and form creates strength, is repeated so swiftly that it becomes imperceptible to the eye. Strength, that like light emitted its own rays, was constantly renewed, destroying and creating form as it went. I saw for myself how the form that was beautiful and fitting overcame the form that was ugly and imprecise. Its distortion invariably implied an opening for the foe and a blurring of the rays of strength....
>
> The form itself must have an extreme adaptability, a matchless flexibility, so that it resembles a series of sculptures created from moment to moment by a fluid body. The continuous radiation of strength must create its own shape, just as a continuous jet of water will maintain the shape of a fountain.
>
> Surely, I felt, the tempering by sun and steel to which I submitted over such a long period was none other than a process of creating this kind of fluid sculpture.[25]

One does not see, look at, the opponent. If one waits to see where and how the other positions himself it will be too late; one must foresee where in a fraction of a second he will be. One also does not see the figure of one's own power; every distance taken from it, to take note of it, subtracts from that power. The victorious combatant is the one who reserves nothing for after, who casts himself wholly into the instant that vanishes from itself, into the unseen hollow he makes of himself.

The victor was the subject of the highest art in Greek classicism. This art was necessary, to make a spectacle of what is a spectacle only through art: supremacy—understood only by combatants, where neither oneself nor the opponent can be a spectator at the moment it occurs. This necessary art formulates the classical judgment that the moment of victory is the supreme moment of existence; there is nothing after it or beyond it.

The Fierce Dark Flames

The insistence on correspondence and fittingness that is in the body is its strength. Courage is the name of this insistence inasmuch as it is an insistence on correspondence in the exposed body seared with pain. In the force of recoil from pain the reiterated insistence on exposure produces clarity of consciousness.

> I had begun to believe that it was the muscles—powerful, statically so well organized and so silent—that were the true source of the clarity of my consciousness. The occasional pain in the muscles of a blow that missed the shield gave rise instantly to a still tougher consciousness that suppressed the pain, and imminent shortage of breath gave rise to a frenzy that conquered it.[26]

Clarity of consciousness, unlike the self-consciousness elaborated with words, is a force. The pain searing the surfaces recoils into oneself, the self-consciousness that arises in this pain is a force that hurls the body forth into the dark clearing it sees. In the fierce dark flames of physical courage, "the flesh beats a steady retreat into its function of self-defense, while it is clear consciousness that controls the decision that sends the body soaring into self-abandonment. It is the ultimate in clarity of consciousness that constitutes one of the strongest contributing factors in self-abandonment."[27]

The fierce dark flames drive the ultimate clarity of consciousness to expose itself to death.

The Image of the Absolute

Victory is only in unconditional combat, in which everything has been cast. In the space of action, the medium of the seen, that which bears down on one when all the pomp with which imagination invests the musculature of the other is dissipated, is death. In the supreme moment, all the surfaces of the powerful body that give it its dignity are shaped by the forces of death they hold.

Without the contiguity with death, this excessive preoccupation with one's own body, on the part of a male, would be only comical. The seriousness of mundane tasks and trials in the daylight world is relative and relativizes every competence and every preoccupation with one's own form with which one objectifies one's competence. The darkness of death that bears down upon the body of the combatant freezes the gaiety of the imagination of the spectators.

"How comic would one find the gaiety and elegance of the bullfighter were his trade divorced from associations with death!"[28]

The surface thought pushes on to the outlying regions, the furthest edges of body and of spirit, seeking there the point of their contact. The point of contact—this is the ultimate principle of Buddhist ontological thought—is not at the origin, the base, the summit, nor even at the end, the telos; it is at the outer limits toward which the forms extend their impermanence. The outer limits of the body are exposure to death. It is to that extremity of exposure that one must go if one is to find within oneself the splintering of the forms and surfaces under the swaying blue sky that, like a fierce bird of prey with wings outstretched, alternatively sweeps down and soars upward to infinity. At its outer limits, where the surface body touches death, it turns into pain, and ignites the most intense clarity of consciousness. At its outer limits the surface body touches the outer limits of consciousness: the extremities of the great serpent meet. The "higher principle that manages to bring the two together and reconcile them...was death."[29]

Victory, where strength creates form and form creates strength, is not an overpowering of death. The glory of this radiant liquid sculpture is a purely worldly glory, this side of death. The supreme moment is ultimate; every effort to relativize it, to use it for the gaiety and elegance of life in comfort and riches—that is, a life preserved from strength and combat—is comical. The victor can only survive for another combat; the vainglory of the victor who commercializes or politicizes his victory makes him ridiculous. What we sense "in the bronze charioteer of Delphi, where the glory, the pride, and the shyness reflected in the moment of victory are given faithful immortality—is the swift approach of the specter of death just on the other side of the victory."[30]

The Contact at the Outer Limits

Mishima saw the great serpent, not in participating in a traditional religious ritual, but the day he boarded the F104, the most advanced supersonic jet fighter of the Japanese air force.

To push his mind, not back into his body, but toward its own outer limits, was to push it outward across the most remote regions of the universe; it was also, Mishima knew, to push it on to its own death. "Motionless before his desk [the thinker] edges his way closer, ever closer, to the borders of the spirit, in constant mortal danger of plunging into the void."[31] Death is not just a negative operator of the dialectical mind, a corrosive acid seeping through all the words the mind forms; the earth is physically surrounded by death, and

Mishima resolved to take his body to this realm of death.

First he had to undergo physiological training for flight. His body was strapped to the apparatus of the pressure chamber, immobilized. He felt the panicked brain crave desperately the air that was being sucked out of the chamber. In this chamber simulating enormous motion, even the movements of his lungs were pushed toward immobility; he felt death stick fast to his lips. This death arced back to the void before birth.

> Erect-angled, the F104, a sharp silver phallus, pointed into the sky. Solitary, spermatozoon-like, I was installed within. Soon, I should know how the spermatozoon felt at the instant of ejaculation.[32]

The plane blazed into the stratosphere of death, ascended to 35,000 feet, passed the speed of sound.

> For a moment, my chest was empty, as though a cascade of water had descended with a great rush and left nothing behind it.... Everything was quiet, majestic, and the surface of the blue sky was flecked with the semen-white of clouds.[33]

At the summit: Mach 1.3, at 45,000 feet:

> The silver fuselage floated in the naked light, the plane maintaining a splendid equilibrium. Once more it became a closed, motionless room. The plane was not moving at all. It had become, simply, an oddly-shaped metal cabin floating quite still in the upper atmosphere.[34]

In the pressure chamber the body, immobilized, pushed up against the limits of motionlessness of the mind; its lungs had to be forced by the mind. Now, enclosed in the fastest engine for motion the technological mind had invented, Mishima found the outer limits of supersonic speed rejoining the absolute rest of the pressure chamber.

> There was no suffocating sensation. My mind was at ease, my thought processes lively. Both the closed room and the open room—two interiors so diametrically opposed—could serve equally, I found, as dwellings for the spirit of one and the same human being. If this stillness was the ultimate end of action—of movement—then the sky about me, the clouds far below, the sea gleaming between the clouds, even the setting sun, might well be events, things, within myself....

Anything that comes into our minds even for the briefest of moments, exists. Even though it may not exist at this actual moment, it has existed somewhere in the past, or will exist at some time in the future....

This simple realm of cloud, sea, and setting sun was a majestic panorama, such as I had never seen before, of my own inner world. At the same time, every event that occurred within me had slipped the fetters of mind and emotion, becoming great letters freely inscribed across the heavens.

It was then that I saw the snake....

If the giant snake-ring that resolves all polarities came into my brain, then it is natural to suppose that it was already in existence.... It was a ring vaster than death, more fragrant than that faint scent of mortality that I had caught in the compression chamber; beyond doubt, it was the principle of oneness that gazed down at us from the shining heavens.[35]

The Most Natural and Decent of All Desires

Mishima finds he has at last come to understand "the desire that lurks to a greater or lesser extent in all human beings to fashion themselves, however unsuccessfully, in the image of the 'absolute' to come."[36]

This "the most natural and decent of all desires" is in fact dual, a desire for action and a desire for eloquence. These desires engender dreams of their realization. The action that desires to surface all its forces in the forms given it by contact with the absolute dreams of a memorial etched out in words to maintain fixed this form. The words that push on to contact with the truth dream that the death that pursues them and that effaces them as they are inscribed is realized in the taciturn and singular body form the words imagine behind themselves. When the words send the body soaring into self-abandonment, and when the departicularized body becomes eloquent with the eloquence of the genus, then "within one body, without flinching," the desire for action dissipates the dreams in eloquence and the desire for eloquence dissipates the dreams in action. The voluptuous images of the absolute, the inner adversary of naturalness and decency, are vanquished.

Something to Be Seen

From now on Mishima will seek to maintain himself in this soaring lucidity and this power without reverie. It will be a struggle waged against two adversaries he now recognizes: time and history—two dyings that threaten to make his presence at his death, his living in the form of his death, derisible.

The years that pass ravage the true face, that of youth, with anxiety and emotion, they undermine strength and fittingness, they emasculate, bloat, and shrivel the body behind the mask and the uniform. The endings of the rays of force stop shorter each time, leaving inglorious traces on the surface and exposed form of the body. The words that dye with gay colors and designs the lengths of fabric washed in the cold waters of time make the eye unable to perceive the true end, that is, the moment of maximum exposure. One ages: death with dignity and in honor, death as "something to be seen," is progressively sapped of the power, the youth, that alone can make it tragic rather than pathetic. Mishima, past forty, determined to end at the hour when the true end is possible. He assumed as his most pressing task the perceiving of the high noon hour when he would step forth to realize the composed and held figure of transparency without shadow delivered definitively to the absolute. Eloquence becomes a problem of time, of being put forth at the right time—the extremity of Mishima's fifteen years of regression toward youth.

This eloquence, like every eloquence, is possible only within a community. The body—whose force works on it a dissolution of individuality, particularity, eccentricity, and whose lucidity sends it soaring into self-abandonment—is a body whose eloquence is a shared pain. Such a body speaks within a community of the flesh open to death. Mishima urgently sought this community of shared suffering.

He recognized in the words selected from ready-made epic and monumental texts—with which some of the letters written on the evening before their last mission by Kamikaze pilots of Etajima were composed—evidence that such a community had once existed. These words were noble words that spurned the construction of monuments based on personal action; their impersonality and monumentality demanded the strict elimination of individuality. They were the splendid language of the flesh, words that themselves bound together a community in shared suffering.

There once were such words; they are lost to us now. The Kamikaze pilots had chosen them from an epic and monumental text inscribed long ago. The flies of history buzzed over its silence. The sharp silver phallus of their fighter planes descended into the silver bodies of flies clustering on their wounds, as their blood flowed away into tropical seas. Mishima understood he could not inscribe the eloquence of the true end he sought in the epic and monumental text of a history that had come to an end simply by shunning the literary use of language. "The demands I made on words became still more strict and exacting. I shunned the latest styles like the plague. Perhaps I was gradually seeking to rediscover the unsullied fortress of words that I had known during the war."[37] He sought the shared suffering of a community open to death; he sought its text with all the eloquence of his body.

The Imagination That Feeds on the Supreme Act

The bloodstained tropical waters of history had washed the epic and monumental text he sought into an irrecoverable past. Mishima desperately demanded from the history that rises on the West the text in which he could inscribe the eloquence he had perceived in the suffering of the history that has sunk away in the land of the rising sun. He sought to inscribe its noblest words in the text being inscribed by Western history. But Western history inscribes an onto-theological text; a transcendent signifier—the word of its God—teleologically destines it toward the death of death. Mishima invoked for himself a transcendent, substantial, transhistorical, subjective God in the Japanese emperor, whose ancestors for a thousand years had been politically impotent, speaking only unintelligible lines from forgotten epics, and whose present incarnation devoted his time to writing monographs on marine fish. He founded and trained a Shield Society, and selected young Masakatsu Morita to head it. Mishima stridently demanded grand politics and history, from which Japan's postwar Constitution had excluded it; he determined to blackmail by his own seppuku the Japanese Self-Defense Forces to force them to become an army of samurai once more. On November 25, 1970, he telephoned his friends in the media to be on hand with their television cameras. With the assembled troops beneath shouting their derision and the police helicopters circling overhead, Yukio Mishima seated himself in the commander's office in the Eastern Division Headquarters in Tokyo, drove his sword across his abdomen, and slumped forward to be beheaded by his second.

The community in shared suffering, his Shield Society, Mishima had gathered about himself, he disbanded the day of his seppuku. The eloquence of his final action he shared only with Masakatsu Morita, who was to second Mishima's seppuku, wielding the sword that was to decapitate him, before committing seppuku himself. The great serpent of Mishima's ultra-eroticism touched at its furthest extremities the fierce longing to die for a cause which had long annealed the body of this young warrior. Mishima had finally found the lover he could make his executioner.

Masakatsu Morita struck with his sword three times before Mishima's head lay on the ground. Oshima later said that it was not that Morita's strength or resolve were wanting, but that the muscles of Mishima's neck were too strong.[38] Mishima's body, anonymous, generic—transparent, peerless power that required no object at all—resisted with its own eloquence the grandiloquent death his mind had improvised.

Victory is a purely worldly glory this side of death; death is not defeated. Death is also the master of its own meaning. One shall not be able to make one's death serve one's own cause—even if it be utterly departicularized, universal—this side of death.

> Here must always arise a discrepancy between the absolute concept of death and the man-made, relativistic concept of righteousness.... We do not possess the standard for choosing to die. The fact that we are alive may mean that we have already been chosen for some purpose, and if life is not something we have chosen for ourselves, then maybe we are not ultimately free to die.[39]

The imagination that feeds on muscles leaves the image reproduced but briefly in the Western press, that of two sword-severed heads, those of Yukio Mishima and Masakatsu Morita.

> And now, left for the very end, the last and most disturbing image—so disturbing that it has rarely been reproduced. On the carpet, no doubt acrylic, of the general's office, two heads placed one next to the other as if they were skittles, almost touching one another. Two motionless heads, two brains in which blood no longer flows, two computers stopped in their work, no longer selecting and no longer decoding the perpetual flow of images, impressions, stimuli, and responses which by the millions pass each day through a human being, constituting what we call the life of the spirit, and even the life of the senses, triggering and directing the movements of the rest of the body. Two severed heads "gone to other worlds where other laws reign," arousing, when we look at them, more stupor than horror. Value judgments, be they moral, political, or aesthetic, are, at least for the moment, reduced to silence in their presence. The idea which imposes itself is more disconcerting and simpler: among the myriads of things which exist and which have existed, these two heads have been; they are. What fills those sightless eyes is no longer the unfurled banner of political slogans, or any other intellectual or carnal image, not even the Void which Honda had contemplated, and which suddenly seems nothing but a concept or symbol too human in spite of everything. Two objects, the already almost inorganic debris of destroyed structures, which once passed through the flame, will be no more than mineral residue and ash, not even subjects for meditation, because we lack the knowledge to meditate on them. Two stones, rolled along by the River of action, which the immense wave has for a moment left upon the sand, and which it then carries away.[40]

Is this the image of Mishima's and Morita's seppuku stripped of all its eloquence by the jeering of the amassed troops and the racket of police and television helicopters? Or is it the image of the impermanence laid bare when the extremities of the great serpent touch, and into whose perilous and lethal glory Mishima had delivered himself?

Western history, now planet-wide, busied itself with inscribing his act on its own text. This figment of a self that found himself in fiction had, they wrote, cut out for himself the papier-mâché mask of a samurai; this son of a defeated army had sought, by theatrics, to inscribe his force in military history. The Japanese were not mesmerized by the Emperor-God he wished to fill the empty skies over Japan with; the death of the death of God that onto-theology had inscribed in the West had never been inscribed over their Scriptures. They were silent, and went back to industry, imported from the West, which now seeks the death of death through technology; they went back to work, accumulating taciturn and beautiful possessions. Mishima's wife secluded herself with the royalties from his books. The community closes in upon itself, against the sinister carnival of Mishima's encounter with the absolute. The *gaijin* feed on cinema images of the sexual pervert, from earliest childhood voluptuously in love with death.

In the ruins of history and in the emptiness of the solar skies Yukio Mishima found in his disindividuated muscles the forces that drove him toward victory, the purely worldly glory this side of the absolute. He failed to find in the inmates of the disciplinary archipelago the community of shared suffering within which his eloquence could speak. Will we be able to find one day, beyond the disciplined discourses in which we are individuated and normalized, the epic and monumental texts of a future glory? Will we be able to find the community open to death in which our docile and delinquent and perverted bodies can share his suffering?

These Alien Feelings That Are Our Own

Classical psychology, invoking the general distinction between agent and patient in the contact between things,[1] conceived of sense-data and sensory affects—pleasures and pains—as effects left by outside agents on the passivity of our sensibility, effects which then our active minds collate and interpret. It did not discern the violent force of our pains and our pleasures, which are not simply passive, but reactive.

In pain the sensitive substance, recoiling from the impact of the outside force, finds itself backed up to itself, and seeks to retreat from or escape itself. Mired in oneself in pain, one's forces deal with the impression left on one by the aggressive blow struck from the outside, with the aftereffect or image of that blow, and not with the aggressor who has passed on.

In a social gathering, one finds oneself exposed to a caustic or demeaning remark cast one's way. The blow passes, the one who thus spoke offensively passes on to other things, to other people. One feels wounded, mortified. The feeling does not pass. One finds oneself unable to be fully present to what is now being said, and, that night, one goes over the wound, probing it, feeling it, verifying the pain. In the pain there lies the image of the aggression. Having been unable to parry the blow at the time or answer it with a counter-blow, one now works on the image: one disparages, denigrates, vituperates the other now, not in his presence, but in his image. It goes on for hours, for days. How much longer and how much stronger resentment is than was the pain felt in the encounter itself! The impotence to engage the aggressive force and discharge the forces of pain prolongs itself in this stoked violence. Resentment secretes a production of images that obscure the view of the present and distort the memory of what had passed. Its force is a positive force of mendacity. This vindictive force weakens one's active forces; one will be less present at the next social gathering, less self-assured, more vulnerable to the next one who probes into one's reserve, whose wit which one does not return becomes aggressive. This reserve presents itself as a substance upon which a coded identity takes. One will be identified as thin-skinned and moody; in reaction one will identify oneself as civilized and sensitive.

Is not the agreeableness with which pleasure conforms itself to what is given also a force of mendacity? The contentment and satisfaction in pleasure obturate the view, turn inward in sodden torpor, sinks into phlegmatic and insensate absorption. The content of its contentment is felt not simply as the annulment of a lack, the neutralization of the agitation of a want, but as a force to maintain itself.

There germinates in contentment a resentment, the force of an impotence, against the passing of pleasure, and against the passing of all things. Sunken into itself, the sensuality maintains the image of that whose touch gratified and passed. It germinates images of enduring content and integral satisfaction, images of happiness. Through its fixed images of contentment it views the patterns that form on the river of time as things that are worth nothing,[2] passing from being into nothingness. Its contentment degrades and devalues.

Pleasure and pain belong, not to the order of passivity, but to that of the forces of impotence. Their conflicts issue in exhaustion. The knowledge they contain is that of images fixed in resentment, content identified in contentment. In the measure that conversely charged images of the same object or person accumulate, the affective charges neutralize. Out of these neutralized images, in the exhaustion of violent feelings, the thought that arises collates, according to Spinoza, its objectified representation of the things and its truth.[3]

In our pains, become rancorous, in our pleasures, become requirements, we address our wants and our demands on others, we formulate our identities as needy and dependent and servile, our bodies as vulnerable and craving contentment; we demand to be protected and to be gratified, we offer ourselves to be used, to be disciplined. We subject our docile bodies to the normalizing individuation, the delinquency, the sexualized identities contemporary micromechanisms of power/knowledge inscribe on them. The forces of our rancor and our vindictiveness that devise their evasions, snares, ambushes, ruses, and mockeries revise and reinscribe the blazons, signs, and values which others inscribe on the substance of our pain. The violence of the cohesive force of our satisfaction—which contrives its body-armor, moats, and securities, which elaborates its deceits and devises its snares for the others—revise and reinscribe the nature the others identify on the substance of our pleasure.

This reactive form of sensibility is not primary. A living organism is a plenum; its hungers, thirsts, and wants that seek fulfillment, its wounds are intermittent and superficial, surface events that are possible because the organism is an intricate system that maintains itself and generates energies. It is a material substance that does not tend to equilibrium and torpor, but maintains a level of tension typical for its species. Its surplus forces seek out forces upon which to discharge themselves. Its sensibility does not consist simply of surfaces exposed to the forces of the environment; the buildup of its forces and their discharge affect themselves, and intensify in an immanent sensuality. This surplus affect that arises in the action of surplus forces is the strong, active form of sensibility. Desperation and exultation, torment and rapture thrust one outward, to encounter alien forces.

It is with laughter and tears, blessing and cursing, Nietzsche wrote,[4] that the strong, active sensibility greets, not the afterimages, but the active forces of things. The primary sensibility, that which first encounters the forces of the real, is hilarity and weeping, consecration and execration.

It is not when, withdrawn from the contact with a woman—left with one's own impressions and the images secreted over them, the pleasure and the pain exhausted—the understanding collates the images and the reason arrays its comparisons, that one then comes to know what one calls objectively the woman one had been involved with. This woman one knows objectively now is but the image of an object fixed out of reach of one's exhausted forces. A woman becomes real not as a pattern that forms in passing among the shapes in the room, but as a vortex of impulses that makes one laugh or cry, and is approached with one's open hands that clear the space, the *templum*, whose presence one recognizes with a curse. The imagination that feeds on muscles knows only the ridiculous figure of the male anatomy set forth as an object. It is in the compacted frenzy of combat when one's blow creates and consecrates a hollow in space in which the fatal blow it execrates and provokes on the part of the opponent fits perfectly, that one knows the mass, position, momentum, rhythms, nerves, insightfulness, and foresightfulness of the opponent. The things among which one dwells, with the contentment of sensing that they serve one silently and do not make demands on one, sink into the inconsistency of images and signals for one's passage through them; it is blessing and curses that feel the obstinate operations of things, laughter and tears that recognize the forces of their alien reality.

The laughter and the tears, the consecration and the execration are not, like the reactivity of pleasure and pain, an acknowledgement of the sense in sense-data—a sense one agrees to in agreeableness, a sense one follows like a signal in pain. They recognize reality and force, and also the concatenation and direction of forces—*sense* in the sense of orientation and direction-directive. This sense is not surveyed, but encountered as an alien thrust, countersensical to our own unbound forces and to the gratuity of our moves.

The laughter that greets the nonsensicality or the absurdity of this countersensical move feels the breakup of our enterprise not as the thwarting and reduction to impotence of our accumulated and swollen forces, but as their release. In the release of laughter there is blessing, a force that feels itself as a gratuitous and generous squandering, that invites the oncoming of the alien force with its own reverberations. The tears that greet the countersensicality or the ruin of what we found or made blessed flow as the force of what knows itself to be good and generous. The cursing is the rationally unjustified conviction in our voice that its very ineffectuality has a force to pursue the sinister ways of the alien to its own lairs. We see the force of our curses that shatter the dignity of the one that we curse, that extinguish the insouciant sparkle from landscapes and the glow from things closed in their self-satisfaction.

There is no laughter without tears, no blessing without cursing. The Himalayan sublimities are also ice storms and avalanches; the spectacles and companions we only laugh at or with are but spectacles and images: the woman who makes you laugh does not become real until she makes you weep. The strong, active affects do not compose into a coalition for the comprehensive embrace of the real; the original sensibility is an anarchy without principles. The strong, active sensibility is primary, infantile and immemorial; but it also resurges in the compounding of the weak, reactive impulses, in the spiraling violences of pleasures and pains.

The action that laughter and tears, blessings and curses contain is an illumination of the forces they encounter with their own ardor, rendering comic the absurd in the emergence of the microcosmic and macrocosmic order and rendering tragic the destruction in the cosmic evolution and among the green weeds stirring in the slight breeze. The laughter and the blessing know themselves as forces that give the alien their light and warmth and good will; the tears and the cursing know themselves, not as impotence and irrelevance as the world goes its way, but as forces that elevate it to somber tragic monumentality.

The course of the seasons and the planets and the galaxies surely offers many things for our smiles and our regret. Laughter and tears do not explode against the inconsequential; they test their strength against adversity and calamity. The force of life in them which exposes its surfaces to the forces of the world and of the others is a force advancing to the adversary, the absolute. The one who laughs or who curses before the firing squad does not defeat death nor devise a resurrection. Blessing the small birds that fly in the face of the cosmic rages, cursing the wrath of the terrible deities does not, and does not aim to ensure one's own salvation. The laughter and the curses in the face of death are themselves ways of discharging one's forces of oneself, of dying.

Our pleasures and our pains exhaust themselves; our laughter and our tears die away; our blessing and our cursing are carried away into the enigmas of the future and the silences of the past. They are of themselves gratuitous outpourings of force, expenditures without return. Their glory is purely worldly; their force does not hold or redeem.

part three

The Libidinal
Economy

Hard Currency

I *say* "I"; the living organism puts forth a sign for itself. This sign is not simply an effect it produces and puts forth; it is that with which it puts itself forth. It does not only make a sign, it makes itself a sign. The sign is a sound uttered with the throat, or a visual mark made by the hand. A contraction in the throat, a diagram of muscular enervation in the fingers and wrist are sustained by the posture held by the whole body, by the sensory-motor nervous circuitry that orients it at the moment, by the respiratory and circulatory system that brings air to the throat and blood to the contracting and extending muscle system. The capacity to signal is everywhere in the corporeal substance. The muscle tonus and sensory thresholds, the rate and force of respiration, and the heartbeat signal; the posture, the muscle tensions and relaxations, the positions of the limbs and of the facial muscles—all diagram signs.

That is, the audible and visual and also the tangible and felt positions and movements of the bodily substance are referential. They are polarized before an objective, which they indicate or designate, which they set up as a recognizable term. In uttering a cry or a coded sound, in forming a gesture with the fingers and the hands, in turning our face and in shifting our posture, we refer a witness to some exterior thing or pattern, we isolate that thing or pattern from the surrounding field, and make it visible to that witness. But it is also by orienting our gaze, by centering and directing our posture, by focusing our receptor surfaces, that we isolate that thing or pattern for ourselves; it is by contracting a certain pace and rhythm in our hand and applying it with a certain pressure that we make the grain of the wood or the texture of the velvet or burlap into a separate pattern; it is by breathing with a certain rate and force and walking with a certain gait that we make the atmosphere and its odors, the landscape and its rhythms into perceivable elements and patterns. It is by making our corporeal substance into referential diagrams that we make the surroundings into referents, objects, objectives.

Uttering a sound, making a gesture, a body calls attention to itself. An immobilized, sleeping body, half-buried in the bedcovers or in the vegetation of the meadow, can still emerge as a referent, a distinct object, because the witness sees it as a substance that can call attention to itself by assembling its parts, now dispersed by gravity, into a referential diagram. But is it not because it can *say* "I," put forth this audible pattern, is it not because our body can gather up its limbs and organs into a distinct diagram of posture that it can become a referent for itself? When we lie collapsed on the hillside or on the bed or floating in the pool, we lose any distinct sense of our body volume and boundaries, and the substance in which sensibility simmers is sunshine, humidity, earth, or liquidity as much as it is ourselves. This state sinks toward the non-self-awareness of sleep. It would seem that we make ourselves into objects for ourselves, as for others, by becoming the referent of a sign we put forth.

It would thus seem that we cannot know objects, cannot structure the environment into distinct patterns, except as the referents of signs, except by making our body positions and movements signs of them. Our corporeal substance cannot figure as a distinct object for itself except by giving itself a sign of itself, making its positions and movements referential of that sign.

A sign is a sensorial pattern that has a referent, and also has a meaning. The meaning, Jaako Hintikka says,[1] is the way the sign refers to its referent. It is, Edmund Husserl says,[2] ideal; a meaning recurs the same. While the real tree or body referred to are physico-chemical and biological complexes in unceasing flux, the perceived tree or body patterns shifting with every shift of our eyes and posture, and while the physical sound or visual mark "tree" or "body" cannot be reproduced or redrawn with physically the same vibration-patterns or visual proportions—what "tree" or "body" are taken to mean is taken to be the same each time they are set forth. To make signs is then not only to make patterns that correspond to specific referents; it is also to idealize, to take the way these patterns refer to recur ideally the same. The real is phenomenologically described by Husserl as that whose determinations are individuated in a determinate place and time; the ideal would be that which can recur anywhere, anytime, the same.

To enter into a relationship with referents through signs is also to idealize the referents themselves. In the limited case of a body alive with feeling on simple contact with the sunlight and the hillside, the exterior hardly forms patterns at all, and the excitations with which sunlight and hillside make themselves felt in the body are vibratory and in flux. Sunlight, a hillside, a pool, become *objects* as the referents of signs. An object is a piece of the exterior which can be recognized to be there in another moment, in another perspective; it is recognized to be one of a family of like objects. The sign that recurs idealizes its referents into objects.

To put forth a sign of oneself is also to idealize oneself. The corporeal substance that breathes, moves, looks, and feels is a field of disparate processes continually shifting, intensifying, and discharging forces. But the body that says "I" takes the physical signifier "I" to be phenomenally the same and takes it to mean the same each time that body utters it—and takes the referent of that "I" to abide, constant, across the flow of duration, and in the intervals between its being attended to. The body that makes a sign of itself, that makes itself a sign, idealizes itself.

A sign also has a value. It belongs to a system of signs, an economic system, where the place and function of each sign is specified by the other signs with which it can be exchanged.

Every referent can be referred to by more than one sign or set of signs; it is the object, the ideally selfsame structure, referred to by signs of different meanings. But in the measure that each sign which refers to that referent has a determinate value in an economy of signs where it can be exchanged for, substituted by, other signs, the referent itself acquires a value, that is, it is taken to belong to an economy of reality in which it is taken as equivalent to what figures in another perspective, at another time. The momentary sensory density, when designated by a sign, is taken to be an object equivalent to another of a class or category or family of objects.

To put forth a sign of oneself is also to valorize oneself. The body that says "I," or that assumes a reading position at a table before a book or that waves to an acquaintance in greeting, sets forth a sign which it takes to be equivalent to and interchangeable with other utterances, stances, or gestures. The utterance "I," the reading-position, the wave in greeting, are taken to be equivalent to and interchangeable with other sounds, other postural positions, other motor patterns of the hand. In addition, the body that makes itself into a sign, that issues utterances, contracts positions, and makes movements, takes itself to be, and makes itself be equivalent to and interchangeable with other bodies that make utterances and contract diagrams of position and movement. The one that says "I," in so saying, designates itself alone, but simultaneously makes itself equivalent to and interchangeable with others that say "I." The one that says "I" enters into an economy of bodies, as a substance whose value is determined by the other bodies, which it can be substituted for or whose places it can take.

The body that makes signs makes itself a sign—makes itself a referent for itself as well as for others; gives itself a meaning and idealizes itself—makes itself mean something abiding and recurring the same; and makes itself a value—makes its utterances, gestures, and stances equivalent to and interchangeable with one another and makes its substance equivalent to and interchangeable with other bodies. Psychoanalysis offers a genetic account of this idealization and this valorization that a body does on itself. Psychoanalysis is a hermeneutics of signs, an interpretation of dreams, an examination of representations taken specifically as symptoms of libido. In the end it considers any representations whatever—even mechanical or engineering graphs, religious symbols, and mathematical formulas—as signs of libidinal impulses and conflicts. The practical moves with which our bodies refer to their objectives are also libidinal gestures; the practical orientation with which our bodies adjust to reality is also an orientation toward pleasure. Conversely, psychoanalysis takes libido in the civilized, that is, repressed, Oedipally triangulated, human species to be productive of signs. Its genetic analysis will then show how the first and primary sign a body sets forth of itself is a libidinal designation, invocation, and demand, how the first and primary idealization a body works on itself is a phallic idealization, and how the first and primary valorization a body works on itself is a virile and paternal valorization.

The Libidinal Idealization

An infant is not a reality to which a sign is attached from the outside in order to designate him in his absence; he figures as a sign before he exists in reality. His[3] reality will be shaped by that sign.

Before he was born, perhaps even before he was conceived, the infant already figured in the parental discourse. What functioned as the signifier of the infant in the parental discourse was not the perceived real fetus, but an image, the "imaged body" of the infant, imagined especially by the mother. The perceived real fetus is invisible, and fragmented, its stirrings and kickings fragmented in space and across time. The image is that of a little prince, innocent redeemer, joy-bringing goblin, an anticipatory and idealized totality. There was an urgent vital reason to fix this imaginary body through signs and to dissimulate the perceived fetus. This imaged referent is what will enable the mother to not live through childbearing as a fragmentation of her body, a dismembering, a loss of part of her substance, or a threat to her existence. Piera Aulangier,[4] who studied the mothers of psychotics, has discovered that for them, in the experience of pregnancy the real feelings of the stirrings and kickings predominate, and they typically speak of the fetus in themselves and spend little time fashioning for themselves the image of the future little child. Psychotics themselves are characterized by a fragmented, dismembered sense of their own bodies and an oppressive sense of the weight of immediate reality, lacking dimensions of the possible, the future, and the ideal.

The infantile sensibility is not at first cognitive, a surface of sense-data that are givens of sense, indicative and informative; the infantile sensibility is productive. This sensibility glows about the oral and anal orifices and diffuses within. The mouth couples onto the maternal breast and the nutritive fluid flows, is held, flows again, filling the soft vesicle of the infantile organism with content, which irradiates contentment. This contentment is productive; the infant, satisfied, saturated, closes its mouth, its eyes, its fists, closes in upon itself, making itself a "body without organs," as Gilles Deleuze and Félix Guattari, following Antonin Artaud, say.[5] The production of this plenum with closed organs Deleuze and Guattari identify with the id, a state of the body. It produces and reproduces itself.

Freud first identified the forces of the id in the compulsive repetition of infantile responses, which the therapy puts an end to by inducing in the patient a memory of the infantile situation (or of the traumatic situation, infantile in its helplessness). Producing a representation of the situation which had provoked those infantile responses replaces and suppresses the actual reproduction of those responses, a phenomenon Freud named "abreaction." The infantile responses would have become repetitive because the original situation that had provoked them had been lost to consciousness. It had been lost because it was unpleasurable; the very representation was unpleasurable, and a force acting on this representation effaced it. There would be a force that, like the force that produces representations, is psychic, but this force which has to select the representations to be effaced, in effacing them engenders unconsciousness, and blindly repetitive infantile responses. In this way Freud came to conceive of the id, not as a state of the body but as a psychic state, and a state conceived negatively, a negative consciousness, un-conscious.

Does not the psychic force that suppresses the representation, the memory, have to contain first a representation of the representation it is to suppress? If the unconscious would not be a contradiction in terms, it would denote an infinite regress.[6]

In his last theory of the instincts, Freud recognized the inadequacy of the hypothesis that the unpleasure which representations can produce precipitates the primary repression constitutive of the unconscious. Is there not a primary repetition compulsion[7] which reinstates not only the pleasurable affects with which past instinctual discharges are marked, but also painful, traumatizing affects? The dreams of patients suffering from traumatic neuroses as a result of an accident or a war experience involving a threat to life repeatedly bring a patient back to the situation of his accident—a situation from which he wakes up in another fright. The child who, suffering from his mother's absence, throws out his toy and then pulls it back (the "Fort-Da" game)[8] is, Freud thinks, trying to master departure and reappearance, but he does repeat the first half of the game—the departure or the disappearance—"far more frequently than the episode in its entirety, with its pleasurable ending."[9] The precocious efflorescence of infantile sexuality is doomed to failure "because its wishes are incompatible with reality and with the inadequate stage of development which the child has reached" and is pursued "in the most distressing circumstances and to the accompaniment of the most painful feelings,"[10] but the frustration only exasperates and intensifies that sexuality, which will not diminish until the Oedipus complex finally opens for it a new channel and a new form. It is then not a psychic force acting to select unpleasurable representations for suppression that produces compulsively repetitive behavior; the repetition compulsion is the primary law of the forces in libidinal as well as thanatos drives.

Deleuze concludes that the force that originally excludes the memory, the representation of a behavior and of the situation that provoked it, is nothing other than the re-presentation, the reenactment of that behavior. It is when the force of repetition in actuality is unrealized that the repetition occurs in representation, that is, in memory. The primary unconscious then is not a system that repeats because it does not remember, because a memory continually forming is continually suppressed, but a system that does not remember, that is, does not represent what has come to pass in it, because it repeats it.[11] It is the psychic closure of contentment that excludes the psychic representation of an act. The repetitive force of instinctual intensities is productive, not of representational sensations, givens of sense that would function as intentional traces of what inscribed them, but of affective sensations, opaque affects of contentment, which obturate the orifices and the organs. This contentment is a force securing a state of the body. The primary unconscious is the positive force of a body that closes in upon itself in the positive production of its contentment.

The primary death drive itself must be conceived positively; it is not the collapse of the organizing forces within the living vesicle which leaves it in the inertia of an inorganic mass,[12] but, Deleuze argues, the force of barren contentment which closes the body upon itself as an anorganic plenum. It is the paralytic and the catatonic, Deleuze and Guattari write, and not the stillness of a mineral mass, which, producers of horror films have known, represent all the vertiginous fascination of death.[13] In the traumatized dreamer who recycles the air raid and exploding bombs, in the child who persists in the distress and pain of sexual frustration, in the infant who vengefully throws away his toys in the absence of his mother, Deleuze and Guattari see the paranoiac machine of a catatonic anorganic body closing in upon itself.[14]

The infantile body, cast outside, coupling its lips and gums to the maternal breast, then closing its orifices and closing off its organs, produces its contentment. The infant also produces surface sensations. Coupled onto the maternal breast, he drools, slavers. He shifts and rolls in the warmth of his excrement. The orifices extend surfaces with their viscous flows and movements. Pleasure-surfaces extend in the uncharted symbiotic medium. Life in him learns to use the excess energies generated in the organ-couplings to produce a pleasure of surfaces, a pleasure of having surfaces, the pleasure of being outside, of being alive on his own. The energies attached to these surfaces resist the craving to return to the womb, to the quiescence of its fluid equilibrium. They function to block the regressive death drive.

It is these pleasures that Freud recognized as the first manifestation of libido. The anaclitic deviation, as Freud put it, of the functional organ-coupling produces an erotogenic surface to his body. The infant that used his mouth to slaver will use his thumb to let his saliva run, will babble and coo, will rub his body parts together and on the warm surfaces of blankets, will slobber his bottle, cuddle his toys and roll them in his excrement. Excitations, unbound intensities,[15] are produced. The excitations generated are contact sensations, and contain information about the surfaces in contact; they are samplings of outside contours and representative of them. But they are freely mobile across the closed surfaces of the body now sated, whose assimilating and ejecting organs are closed to the outside. They do not function to inform the core body and activate it, as representations of objectives or threats. This infantile sensuality does not consist of drives, wants, or intentions. Planes of pleasure extend, intensify, collide, and merge. Their representative content accumulates and polarizes, forming phantasmal patterns. They intensify by reciprocal induction and irradiation. Surface eddies form, which intensify and affect themselves: eddies of egoism. Excitations discharge, are consumed, in surface eddies of egoism.

The surface sensuality of the infant is already called erotogenic by Freud;

he conceives its movement after the model of genital discharge. Freely mobile excitations function, not to inform an ego, but to produce an eddy of egoism by affecting themselves with their own intensities—feelings that feel themselves. This surface node of egoism is also the locus where they are consumed, in spasms of voluptuous gratuity. In the discharge the surface of freely mobile excitations returns to a state of quiescence, with a death drive that was internal to them. Freud also recognized that the erotogenic sensuality, even in a shattering of its psychophysiological organization and ego–control, seeks to repeat and even intensify itself.[16] The local, episodic, and ephemeral egoisms that form and are consumed resist the "partial deadening of the outer layers of the soft vesicle" that form against massive influxes of stimuli that would crush it. The conflagration of a voluptuous spasm lights fires elsewhere.

Infantile sensibility is a sensuality; the structure of signification is not to be projected back into it. The excitations are not sensations, sense–data, givens of meaning and direction. They are not intentional; they do not aim at recognizing objects. They are contact–phenomena; they extend surfaces whose concavity is informative of its convexity. Through them the infant lives, not in a world of objects–objectives, but in a kaleidoscope–medium where pleasure–surfaces form and evolve phantasmally. They are not signals by which the infant makes known his wants and needs to another; they spread an erotogenic surface where the pleasure that simmers is indistinguishably that of the infant and of the mother. On the surface of a sated and contented closed plenum, the infantile sensuality is productive—productive of surfaces, productive of pleasures, productive of consuming egoisms. These egoisms are loci of incandescence and not of computation, loci of the discharge of surplus energies and not loci where the demand for compensation is formulated. The infantile body, closed plenum and erotogenic surface, is insignificant or nonsignifying.

The contact breaks; the mother pulls away. She satisfies the infant's needs and departs. The Moebius strip of the erotogenic surface splits; the infant discovers distance and otherness. This distance and otherness are not yet that of the object–objective; the convex face of a pleasure–surface becomes out of reach in a space without paths of access for a body without mobile powers. The infant can only sense this alternating presence and absence of the mother as a zone of arbitrariness and capriciousness, extending the distance between impotence and omnipotence. What Freud called the infantile phantasm of the omnipotence of the ego is first not that of his own ego, but that of the mother. Corresponding to it, there arises in the infant the demand for the pure gift of total fulfillment, what Jacques Lacan called the demand for love.[17] The dissension between need and demand[18] is implanted in the infantile sensibility. The satisfaction of need in a particular moment functions as a refusal of the demand for love, for the pure gift of total fulfillment. For the mother satisfies the infant's needs in order to depart. The infant is given the bottle and put to sleep. But the demand for love does not cease being formulated in the somnolent organism; the language—the hieroglyphics and the rebuses[19]—of the infantile dream continues already and henceforth to formulate the demand still addressed to alterity in the figure of phantasmal omnipotence.

How will this demand, how will this infancy now addressed to alterity, be able to break outside, leave the closure of its somnolence and its dreams, in order to speak? One can enter language only as an element of language, a sign. How will the infantile life, this primary-process libido—this closed plenum, and this surface production intensifying and discharging without recompense or response—come to be doubled up with a signifier for itself or turn into a sign?

Growth progressively empowers sectors of the neuromuscular system, and with them the pleasure-surfaces extend further. The infant experiences his kinesthetic body in fragments, in which scintillate nomadic and episodic eddies of egoism. Then, sometime after the age of six months, the infant discovers an entirely different surface-body of himself: a visual expanse extended, whole and entire, across a distance in a mirror. He is fascinated and delighted.[20]

It would be a mistake to suppose he discovers here an object or discovers that he is an object. An object is something that remains fixed and turns different faces of itself to the exploration that turns about it.

His fascination is not that of simply another pleasure-surface he can touch and caress. It is the fascination of identification: he identifies himself with it. It is a specifically human identification and a specifically human fascination. The infant recognizes his father visually reproduced by looking from the mirror to his father standing by him; then his father points to the image and says: That is you! The infant tests it by moving himself, sees the image disappear and return to the mirror, and laughs with pleasure. Siamese beta fish and birds see in their mirror-image the visual appearance of another animal; apes, after they find their hand stopped by the glass of the mirror, reach behind it, find nothing, and lose interest. In fact the infant cannot identify the mirror image by comparing it visually with the original. He knows himself as a core of feelings and motor vectors, and a surface of excitations; only his extremities, intermittently and fragmented, are visual phenomena. The mirror puts in front of him, on a surface he does not feel or move, a visual pattern. Faced with the mirror, his corporeal substance splits. In a leap of pleasure he closes the split, he identifies himself.

The distance the mirror reveals between his kinesthetic-affective here-now and his visual shape is also a distance of time. The mirror presents the infant with an anticipated composition of the fragments of his body into a subsistent totality; in pleasure the infant identifies with this ego-ideal. The identification will function vitally as a factor of integration. The identification of the mirror image as himself is not simply a judgmental predicative synthesis— "That is me!"—it is a projective identification: not an identification of it, but a vertiginous identification with it. The pleasure is both a tearing asunder, the rending of a projection out of his motor-affective core, and a swelling up of himself into the anticipated now-visualized totality—an ecstatic contentment.

The representation of oneself that the mirror offers is not then, for the infant or for the adult, a copy, a replica, or a facsimile. For the adult too knows the enigmas of the mirror, which reverses his right and left side without reversing top and bottom, and shows something different from the sum of the visual surfaces he can obtain by turning his eyes upon his body. And he knows the affective charge he seeks in vain to suspend in order to "see how he really looks."

The stage of fascination with the mirror image is the stage of the original narcissism. For it is also a suicide, a losing oneself in the stagnant element of the image. The infant is captivated by his image, alienated from the episodic and fragmentary flux of his own experience of himself to identify himself with this figure posited at a distance, integral and identical, substantive and ineffectual.

The captivation by the mirror image is also his entry into discourse. Now there is a material element—the mirror image—which can be referred to, by the child as by others, as a signifier of his kinesthetic-affective substance. The parent that has pointed to the visual image in the mirror and said, "That is you!" has known that image, and has spoken about it all along; it has been for him or her what they named in speaking of their child, the materialization of what they conjured up and named in speaking of him before he was born. Gradually the child learns that each time they named him, it was this image they saw. In identifying with it, he identifies with his name in language, which is never an index of private phenomena. He enters discourse.

Freud detected the first infantile discovery of the semiotic system in the "Fort-Da" game of his grandson.[21] The infant, left alone by the departure of his mother, throws his toy out of the cradle with a cry. Freud, babysitting, retrieves it; the infant greets it with pleasure and another cry. But he tosses it out again.... Freud understood that the infant had formulated a true semiotic system, two differentiated cries, to designate "Fort"—Gone! Absent!—and "Da"—Here! Present! (In the English world: Peek-a-Boo!) Indeed every semiotic system is built on the progressive articulation of this dyad. The proof that the system was in place was that the infant greeted the return of his mother with the "Da" cry—and from then on took great pleasure in repeating the game with other toys, with the appearance and concealment of others and of himself. The parents, playing Peek-a-Boo with him, adopt his nomenclature, and teach him theirs. The mirror stage is the moment when the infant acquires a sense of the difference between his own kinesthetic-affective experience of himself and the visual experience others have of him. Acquiring access to the mirror image, he acquires a signifier for himself, and himself enters into the semiotic system.

As the "imaged body" of the infant still hidden in the womb served for the parents as a regulatory sign for their conduct then, now they make this image function as a regulatory sign for him. "What are you doing? Just look at yourself!" As he learns to use this image to regulate the behavior they want, he also learns to use it to obtain from them the behavior he wants. He finds it everywhere before him, extended on the shining surface of their eyes. There this image can be maintained, adjusted, combined with other images; the child starts to strike poses, decorate himself, parade about. No longer is this image conjured up only with the words of their sentences.

The signifier for himself that the child has acquired has a metonymic form: a signifier for a part of the child (the future totality) has been substituted for the actual and present reality—his fragmented kinesthetic forces and in-fantile, non-signifying, sensitivity.

The mirror has given him, suddenly, capriciously, the totality of himself; he voluptuously identifies with it, and uses it to signify the demand for love he has not ceased to address to the other. The image with which the child identifies and which he animates is not just represented to himself, an indicative and informative diagram, but addressed to others; it is a vocative and imperative signifier.

But once the child enters into the parental discourse, he finds himself subject to its law. Discourse requires that the child detach himself from his primary-process reality as a closed anorganic body-plenum and an erotogenic surface, to identify himself with the reflected surface of a signifier. To relate to things by signifiers is no longer to sense them by contact as pleasure-surfaces but to designate them as terms at a distance, nexuses of properties that are the same for other speakers as for oneself—objects.

Verbal signifiers are identifiable by their phonetic contrasts with one another. In the formulations of discourse each signifier designates an object by invoking contrasting signifiers for other objects; as soon as one relates to an object with a signifier one enters into an open-ended field of objects. In discourse the signifier for an object requires a signifier for a subject that issues signifiers for those other objects and can thus maintain this object determinate. The signifier for the speaker functions as a vocative and imperative sign that requires and calls upon signifiers for objects, which themselves call for further signifiers for objects in ordered chains. Discourse extends the field of objects indefinitely, and calls for the child to identify himself with the signifier for a subject continuously.

There is a law, a prohibition, that governs the order of discourse; the movement that makes each term refer to, call for, require a further term is that which divests that term of its terminated reality and makes it figure as an objective, and not as a presence and a satisfaction. The movement that makes all the terms of discourse references to and demands for further objects is an operation that divests exterior realities of contact plenitude; it makes them be there as objectives at a distance indicating further objects at more remote distances. The order that positively articulates an indefinitely extended field of objects is also, negatively, the law that prohibits them from crowding in on us with their promiscuous surfaces. In discourse, the child is no longer an infantile libido contented by the flows of sustenance and excited by sensorial surfaces in tangency and contact, but a longing for objects, that is, for the referents of signifiers, which are there as but relay points toward yet more remote objectives. This longing Lacan identifies with the Hegelian-Kojèvian term "desire," understanding by this term an orientation that is without end, for its ends, its correlates, are but symbols for still further ends, and for an ideal end which is only dissimulated and not articulated by these objectives. The law of discourse does not then simply regulate the primary processes of infantile life; it reconstitutes that libido as desire. Thus we have to understand not simply how the child, with the evolution of his sensory-motor integration, comes to reach for and effectively take hold of substances and pleasure-surfaces initially out of reach, but how the infantile libido is detached from the surfaces of its primary-process immediate gratifications and turned into a longing for objects-objectives articulated in, and as, symbols.

The order that regulates the predication of interminable ordered chains of objects to this subject is also the law that demands that he divest himself of his pleasure-surfaces and identify himself wholly with the signifier he is for others and is for himself in discourse. It is as one excoriated of his surfaces of erotogenic pleasure, identified with a vocative and imperative signifier, that the libidinal substance enters discourse. Infantile libido becomes significant, speaks, articulates an interminable field of objects that are symbolic objectives; it appeals to and puts demands on others. How does it come to pass that the infantile libido is evacuated of its anorganic contentment, excoriated of its primary-process erotogenic surfaces, and induced to invest itself wholly in the vocative and imperative surface of a sign?

The law is paternal; it is the word of the father. The father intervenes to counter the phantasm of maternal omnipotence with the supremacy of his word; he prohibits the child the maternal surfaces as surfaces of contact pleasure. He simultaneously puts the infantile body as a surface of immediate, contact, gratification under interdiction. The word of the father orders that the child's body as a pleasure-surface be taken out of his hands, requires renunciation of masturbation, requires castration, excoriation of the surfaces of erotogenic contact gratification.

Discourse is imperative before it is indicative; its order forms the subject, subjects him, before it informs him about objects. The paternal imperative has a categorical form; it is only once the infantile life is detached from the immediacy of surface gratifications that its desire can come to understand objectives, means, reasons, and motives.

The child laughs at the castration threats, empirically more frequently formulated in the name of the father by the mother. Yet his laughter is troubled by a question he pursues, the question that takes him out of infancy, what Freud identified as the first question: Where do children come from? He has come to understand they come from the bosom of the mother. When the veil that covers it lifts, his laughter will freeze: he discovers, with horror, the castration of the mother.

This horror fascinates, with a fascination that will subject him to the law of discourse. For in his foreboding horror before the discovery of the maternal mutilation, the child feels both the seriousness of the eventuality with which he is himself threatened and the chance he is. For he now also understands the voracious intensity of the ardent eyes the mother turns on him, understands why all this time she has been holding him close to herself, fondling him possessively; he understands she looks to him as to the missing part of which she has been castrated.

There thus arises the phallus—that which is signified by the desire of the other, that which is addressed in the desire of the mother the child has felt by feeling it turned in his direction. There arises in the child the mesmerizing idea of being a phallus for his mother—in order not simply to be able to torment her with his importunate cries for the satisfaction of particular needs, but to be able to demand of her the absolute devotion of all her substance: love.

What the son now sees reflected in his mother's eyes is not simply his visual reflection, but a demand for him as the phantom part of which she has been amputated. The phallus arises as a pure signification and original absence. What the son takes it to designate is himself shaped entirely as a penis, functioning not as a pleasure surface, but as that which would make the mother whole. For him to be that, he would have to project himself wholly into this absence, to materialize a visibility there turned away from himself. But in doing so, he would then demand her total devotion; he would exist as that demand, a vocative and imperative sign.

It is this prospect he catches sight of that makes possible for him to give up his penis as an immediate pleasure-surface. He can then subject himself to the law of the father, no longer find himself in contact gratification, excoriate himself of his erotogenetic surfaces, and project himself wholly into the vocative and imperative phallic sign.

In making himself a phallic sign, the son internalizes the paternal law as the law of his inner libidinal economy, speaks in the name of the father, engenders a superego, engenders his own father, puts his father in place of himself. The fear of the father converts into a libidinal investment in him. The polymorphously perverse sensuality of infancy is polarized into bisexuality.

The libidinal pleasure mutates into erotic excitement. With this term we wish to designate the pleasure in the shattering of psychophysiological and ego-control structures that result in greater tension and the longing for greater tension.[22] Although Freud tended to equate all erotic pleasure with the concept of tension release, modeled after the physiological diagram of genital discharge, he observed that "all comparatively intense affective processes, including even terrifying ones, trench upon sexuality."[23] It is precisely "in the most distressing circumstances and to the accompaniment of the most painful feelings" that the sexuality of childhood, he wrote, shows its efflorescence.[24] There is perhaps a biological finality in this; the individual is carried through the experience of psychic shattering, a threat to the stability and integrity of the self, by the pleasure of erotic excitement, a pleasure inherently masochist.[25] Leo Bersani writes: "Sexuality manifests itself in a variety of sexual acts *and* in a variety of presumably nonsexual acts, but its constitutive *excitement* is the same in the loving copulation between two adults, the thrashing of a boundlessly submissive slave by his pitiless master, and the masturbation of the fetishist carried away by an ardently fondled silver slipper."[26] But it seems to us that the Oedipus complex, which results in the definitive split of the subject detached from its erotogenic surfaces and invested in the phallic phantasm, its libidinal attachment now bisexually polarized, is the theater where erotic excitement is originally generated.

The primary-process libido of immediate contact gratification is insignificant and without communicative value; it is not addressed to another, makes no appeal to and puts no demand on another, envisages no alterity beyond the surfaces of contact. The phallic libido is the body wholly made into a sign, a response to the appeal of the other, a demand put on another. It is simultaneously the sign of wholeness, integrity, plenitude, the object of the exorbitant and unceasing desire divined in another, and the sign of prohibition, castration, renunciation of immediate gratification.

The development of perceptual discernment and motor agility makes the positions, gestures, and movements of the infantile body capture the forms of things before making contact with them; a witness can thus see them as indicating objectives. A witness will so see them when he recognizes those objectives as the objectives of the needs and wants of his own organism. But the gestures of the infant are not elements of discourse until they address demands to and respond to the demands of the other. The cries of infancy appeal to the other simply as the breast that responds to his needs. But the mother satisfies needs in order to withdraw; the infantile dream formulates an unrestricted demand for the love of the mother. This total demand will be expressed when the child forms himself wholly as the phallus she lacks. Then his positions, gestures, and movements all have vocative and imperative force in their indicative forms. With all the surfaces out of reach which the child's informed and indicative gestures designate, they designate also a love that withdraws behind all the objectives which his moves reach out for.

With the castration complex, psychoanalysis claims to explain how the infantile libido becomes significant and comes to speak. Identifying itself as a phallus, it makes itself into a sign, an appeal addressed to another, a demand put on another. Psychoanalysis also claims to bring to light the libidinal force and function of the idealization of objects—the idealization that constitutes sensible surfaces into objects.

Phenomenology, Sartre explained, identified the objectivity of objects with the total set of concordant variants a phenomenal pattern offers perception.[27] A perceiver can perceive sensible things only by being among them, himself or herself a sensible thing, and can be open to them only by not perceiving all the opacity of his or her own substance.[28] The perceiving body perceives itself marginally and the things before it only frontally, perceives them as surfaces occluding a depth. However, it grasps the axes and dimensions about which the pattern given at any moment is variable in an ordered way—and thus has an anticipatory perception of the total series. Each surface is perceived from a specific position of the perceiver; surfaces coalesce as surfaces of a sensible thing for a perceiver that varies his or her position. The active orientation toward consistent and coherent things is brought about by the development of neurological and motor coordination in the child's body. Sensory surfaces coalesce as the surfaces of a thing open to anyone as the perceiver successively occupies positions other perceivers do or can occupy. For the total series of perceivable surfaces of any one thing to be given, all the possible viewpoints from which it could be viewed would have to be perceived and occupied; the objectivity of an object is the correlate of a sensibility that would displace itself indefinitely, exchange viewpoints with others indefinitely. Were but one of these objects perception aims for to be given, all possible surfaces of all possible objects would have to be given with it. This is unrealizable not only because time and the energies of the perceiver are wanting; such a total objectification of the sensorial field would exclude the subject of perception, which can be open to outside things only by not perceiving all the opacity of its own substance stationed in the midst of them.

The terms of language designate things as objects—that is, they designate the inner coherence of the total series of perceivable surfaces a thing can show. But, signalling them by the sensible patterns of verbal signifiers, they posit objects only ideally. Speech acts are gestures that synopsize the indefinite series of displacements with which a perceiving body would record all the perceivable surfaces of an object. For Merleau-Ponty, speech is a superstructure built on perception and motility; it is the discernment and agility of gestures that seek with others what perception reaches for.

Psychoanalysis argues that the object as a cognitive structure is based on the object as a libidinal objective. In the infantile body the development of neurological and motor coordination serves to extend ever further the array of pleasure-surfaces. A sensible substance does not become an object in prolonged fondlings of sensuous contact. For a sensuous pattern to become a *perceived* surface, it must already have become detached from contact with the erotogenic surface it excited. We must then distinguish between a voracious sensibility that would strive to extend itself ever further down the surfaces of contact gratification, and an objectifying intention that does not adhere to surfaces but posits them at a distance, referring, for their determination, to ever further objects. The objectifying movement is the positive or positing side of a continually reiterated movement of detachment from every surface and every surface-pleasure. Yet the objectifying movement also issues from the pleasure principle. For each time a partial pleasure is sacrificed in anticipation of a total pleasure, which is indefinitely deferred. The desire that seeks objects is frustrated by all its surface contacts; it takes every surface contact as a frustration of the contact with the total or the absolute it seeks. The object-structure of the cognitive object does not then emerge out of the development of our praktognosis; it emerges out of a fundamental change in our pleasures. The object lures us, not as a quantitatively extended expanse of the surface under our sensuous touch, but as a symbol for something else—not a totality toward which the given surface contributes, but a totality the given surface frustrates.

In an object the sensible pattern with which a being is given to me is there as though it were not given to me; it is detached from sensuous adhesion and has become a relay for my longing. In all the other sides and aspects implicated in the side perceptible to me the object hovers as a lure for multiple and exterior longings. The substances at hand lure me as the objectives of this refracted and reiterated desire; their sides turned from me interest me, not as objective through others, but as objectives for others. We are not first drawn to others cognitively, in order to appropriate from them the missing sides of the object we aim to constitute; objects are what we desire when we seek outside lures to captivate the libido of others. We are relayed from aspect to aspect toward an object and from object to object without end because what we seek in objects is not sustenance and not excitations, immediate surface gratification, but the means to captivate the desire of the other.

In appropriating the surfaces of things turned from me I mean to hold on myself the objectives of alien desire. In this appropriation my phantasmal phallic identity is arrayed with visible and tangible forms, and the perceptible patterns acquire the vocative and imperative force of phallic relays. It is as phallic symbols, relays for a desire that is total and insatiable, that sensory surfaces are constituted as objects.

What psychoanalysis finds as a condition for the possibility of the constitution of objects is not a transcendental subject of cognitive syntheses, but a phallic identity.[29] For phenomenology, the common terms of language designate a space and time extended beyond the scope or my, or any, human vision, in which all the sides of an object are arrayed. For psychoanalysis, they designate lures for that invisible, impalpable absolute which is the desire of the other. For psychoanalysis, speech is not a perception and language is not an instrument: speech is seduction.

In putting his real penis in the place of the phallus, in putting himself in the place of the father, the libido acquires its ideal identity. This identity is no longer that of the episodic and nomadic egoisms which form in eddies of surface gratification. It is not that of a pleasure which vibrates on, illuminates, and affirms an intensity which is already discharging itself, already passing. The egoisms that form in the primary-process erotogenic zone form in closed moments of a now without memory and without expectations. The phallic identity is set forth in a horizon of time extended beyond birth and beyond death. The son abandons the masturbatory surfaces which materialized and extended in the now of contact; he castrates and excoriates himself, in order to identity himself with the phallus the castrated mother had, the phallus he was before birth. When one day he approaches the surfaces and the orifices of a woman again, it will not be to sink into the closed now of pleasure; she will reproduce the child he will appropriate, that will bear his name, the child upon which the prohibition of the father can be extended.[30] Beyond his own death, his assassination at the hands of his son, he will find his identity—his name, his law—in his son. The final libidinal identity subsists in a time-axis of unending recurrence, the ideal or infinite time of signs.

The Libidinal Economy

As an object, a sensory pattern no longer consumed in pleasure has value; it is put in the place of the phallus, the ideal term of desire. The phallus itself is a value and not only an ideal signification; it is a good that figures in human commerce. Psychoanalysis addresses itself also to the question of value: how is a term originally constituted as equivalent to and interchangeable with another term in a system of exchanges, an economy? How does the human corporeal substance constitute itself as a value?

For there is an inner economy in the man that participates in political economy, the economy of the *polis*. It is by reason of his organism structure that man is Homo oeconomicus. There are operations, whose rhetorical tropes we have to exhibit, by which man acquires a sense of the values of things in first acquiring a sense of himself as a value.

When we call the infantile body an organism, the term is anticipatory; it invokes an integrated neuromuscular organization that is still wanting. Deleuze and Guattari conceive of the fragmented body the infant experiences in positive terms. Their notion of the anorganic body depicts a closed plenum upon which the organs are attached; these are not integrated by a postural schema in focused and integrated sensory-motor operations. The orifices can couple onto other orifices, can draw in nutritive fluids in gulps, can open to excrete wastes, and can also operate disconnected from the nutritive function, producing pleasure-surfaces where peripheral and episodic egoisms form. The organs are susceptible of several usages. A mouth is a coupling that draws in the fluid but can also slobber or vomit it out forcibly, that gurgles and babbles, can spit, grimace, smile, pout, and kiss. The anus is an orifice that ejects the segments of flow but also holds them in, ejects vapors, noise, can be coaxed, refuses, defies, and defiles. The organs can substitute for one another; the mouth can excrete fluids as the anus can pout. The fingers can hold onto the maternal breast as the mouth couples onto the nipple; they can be inserted into the mouth to be sucked and slavered; they can spread the saliva and the excrement.

The infantile organs, attached to the plenum of the body rather than functionally integrated in its service, drool, slaver, babble, let the viscous and vaporous fluids flow, spreading surfaces of excess and surface effects of pleasure. The excrement is gratuity and gift, the archetypal gift, which is transfer without recompense, not of one's possessions, one's things, but of one's substance, oneself. If there is an economy in the infantile body of organs exchanged for one another, it is an economy of supply without demand. The mother too gives her fluids, her warmth, her lullabies in uncalculated abundance and pleasure.

It is about the anal production that an economy of supply and demand is first established. The mother, the convex surface of the expanses of infantile pleasure, withdraws. A demand is put on a production the infant thinks only to give freely. The infantile production of fluids, vapors, and scents is not to be shared in every contact, spread around on all the surfaces; it is to be retained, held back, hidden, covered, privatized, constituted into private property, in order to be then given over, not freely but in exchange. The symbiotic couple draws apart behind closed doors to strike a deal, bargaining to extend the time of the transaction in order that the quality and substance of the merchandise can be brought out in detail for suitable appraisal. Come on, do it in the potty! Let Mummy see! How pleased Mummy is! Human commerce begins, the libido is economized, capital is constituted—in the men's room, and in the infantile soul. The outside agitator seduces the infant with the lure of primitive communism: he is persuaded to give of his own substance in exchange for love, for symbiosis with the other, the omnipotent one, which she has suspended. Elementary form of exchange-value: trope—metaphor.

Yet what is given are but signs of these goods, these absolutes: How pleased Mummy is! Come sit by Mummy! Mummy will give you some candy! Tokens for tokens. In fact she is not interested in what he can contribute to the potty, and only wants to buy time for herself. The golden baby feces are to be exchanged for maternal love on the installment plan. The baby for his part no longer gives himself; he holds back for this transaction, holds back now in this transaction. After much badgering and coaxing, he wryly gets off the potty having deposited only some token measure of currency. Soon he will be leaving with a hug, a brief kiss, a word, leaving his card, a traveller's check. He puts some of his liquid assets into circulation at every rest stop, keeping hard assets in the cloacal vaults. He is building up character, Freud says—that is, compulsive orderliness, cleanliness, and parsimony.[31] He takes a part of himself to be exchangeable with any of an open-ended series of goods. It is what Marx named the extended form of exchange-value: trope—metonymy. The mother looks, verifies that what he has left in the potty is equivalent to what was left yesterday, gives him a kiss and a toy and goes off to make lunch for herself. Making his whole substance representable by a part and exchangeable, the infant makes himself equivalent to anyone else, interchangeable with just anyone. He makes himself a unit of servile society.

Exchange-value attains what Marx calls its generalized form when one commodity is taken as the measure of value. Each good is designated not for its own properties, but seen as the multiple or fraction of the standard commodity for which it is held equivalent, by what Hayden White has identified as the rhetorical trope of synecdoche.[32] In feudal society one kind of human substance is set up as the measure of value of each; each man is valued according to the degree that he shares in or reflects the state of the lord. The Oedipus complex functions to reorganize the inner servile economy of infantile libido into a feudal form.

The change in the superstructure is prepared by developments in the infrastructure. The libidinal production is shifted from anal to penile material. The penis, which appears as an exterior prolongation of the roll of feces felt hardening pleasurably within, acquires the value of the gold of feces. By himself the child discovers the pleasure of wasting his seed; he produces a surface of waste again, and surface effects of pleasure. A viscous surface of pleasure that, like the oral and anal erotogenic surfaces, exposes itself to the maternal contact.

The father perceives this gratuitous production as a dumping apt eventually to interest his, the father's, wife. The son is ordered to close down the pleasure production of his erotogenic surfaces now specialized in the penis; he is ordered to remove his penis from the pleasure-producing zone, take it definitively out of anyone's reach, castrate himself. The father categorically refuses to bargain, offers no compensation for this expropriation.

The son can agree to his massive excoriation, this massive loss of pleasure, only when he discovers the chance he represents of answering a demand for which everything will be returned to him superabundantly. He has understood that his mother satisfies his needs in order to frustrate his own demand for absolute satisfaction, for love. He now comes to understand the cupidity in her adorable eyes. He will exchange all his wants in order to be, not the jewel, the apple of her eye, but her phallus. He can agree now to sacrifice his real penis, as a pleasure-surface immediately on hand, and the whole of the polymorphously perverse erotogenic surface production about it, as his father had demanded. He will exchange all that reality for the ideal phallus, absent really from the mother's corporeal substance, and absent from his own vision and touch, a transcendental ideality maintained by the total and unceasing craving in the eyes of another.

The phallus is the absent part, the part only signaled, signified in the eyes of the other, in the desire of the other, put in the place of the whole erotogenic reality of the child. It is the value—an exchange-value, the phenomenal form of value—that covers over and excludes from consciousness the carnal surfaces as utilizable for the production of pleasure. It is the generalized form, the ideal identity, of value, the commodity for which every good and every pleasure is exchanged. Every good and every pleasure and every body part will have value inasmuch as they are designated in terms of their phallic equivalent and perceived in terms of their phallic content. Every object negotiated for will be prized as an accouterment of the phallic image, another visible and tangible lure put in the place of its ideal insubstantiality. The use-value of pleasure-surfaces is exchanged for the exchange-value of commodities in which one sees not one's needs but one's worth.

When a commodity of no use-value is selected as that with which the value of all commodities are measured and for which they are exchanged, money is created, a value constituted, Hayden White says, in the trope of irony. Gold is of all the available metals that of the least use-value, both by reason of its properties and by reason of its scarcity; were it abundant one could, like the Aztecs, panel one's walls with it, for though it is too soft to use in implements, it is as durable and washable as plaster. In monetary economy to perceive value in goods is to perceive gold, and not labor, in them. As the ideal and phantasmal figure of absence, constituted in castration, a phantasm invoked by the spectacle of the castration of the mother and calling for the castration of the son, the phallic body is without use-value for the production of voluptuous pleasure; with it, one enters into a monetary economy.

The phallic libido has yet to acquire value in a reproductive economy. The passage from the phallic stage to the genital has the form of the son taking the place of the father—assassinating the father—and becoming a father— engendering a son to castrate in turn. He will effectively take the place of the father when he enters into contract with the other, the woman—not the symbiotic reality of the mother of infancy, from which he has been severed, but her representative, represented as the father represented that woman to himself. He seeks this replacement woman not in order to indulge the infantile, insignificant and uneconomic gratification of erotogenic surfaces, but to put his real penis in the place of the ideal phallus, giving it the value of the phallus—in return for an absolute of gratification, which she will pay on the installment plan. But his penis is not the phallus the wife lacked to become whole; she will use it not to extend her own surfaces of infantile, insignificant and uneconomic contact gratification, but to reproduce. Each enters the contract with an eye to his or her own interest; he offers his penis as a check drawn on a phallic mortgage and demands an absolute of gratification; she sees in his penis the means to acquire the unconditional love of an infant. Money that begets money; the phallus is the fetishist commodity of a capitalist libidinal economy.

In the contract his erect penis will have value, not as an instrument for the excitation of anonymous erotogenic surfaces, but as an instrument of dereal-ization, castration, idealization. The penis cannot maintain upon itself the value of the phallus unless it bears the paternal interdiction. The wife engenders a child to reconstitute her wholeness, but the father appropriates the son, pro-duces a son to bear his name and his law, to castrate in turn.

The paternal body presents itself as the supreme value in human commerce, the incarnation of law, reason, and ideals, in the measure that it incarnates renunciation of the productive libido—infantile, insignificant and uneconom-ic—the libido without character—disordered, contaminating, squandering. It governs a domestic economy in which commodities are accumulated as accou-terments of the phallic order. It is extended into a public field in which econ-omy has evolved into its monetary form.

The Marxist theory of alienation sees in capitalism a fetishism of money, and denounces as cynicism the irony of all things measured by the value of this substance of no use-value, which negates the productive substance of the human body. Whereas in feudal economy the value of the lord's body mea-sures the worth of the realm he incarnates and the exchange-value of the commodities and serfs it contains, capitalism would be the universal devalua-tion of the human body, which would possess value only inasmuch as its forces could be exchanged for money. But in the desacralized world of late capitalism, do we not also see a hypervaluation of human bodies? Late capitalism depends, for its necessary acceleration, on an enormous anti-production[33]—the produc-tion of sterile consumption and the destruction of unmarketable products. The military industry which, in an arms race that functions to deter war and the actual destruction of factories, produces weapons to become obsolete before they have time to rust, but which also produces weapons to be used in wars upon the systematically impoverished of the Third World and upon domestic urban guerillas—serves this purpose. Human bodies whose cupidity is heated up by advertising serve as the pyres upon which an excess production of industrial commodities is destroyed. In addition, there are produced sterile and voluptuous bodies whose role is to serve as fetishes, whose monetary worth knows no limits. Marxists would reply that holders of capital are willing to channel vast sums to the Queen of England, Imelda Marcos, Donald Trump, media celebrities, and athletes because these bodies serve as logos of corporate enterprises, and the wealth diverted to them is an investment.

Still, it remains to be understood how it is that for the sterile phallic fixa-tion upon a voluptuous body, sums that would rescue whole populations from famine are potlatched. It remains to be understood how a body can acquire the value of a fetish, a phallus.

Nightclub performers, air-hostesses, salespersons in boutiques, and prostitutes figure in the economy as bodies valued not for their labor but for their sensuality. The ordinary methods of monetary evaluation in capitalism also determine the monetary worth of voluptuous carnality—the worth of an hour of a streetwalker's time, of a few minutes of an flight attendant's graciousness, or of thirty seconds of an athlete's body televised with a car, a refrigerator, or a Marlboro cigarette. A streetwalker is paid not a sum approximating the incomparable quantity of the pleasure she gives, but, like any working woman, a sum determined by the law of supply and demand, that is, the minimum the client can get agreed to by the surplus of unoccupied streetwalkers, but not below the sum she needs to keep fed and keep working.

When the monetary worth of a voluptuous body knows no limits, a reversal occurs; the money that no longer measures the worth of that body is measured by it. Sade, writing at the end of the feudal order where blood and bloodlines were the measure of value, gives us in his heroine Juliette the figure of a body that becomes the measure of value in the coming epoch in which the most heavenly ecstasies of religious fervor, chivalrous enthusiasm, and Philistine sentimentalism will have been drowned in the icy water of egotistical calculation. By training herself in the contempt for the bounds fixed by the laws of morality and decency, Juliette has become allied to the supreme ruling powers and immeasurably rich; now, not out of need but out of extravagant riches, she prostitutes herself. Yet she demands to be paid. Her career in transgressing the array of social and institutional laws has prepared her for every debauchery anyone can imagine; the degradations to which she submits her body only exasperate the longing of her clients for possession of her. For the exasperated unsatisfaction they will know on her body, she requires to be paid sums that would rescue whole populations from famine—and she boasts never to have parted with a sou to alleviate any case of human misery. By measuring her own worth in terms of the use-value of goods needed by millions, by giving nothing of use-value in return for the esteem in which she is held, she has not converted her body's capacity to produce voluptuous pleasure into means to earn money, but has turned it into money. She makes herself the gold-standard of the monetary system; she, Pierre Klossowski said,[34] makes herself legal tender, her body live currency, on which the inert currency of coins and banknotes are drawn.

Late capitalism is the theater of an unprecedented fetishization of voluptuous celebrities. It is also that of an undiminishing appeal to the value of the nuclear, Oedipal family.

Industrialized capitalism has divested the family of its function of being the essential institution with which production and commerce are organized.

The competition-driven inventiveness of capitalist production devalues the experience of the fathers before the freedom from preconceptions and the boldness of the sons. But the family remains the original mechanism with which what we recognize as a civilized body acquires value. The virile body figures as the incarnation of law, reason, power, direction, and directives, not because of the use-value of the specifically male nervous circuitry and musculature, but because of its force as the incarnate sign of civilization. The worth of the family is measured by the goods and commodities that are invested in it—it requires all, requires all production to represent but its reproduction. The worth of the family is measured by the quantity of labor time invested in those goods and commodities, by the quantity of voluptuous substance it renders unused and unutilizable.

How many other economies are yet possible?

Fluid Economy

Metaphoric Economy, Metonymic Economy

Out of the basic elements of life in common, the various possible consistent configurations into which they can be composed determine an array of possible forms of society. Shirley Lindenbaum[1] distinguishes, in the Melanesian cultural arena, three forms of society. In these societies where the division of labor and the organization of authority are gender based, the primary social act is that of the man who goes to another compound to transact for a woman. The transaction is with her father and brothers. For the woman given, a woman must be returned.

In a first configuration, the paradigm would be men who exchange their sisters. This configuration is found in the egalitarian communities of the Malekula and the Small Islands, the Southwest Papuan Gulf, and the Great Papuan Plateau. The system in force among the Sambia (who emigrated from the Great Papuan Plateau), where typically the brother receives for his sister his niece for his son, would be a variant of the sister-exchange paradigm.

Nature unfortunately does not dispose of the distribution of differently sexed children in a correspondingly systematic way. Human engineering, in the form practiced by the Banaro, where infanticide of children of undesirable sex is the rule, would compensate for the nonsystematicity of nature.[2] Delayed exchange plays on time to correct inequalities. At the time the bridegroom will give to the men from whom he receives a woman the equivalent of himself, his male essence; in the next generation his daughter will be returned for his brother-in-law's son.

The immediate exchange is metonymic; for his bride, the bridegroom will give her brothers a part, more exactly, a portion, of his own male fluid in which his productive power is materialized. He will give them, in fellatio, a portion of his male essence; he will be the man in their compound that produces men.

These are societies with a dual economy: agriculture, the domain of female labor, and hunting and fishing, the reserve of male prowess. Married men eat male food, drink the milk sap of the pandanus trees they cultivate and tend and eat the game they hunt. They cook and eat together in the men's house. Relations among men are fiercely egalitarian. Women garden and eat their own food. The productive existence of men and that of women are, like their bodies, more parallel than complementary. A wife remains bound to her own family, and in time of conflict she may lend her force to theirs. The infant is their coproduction. The parents do not educate their sons into the skills of men and of women; they will be initiated by the whole clan into the skills and tasks of each stage of their development. In the basic social transaction, the man who goes to the adjacent hamlet does not receive the whole woman, an assistant in his productive or political existence, nor someone who will produce children and give them to him, or educate them. What he receives is essentially a supplier of female milk for their coproduced children, and in return he contracts to give his male milk to her younger brothers. The fundamental act of association which organizes society is a transaction with portions of the self, fluid portions of a fluid self.

A second form of society, which we find in the Eastern Highlands of Papua New Guinea, is characterized by bride-price. For his bride, the husband gives to her brothers, not his male milk, but a bride-price consisting of the products of male power, that is, of the hunt: tusks, fangs, fur, plumes, shells. Among the Sambia, a people of Lowland origin who immigrated to the Eastern Highlands, the milk sap ingested from trees becomes male fluid; there is then in the forest an equivalent for male fluid, and it figures in conjugal commerce. But the conversion to the prime substance of male power takes place within the body.

The form of society characterized by this kind of bride-price is found where the distinction between the female sphere, agriculture, and the male sphere is strongly felt. Men devote themselves exclusively to the hunt and war—more exactly, head-hunting, since the combats are not for territory, booty, or women. The head-hunter is not protecting the women, who are nowise being threatened; the men are pursuing combats of prestige and cannibalism among themselves. There are no war-chiefs or concerted battle strategies; each male arrayed in tusks, fangs, and spectacular headdresses of the shimmering plumes of the bird-of-paradise is seeking out the most powerful, spectacular, and brave male in order to cannibalize his body and thus incorporate his spirit.

The bride-price the bridegroom gives the bride's father and brothers is economically unproductive; it is not wealth that they will use to increase wealth. The tusks, fangs, and plumes offered by the husband will be *incorporated* into the nostrils, ears, arms, heads of the father and the brothers, enhancing their male power as hunters, incorporating in them the weapons and power of the most lordly animals of the jungle. It is not a boy but a man who comes to transact for a woman; the tusks he bears in his nostrils, the fangs in his face and ears, the plumes in his hair are not symbols of male power, but parts of his hunter and warrior body. They are the detachable parts he can pass over to be incorporated in the bodies of the father and brothers. The fundamental social transaction is with parts of the self.

A third type of society, found in the Western Highlands of New Guinea, is characterized by bride-price that is a true price, objects obtained by male power and which remain external to the body, objects useful, ceremonial, or decorative. The bridegroom will offer the bride's father and brothers quantities of rare shells, ritual objects or insignia of status, or else large quantities of foodstuffs, pigs, beverages, which cannot be kept but will be consumed in potlatch feasts in which the connections of and obligations to the father-in-law's family will be increased. Here the exchange has become metaphorical: for the possession of a wife, the husband gives not a part of himself but a representative of himself.

These are societies in which the herding of pigs and extensive cultivation of crops make female labor not complementary to male hunting but in disequilibrium with it. The sphere of male power is that of status in the political organization, control of ritual and of the ideological superstructure. With their political organization, the men control the surplus agricultural production and engage in financial transactions that issue in the concentration of wealth. The male economy is organized such that men can traffic with other men for the acquisition of many women. The dominant discourse concerns, not women's generative role in social reproduction, but women as producers of external wealth.

In these societies, the male culture produces not men, but "big men." The idea that men create men gives way to the notion that men "give birth to" key wealth.[3] Homosexual transactions disappear in these societies. Male lactation, male breeding of men, is here no longer a sociosexual concern. The tolerance for gender ambiguity diminishes as erotic attention is directed to the trappings and blazons of the self, rather than to treasured internal substance.

In this century such Melanesian societies have entered into relationship with Western societies. Food production in the village is supplied by the women; with game scarce and headhunting suppressed, the young men are drawn off to the plantations and the mines of the white men. But there they do not enter into a productive economy themselves; they work for wages while the white men control the productive resources and the tools. They really cannot use their wages to acquire productive wealth, plantations or mines; the profitable plants cannot be grown in their Highland homes. They use their wages to acquire male regalia: metal-buckled belts, wrist watches, gaudy and macho clothing, eventually motorcycles, which they will take back to their villages to offer as bride-price in exchange for women, the local wealth producers. The fathers-in-law then hoard these things as prestige objects, representatives of their status within male society. Filling his compound with the sumptuary objects of white male prestige, the father extends his prestige to white male society also. For the greatest male power a father can have is to be the headman of the village with which the white labor-recruiter will have to deal.

The white men themselves have a society in the region. In their associations they do not transact with body portions or body parts that produce girls out of infants and men out of boys; they transact with money and productive property. They transact not with other white men for wealth-producing women, but with the black "big men" for black laborers for their plantations and their mines. Among themselves, they transact for the raw materials they manufacture, the commodities they market for a profit, the wages they invest for a profit. The fundamental social transaction is not for the reproductive body of a woman but for things that produce more things; the transactions among white men produce not men, but "big men." For these things that produce more things are also prestige objects. As resources they supply one's needs; as property that produces more property they materialize one's independence, freedom of initiative, and status. They are representatives of the self. But the self in question is in turn a representative. The prestige objects are representatives not of one's body but of one's training, education, business acumen, and connections. By entering into social commerce, one builds up a business, one builds a home that represents success. With these one has credit, can get loans, one can transact for more productive wealth. The business, the home, represent one—not oneself as a body, but as a name that means something in the real world.

The Sambia

I receive, from the other settlement, which we had long viewed with suspicion, a young wife. When she comes to dwell in my house, I enter into a pact with her family. Her younger brothers will daily kneel before me, and will open their mouths for my penis, and will drink my male fluids.

I stand before my wife kneeling before me, before her brothers kneeling before me, as they harden and suckle my penis. I lower myself over my wife, laid over the forest mosses and ferns, and pump my fluids into her. I withdraw glistening with pleasure and power in the sun.

I see my fluids drunk by my wife bringing her to menarche and fertility; poured into her vagina, day after day, they coagulate into the bones, organs, and flesh of our child. My fluids drunk by her brothers make them strong: I see their boyish frames harden with muscles, their faces grow beards, their penises grow and harden. With my fluids I pour a protective spirit into the fetus forming in the hollows of my wife's body; with my fluids I pour a virile soul into the hollows in her brothers' tender bodies.

Day after day I pour forth fluids. As my fluids drain from me my own strength flows out with them. My body, now hard as the trunk of a tree, grows no more; I see it destined to shrivel and bend like the bodies of old men given over to death. I go in secret to the pandanus tree and drink from the aerial roots hanging from its trunk the breast milk of the land my fathers five generations ago took possession of before it took possession of their bones and fluids. I find the milk of the trees flowing again from my penis. I breast-feed my wife with the milk of my penis. I breast-feed my wife's brothers with the milk of my penis. My wife breast-feeds the child whose bones, organs, and muscles formed in the male milk I poured into her womb.

Who am I? Call me a Sambia. Where we live few outsiders have ever ventured. We call it the nest of the high-ranging eagle. From the heights of our terrible isolation we see the cliffs lifting the voracious jungle over the roaring cascades below to the oceans vaulting above. For nine months of the year the rains descend upon the mountains, the jungle, our small thatched shelters, our bodies. Our settlements perch on mountain spurs rising steeply from the valley floor; the sides of the ridges deteriorate rapidly into small streams draining from the mountains, making our steps treacherous, but also fortifying our hamlets with deep gullies and watercourses against the approach of our enemies. Often we feel the earth below tremble and the mountains shift. The jungle surges with oak, pine, beech, and broad-leafed trees; bright orchids float in the rain pools caught in the crotches of their limbs, their branches streaming with vines and creepers. Above our settlements the forest thins out to a single layer of gnarled and crooked trees whose branches are hoary with liverworts and ferns drifting in the cold fog. The trails from our homes and our gardens into the green summits above weave around aerial roots, limestone outcrops, banks of vines and lianas, often passing over slick tree bridges suspended over streams and rivers hurtling down ever-deeper gorges. Over them we circulate, conduits of blood, breast milk, penis milk.

Who are the Sambia? Gilbert Herdt, the Stanford anthropologist who lived among them in 1974–1976, and again in 1979 and 1981, does not reveal to us their real name, and has taken pains to conceal their exact location, somewhere in the Eastern Highlands of Papua New Guinea, in order to protect them and their secret institutionalized homosexuality. He tells of them in his book *Guardians of the Flutes: Idioms of Masculinity*, and in the books he edited, *Rituals of Manhood* and *Ritualized Homosexuality in Melanesia*,[4] books that have made this minuscule and isolated population and its culture the key to unlocking the meaning of gender identity forged in diverse but related male rituals among perhaps up to twenty percent of the known cultures of Melanesia.

The Sambia number about 2,300; they live in small hamlets in six population clusters. Gardening, mainly sweet potatoes and taro, and hunting are the main economic pursuits. Women do most of the garden work. Men do all the hunting, primarily for possum, tree kangaroos, cassowaries, other birds, and eels. A strict division of labor and ritual taboos forbid men and women from doing one another's tasks; a hamlet, and each house, is divided into male and female spaces; the spaces between houses and the gardens about them, the valleys below and the forests above are traversed on paths reserved for each sex and taboo to the other. Late arrivals in the Eastern Highlands from the Great Papuan Plateau, the Sambia lived subject to raids and ambushes; with only his hand weapons between each individual and his and his family's death, each man could count only on his bare physical strength and personal valor to survive and protect his home. Men are even now seen as destined to be warriors, and the qualities of a warrior—strength, endurance, a fund of violent emotions, bravery, and individual cunning—are perceived to constitute maleness.

Females are perceived to mature "naturally," without external aids, for their bodies contain a menstrual-blood organ (*tingu*), whose flowing pool of blood feeds their physical and mental development. Their bodies are hot with their superabundant blood, and survive infancy better, acquire motor and linguistic skills earlier, mature earlier, are stronger, and live longer than those of males. Boys possess *kereku-kerekus*, or semen-organs. This organ is not functional at birth; it contains no semen naturally, and can only store semen, never produce it. Only oral insemination, Sambia declare, can activate the boy's semen organ and develop the musculature, hirsute face, voice, and genitals of virility.

The girls progressively associate with and master the skills of women as they grow. Boys, however, are allowed to roam freely with their age-mates, acquiring their own skills and amusements. They are not educated into male gender identity, the masculine social persona, nor the skills of virile professions; they are initiated.[5]

The first three initiations, at ages seven to ten, at eleven to thirteen, and at fourteen to sixteen, function to forcibly break the boys from their long association with their mothers, and their milk. At the first initiation, the seven- to ten-year-old boys are weaned from their mothers' milk and foods to male foods and the penis milk of youths of their brothers-in-law's clan. After the third initiation, they will serve as fellateds to feed semen into first- and second-stage boy initiates. The fourth initiation purifies the youth and issues in cohabitation with his wife; he will henceforth have to inseminate his wife orally to bring her to menarche. The fifth-stage initiation comes at the wife's menarche; the husband will have to henceforth inseminate her vaginally, and is given the highly secret practices, especially his breast-feeding from the white milk sap of thirteen species of trees, to compensate for the semen depletion vaginal intercourse will entail. Sixth-stage initiation comes upon the birth of the first child; it endows the father with the social personhood of one responsible for the production and the reproduction of the clan. But he will have achieved not only masculine personhood but male gender identity, indeed physical maleness, and these attainments, which semen-depletion in the years ahead will undermine, are maintained only in the giving. He must, with his semen, give masculine personhood, male gender identity, indeed physical maleness to his wife's real or classificatory younger brothers.

Sambia do not conceive semen as so many little seeds but one of which is required to germinate in order for the fetus to form. They conceive the womb as a receptacle, into which blood flows from the *tingu*, the menstrual-blood organ. When it is kept full of male fluids, the fetus can form, coagulating in the mix of maternal blood and male fluid. Consequently, to form a fetus a male must inject his fluids into his wife constantly, up to the last stage of pregnancy. (It is then misleading for us to speak of semen or sperm.) The womb is a container and transformer of fluids; there male fluids change into the bones, internal organs, muscles, and skin of a fetus. Only the circulatory blood in the fetus comes from the mother. Some of the mother's menstrual blood is transmitted to the female fetus's *tingu*; this blood will be the innate or "natural" source of her psychobiological feminization.

To give male fluids in fellatio is *pinu pungooglumonjapi*—pushing to grow. Male fluid, ingested orally by the mother, is conducted to her breasts and there transformed into mother's milk, which grows the infant's soft body. Growth is aided by eating pandanus nuts, and it is part of the work of procreation for the father to tend pandanus trees and scale them to obtain the nuts.

After weaning, girls continue to grow without further external human fluids, whereas boys falter, staying puny, soft, and weak. Male growth after weaning comes from fellatio, which is male breast-feeding (*monjapi'u*). A portion of the ingested male fluid is stored in the boy's *kereku-kereku*, and drawn on after puberty to produce the new growth of musculature, body hair, and genitals. The strength—size, valor, and force of speech—of men comes from the male fluids they have received from other men.

The male fluid taken from other males and stored in the boy's *kereku-kereku* will also provide the youth with male fluid for his own later sexual couplings. The first sign of surplus male fluid in the body comes in emissions in wet dreams.

How utterly anomalous seems a society that could make of the whole period of the boy's development from childhood to adulthood a period of exclusive, positively valued and erotically exciting homosexuality, could make of this homosexuality the royal road to heterosexuality! For us such a society could only risk its reproduction and such a culture its coherence.

The Liquid Currency of Social Transactions

In our conception, body fluids flow, quite outside of, and beneath, our political economy—fluids enter our bodies naturally, unnoticed by our conscious surveillance and uncoded by our social codes, and evaporate or are discharged in the extreme privacy of our closed-door bathrooms and our dark bedsheets as we retire alone, an emission outside of social laws, unmentionable in our socially significant discourse. We would inquire into how and why they are produced, or where and when they are consumed and discarded, or by whom, only in the biological or medical discourse in which our organisms figure only as entities of anonymous and silent nature.

For the Sambia, the vital fluids transubstantiate as they pass from one conduit to another.[6] They are the scarce resources of the life, growth, strength, and spirituality of the clan. Among the Sambia, body fluids do not flow; they are transmitted from socius to socius, metered out in social transactions. Sambia society is fundamentally constituted by these transactions.

Trees are regarded as of female sex; the white milk sap of pandanus trees is obtained from the thick hanging aerial roots, which are the breasts of the trees. The strength of trees, of female nature, is transubstantiated into male fluid in the bodies of the men who suckled them. The pandanus trees are carefully planted and tended by the clan on patrilinear territory, and the fathers regulate the distribution of this milk to the fifth-stage initiates in secret ritual practices.

The abundance of male fluid produced in the men is transmitted to the mouths of boys, where it masculinizes them by being stored in their innately empty *kereku-kereku*s. It is marriages contracted for that determine which boys have access to the male fluid of which men. A man who contracts for a wife contracts an obligation to give his male fluid to the mouths of her real or classificatory younger brothers. Boys who have received enough male fluid so that the abundance begins to flow from them in ejaculations enter into the obligation, marked by the third-stage initiation, to give their excess to a regulated set of younger boys.

The fourth-stage initiation puts youths under the obligation to give their penises to their wives to suck. Transmitted into the mouths of women, their male fluid transubstantiates into female milk. When the breasts of the young bride swell with its abundance and she reaches menarche, the fifth-stage initiation orders his male fluid to be transmitted into her vagina where it transubsantiates into the bones, internal organs, muscles, and skin of a fetus. Sambia do not recognize unproductive orgasm with her as the end of vaginal intercourse, and they show no concern with bringing their wives to orgasm.[7]

While men sometimes masturbate in preparation for being fellated, solitary or reciprocal masturbation to orgasm is, as far as Herdt has been able to determine, quite unknown among them.[8] Male-fluid emissions in wet dreams are regarded as fellatio with spirits, and come under the category of play since they are not productive—spirits are not engendered through them. Nocturnal emissions are regarded with some anxiety, for the spirits drain and deplete the male-fluid storers they suck, and probably wish to harm them.[9]

The discharge of blood is also completely socialized. The female *tingu* is a fountain of blood; women's bodies give forth blood in a superabundance that is disquieting to the men.

> Blood keeps the body cool; sickness goes into a hot body. Women have cold skins *from too much blood.* Men are hot-skinned *from too little blood....* Women hold the source [*kablu*: tree base] of blood. They have a blood pool [*boongu*].... Sickness avoids women, their coldness chases it away. Women don't die quickly, they are never ill. We men have small buttocks, we go up trees. Women have big buttocks, like tree trunks, they live a long time. (Tali, a Sambia informant.)[10]

All menstrual flows are regulated with detailed ritual anxiety. Bloodstains left on the ground are highly taboo. The menstrual blood of the mother belongs to the fetus that will form in it; the surplus blood production is required by the female fetus, for from the blood infused and stored in her *tingu* all her biological and social growth and maturation will depend. Men spit immediately after vaginal intercourse, to expel any bloodstains left on them. The excess blood that pours from a vagina, rather than being absorbed in a fetus, breaks the chain from socius to socius; the shamed woman must withdraw to a menstrual hut outside the confines of the settlement and undergo ritual reintegration to return.[11]

After battles, shamanist ceremonies expurgate the blood of slain enemies from the weapons and bodies of warriors, delivering it back to the ghosts of the slain. This purge, when completely successful, would disconnect the circuit of reprisal attacks by the exsanguine ghosts of the victims.[12]

Finally the transmission of breast milk is always a social transaction. Lactation in a woman is not an anonymous biological process; it is marriage and the husband who pours male fluid into her mouth that instigates and maintains the milk flow destined for the mouth of the child.

Fluid Value

Male fluid, blood, and breast milk are resources given and received; we must differentiate, then, between their use-value and their exchange-value. When commodities are transferred to be of utility to the other party who offers another kind of commodity or service in exchange, or who transfers them in turn to a third party, or when a delay intervenes before the exchange, they may acquire a value supplemental to their perceived utility. Male fluid, blood, and breast milk are values in an economy.

Marriages are arranged, preferably among infants, betrothed by their fathers, normatively between clans, preferably of different hamlets, which are potential enemies. Homosexual contacts are prohibited between all clansmen, matrilateral kin, age-mates, and with ritual sponsors. The clan that donates the wife also confers the husband's homosexual partners, her real or classificatory younger brothers. The male-fluid transaction ties the unrelated groups; one does not give or receive male fluid from true, intertribal enemies, only from potential enemies. Male-fluid transactions dis*tingu*ish kin from nonkin, and friendly from hostile persons. Thus to the male-fluid transaction the value of political and economic alliance is added.

For his male fluid his work makes available to her—work of multiple, regular male-fluid prestations, and work of tending the pandanus trees and procuring their milk-white nuts to supplement breast milk for her growing children—the donor receives in exchange the work of his wife, producer of garden products and producer of his children. The potential for male-fluid donation is the basis for ownership of persons; wives are inalienably owned by their husbands and their clans; in case of warfare, all ties of the wife with her clan are abolished. Adultery is seen as "stealing another woman's male fluid," and is called *kweikoonmulu*, "male-fluid fight."[13] Thus while a wife becomes her husband's exclusive sexual property and her labor—complementary to, rather than cooperative with, his—belongs to him, she acquires exclusive property rights over that scarce resource, his male fluid.

Not only the capacity to give male fluid, but also the way of giving invests the donor with power. Sexual contacts are effected privately in the forest in the evening. Sambia use only one position, the standing one, for fellatio with boys or women, and husbands use only the "missionary position" with their wives for vaginal intercourse. "Foreplay," caresses, body contact, is minimal; the male-fluid donor withdraws quickly after ejaculation. Orgasmic pleasure, then, comes with male-fluid donation, in body-positions that materialize instant freedom to withdraw at will. Boys rarely experience erection or orgasm while serving as fellators; women rarely, or never, experience orgasm in intercourse—their orgasmic pleasure comes in breast-feeding their children. Direct male-fluid transactions are asymmetrical; the donor materializes as power, the recipient absorbs growth, strength, spirituality. (And yet—men view sexually experienced women as consumed by insatiable erotic appetites, and do know that boys relish the savor and texture of abundant male fluid in the youths the boys court.[14])

There is a collective male-fluid pool, contained in the bodies of all men living within neighboring hamlets. As a boy draws strength from numerous men, who deposit their male fluid in his reserve for his future use, so men are kept strong by having their male fluid safely contained in many boys. This explains why, for the Sambia, homosexual contacts are less depleting than heterosexual—and why there is no ritual concern with replenishing one's male-fluid supply by ingesting the white milk-sap of the breasts of trees until the fifth and sixth stages of initiation, which initiate a male into heterosexual intercourse.[15] Since recipients harbor portions of one's male fluid (strength and spirituality) inside them, one is kept healthy in them—through sympathetic-contagious magic. A woman lacks this protection; she is not a cult initiate, and her male fluid comes from only one man, her husband. Nor is a man protected by depositing his male fluid in women or creating children. This is a conception quite the opposite of ours; our sympathetic-contagious magic thought finds the prolongation and maintenance of our virile life, strength, and spirit in our children.

In mediated transactions, male fluid is transmitted to someone whose body transforms it into something else useful to a third party. Thus the male transmits male fluid to the woman vaginally, whose body stores and transforms it into the bones, organs, muscles, and skin of the fetus. His male fluid also infuses a soul and conveys the spirit familiars to her male fetus. He transmits male fluid to the woman orally, whose body transforms it into breast milk, used by the infant for its sustenance.

A boy ingests male fluid from his real or classificatory brothers-in-law, who relay his father as male-fluid—growth, strength, and spirituality—donors. When this son becomes a male-fluid donor in turn, he will trade his sister for a wife, and his male-fluid-fed strength and spirituality will be transmitted to her and her offspring, as well as to her immature real and classificatory brothers.

Finally, the milk sap of thirteen species of trees is received by the male, who transforms this breast milk into male fluid, in order to give it in turn to his brothers-in-law, his wife, and through her, to his child.

In these transactions which benefit a third party, the breast milk of trees and male fluid acquire the supplemental value of fetal tissue, spirit familiars, breast milk.

Interest Accrued Over Time

A man from one clan obtains from another clan in an adjacent, potentially hostile, settlement, a woman, a garden producer and coproducer of babies, who will perpetuate his clan. His real and classificatory brothers-in-law receive male fluid from him. The husband may give one of them his sister for marriage. Or he will give one of their sons his daughter for betrothal in infancy; they will trade her for a wife from a third, related group. Thus the male-fluid transactions acquire the supplemental exchange-value of a promissory note to be redeemed in the next generation.[16]

The exchangist politico-economic structure of the transmissions of body fluids coded and metered in Sambia culture fashions time cyclically. Resources that flow out of one group are destined to find their way back, if not in this generation, then in the next.

The establishment of a ritualized social economy of closed exchanges of the equivalent has the paradoxical effect of giving time a value-producing force. The time a return can be delayed will add or subtract a supplement of value to what is exchanged. For example, in a society whose codes of honor determine that offenses each require a specific revenge, the one on whom a certain vengeance is obligatory can maximize the force of the vengeance by determining that it fall at once or perhaps that it be long delayed. Among the Sambia, where every transmission of male fluid, blood, and milk is regulated and its direct and indirect exchange-values coded, the individual's own initiatives consist in being able to maximize his or her resources by delaying or accelerating the obligatory return in transactions in which they have value.[17]

An individual is not a producer of his or her own resources that have value in social transactions, nor the seat of initiative that determines their use and exchange-value. The individuality of the individual consists in the possession of strategies that manipulate the productive force of time, in the initiatives at his or her disposal to create a supplement of value by manipulating the delay of the obligatory return. The Sambia have a fluid individuality, forming and dissolving in the force of the flow of time.

The Mystification-Value of Fluid Commodities

In transactions with male fluids—as with detachable parts of male bodies and with representatives of self—the exchange-value of these commodities doubles up with a symbolic—a rationalizing and mystifying—function. The economics of fluid-exchange is also a political system. Every exercise of political power, Foucault wrote, depends on masking a substantial part of itself.[18]

The dumbfounding and perhaps overdetermined secrecy of the Sambia homosexual years is not easily interpreted. How extraordinary that it was only in 1974, among the minuscule population of the Sambia, that a practice was discovered that has since been found to be pervasive throughout Melanesia— an enormous geographical area which covers tens of thousands of square miles, from Fiji in the east to the offshore islands of Irian Jaya far to the west![19] Up to 20 percent of known Melanesian cultures have at this very late date been found to enjoin homosexual practices on all males. Herdt himself lived five months among the Sambia, slept for weeks in the men's house, without suspecting that all males from ages seven to ten practiced homosexual fellatio virtually daily for the next ten to fifteen years, and some continue throughout life.

The practice is not only kept secret from outsiders, from anthropologists, whom the local people quickly sense would use it immediately as a rationalization of their white contempt. Among Sambia themselves, at the first initiation, when fellatio is enjoined, the boys are threatened with immediate death if they reveal it to uninitiated boys or to any female. What is the reason for this secrecy, and what is the secret the reason rationalizes?

Sambia men are warriors. The defense of the community, by hand-to-hand combat with rudimentary weapons, where treachery, ambushes, and raids have to be met with bare physical prowess, audacity, and the ability to take pain, is the obligation of every male. Women, drawn from potentially hostile neighboring communities, retain contact with and share the political interests of their brothers and their clans; they remain potential spies in the households of their husbands. Groups are small enough to be highly vulnerable internally.

By the coding of male fluid as a valued resource, men are placed firmly in control of their part of the means of socio-biological reproduction. The metering of male fluids keeps women and also boys in their socio-economic place. If male fluid were free or easily at hand, its value would deflate. The coding that makes of body fluids commodities and regulates body-fluid transactions keeps in place political networks through which senior men make peace, negotiate marriages, and carry on exchanges.

The Sambia coding, cast in physical-cosmological terms, says that what men produce is men, who are not engendered and matured by natural processes, but produced through isolation and ordeal, initiation, revelation of male secrets, and male breast-feeding. But the coded procedures of the production of men also produce a cultural order. Women's sexuality and reproductive powers are natural, uncontrolled, and threatening to this order. The women's physical control over reproductive processes and emotional control over their sons must be overcome by secrecy, taboo legislation, and dramatized male power. For us, the Sambia coding dissimulates a politico-economic project which employs ordeal, fear, and cruelty and produces domination; legislation and religion function as ideology. The coding "naturalizes" and "celestializes," as Marx would put it, an order that is cultural and historical. The male ideology and initiations function to ensure male power over female resources—periodicity, fertility, child care, and labor.

The initiation system requires that those who submitted to psychologically traumatic and physically painful initiations as boys cruelly inflict these ordeals upon the succeeding generation in the service of a cult ideology whose cruel motivations and partly fraudulent ritual trappings have been discovered by them in the male initiations procedures. Is not bad faith constitutive of their codings?[20]

Such systems, Roger Keesing writes sternly,[21] are fraught with contradiction from within. These men depend for their physical survival on the labor of the women they exclude and demean. By separating the men's realm from the women's to create male solidarity, their system leaves beyond male control the everyday lives—and minds—of women. Do they not know this?

It seems hard to believe that in cultures so restricted—one closely studied Papuan culture, the Baktaman, comprises but a few hundred people[22]—the women really could know nothing whatever about the daily practices of their men and their sons. That there is deception built into their codings, and self-deception also, seems evident.

Herdt, as most male anthropologists, had no access to the female ideology, culture, experience, and judgments. Terence and Patricia Hays did, in their research among the Ndumba, an Eastern Highlands people who show some influences from the Sambia. They ask, "Why do Ndumba women thus actively cooperate in the performance of ceremonies whose central meanings consign them to subservient positions in society and whose main theme appears to be misogynistic?" Their research concludes that "Ndumba women believe in their mystical powers and the dangers they pose to males as fully as do the men and...they also see the need to control these powers if men and society are to survive. For the common good, women must educate girls and remind each other that they possess forces that are so powerful that men cannot, working alone, safeguard themselves.... To possess such awesome forces is a heavy responsibility and, perhaps, one that carries its own satisfactions."[23]

The Experience, and Use of Male Bodies

To denounce the cognitive content of a culture as an ideology is to interpret its positive ideal negatively. The reverse reading employs concepts that come from the cognitive content of another culture. One interprets the maleness Sambia initiation procedures produce and male culture celebrates as envy of female powers and as death drive. The validity of the interpretation depends on showing that these concepts fit better the Sambia inner experience of their bodies and the warrior use of their male bodies.

Bruno Bettleheim could see in the subincision practiced on their penises by Australian aborigines[24] a procedure to give to male bodies by culture the missing organs of female fertility. Is the institutional secrecy of Sambia male society and culture the institutional projection of an unconscious censorship which both dissimulates and reveals envy of women? Does it betray male envy of female bodies, of their superabundant blood, their superior health, their superior work capacity, their greater longevity; male envy of their reproductive and nutritive resources; male envy of the cosmic periodicity of their vitality—which men compensate for with the construction of an exchangist politico-social economy which engenders a cyclical time of the cultural order; male envy of that biopsychic and conflict-free pre-Oedipal stage which characterizes, according to psychoanalyst Robert Stoller,[25] the first months of the infant's symbiotic life in the bosom of its mother—for which men compensate with the construction of male warrior solidarity?

For us, male and female bodies are morphologically complementary, and we use the dyad active/passive to conceive them as functionally complementary (male musculature/female glands and curves; male erection/female orifice). The inner states of individuals—sexual attraction, revulsion, fear, envy—must differ where the inner and outer perceptions of male and female bodies differ. The terms "sexual antagonism" and "death drive" used to characterize the inner states of men in Melanesia in their relations with women and with other men cannot mean what these terms mean for us, who do not have the same perceptions of our bodies and have not had the kinds of sexual couplings and combats they engage in.

For the Sambia, male and female bodies are parallel, analogous conduits of vital fluids; the individual body is but a local conduit of their flow across nature and the human community. This fundamental concept of their system of thought must express the distinctive focus of their inner experience of themselves, which precedes and makes possible their system of thought. The female body is not privileged with organs for conception; there is in fact no real notion of conception, the fetus coagulates in the receptacle of the womb when it is filled with a mix of maternal blood and male fluid. In fact, our notion of conception, which makes the male action transitive, though minimal and brief, is a recent notion, and it is not an experiential notion but one derived from empirical induction.

In morphologically parallel conduits for fluids, the fluids must flow. The female body contains a pool of superabundant blood, stored in the *tingu* of the female fetus prenatally and released over time; the bodies of boys have an empty and inactive *kereku-kereku* which has to be filled from the outside. For fluid to flow in their conduit bodies, boys must draw upon the male fluid of mature males, and upon the white milk sap of pandanus trees. They are not trying to annex to themselves the specific organ of females, but making their own organ functional. For Sambia, fellatio among men does not transfer female nutritive powers to males; it forges male identity in a body lacking it innately. The experience of maturity in being a male fluid donor must be fundamental, and give its specific sense to what boys are perceived to lack.

The initiation through sexual practices that are psychologically traumatizing and physically painful is, positively, a promotion to the pride and solidarity of warriors. Herdt, however, conceives war psychoanalytically as an exteriorization of the death drive.

> Twentieth-century intellectualized researchers have not emphasized
> how catastrophic war can be, socially, economically, and psychologically,
> especially that primitive form of warfare that depends on stone-age
> weaponry—through man-to-man combat—which we have never known.

Such facts relentlessly condition the very meaning of male existence.

War had been, after all, chronic, pervasive, and destructive. How is it really possible, now, even to attempt to recapture the sense in which a Sambia man lived life in the face of the day-to-day possibility that he could be snipered in his gardens, be cut down in battle and axed to death, or have his wife stolen by another man, physical strength and stamina his only steady insurance against such threats? How is it possible to forget past battles and brushes with death? And nothing can erase the memory of brutally massacred comrades and kinsmen and friends.... On the raid, no less than in the battle, a man had to demonstrate his masculine "strength" or face destruction. This demonstration might mean a show of aggressive bravado, seeking thrills and quick-witted demonstrations of virility through physical action.... In what follows, we must remember that man's myths and idiom belong to that stark reality.[26]

But the term warfare is in the end ethnocentric and inappropriate in our discourse about them; their raids and battles do not result in economic conquest or political domination. What Kenneth Read observes of the Gehuku-Gama is also true of the Sambia:

The constantly recurring (and tedious) chronicles of intertribal warfare epitomized one aspect of the dominating ethos; for unbridled warfare (*rova*), as distinct from feuding (*hina*), required no precipitating event (though often some were cited). Warfare did not lead to conquest (in the sense of extending boundaries or imposing sovereignty over others), though one of its aims was to destroy the villages of enemy groups and force their inhabitants to seek temporary sanctuary elsewhere. But in the course of time, the defeated (who always intended to return) were commonly invited back to serve once more as a foil for testing and demonstrating the ultimate expression of strength and masculinity.[27]

Male ontogeny in Sambia tends, Herdt observes, to the implantation of overweening, vain, male susceptibility, given to acerbity and brute and fiery violence.[28] This is perhaps too impressionistic an appraisal. Sambia warriors apply to the shaman after the battle that he purge them of the blood shed and return it to the ghosts of those fallen in battle. Must not the fact that each boy has spent his formative years drinking of the male fluid of his potential enemies determine the deep structure of his warrior character?

Combat among Sambia is not only eroticized as hatred and a death drive directed outward and given full sanction by the culture; it is also a relation between males whose first bond was that of a reciprocal donation of male substance, a donation intensely eroticized, the sole voluptuousness of the formative ten to fifteen years of their lives. The contests in which these males will spend their adult lives as professional warriors must also be an eroticized form of male-fluid circulation. What is at stake, erotically, in the return of the defeated in an interminable and self-perpetuating cycle of bloodletting must have the same circulatory diagram as their domestic vital-fluid transactions.

Fluid Erotics

In the mountain fastness of the jungle drenched by rain nine months of the year, the Sambia live in intense awareness of their own fluids, blood, male fluid, milk—these inconstant resources of life, society, and culture. To speak of the specific force of the erotic exploration of the self and of others among the Sambia, the erotic quality of their lives, the inner erotic states, we have to divine them as they must be lived in the perceptions they have of their bodies, or rather "fetishized" body parts, and in their erotic transactions, with portions of the self rather than with representations of the self.

The release of a surplus tension was for Freud the diagram of orgasm, the greatest pleasure our kind can know, and also the model for every pleasure. The release of the superabundant semen produced in the male body, spermatozoa in incalculable numbers when but a half-dozen are needed for the reproductive capacities of a woman's lifetime, is the material substance of this pleasure; Bataille built on this superfluity his erotics and ethics of excess, of expenditure at a loss, of gratuitous discharge.[29] For us, the excesses of semen in the male give him the inward sense of maleness, male power and male passion, as a gratuitous excess to be discharged in transgression and in glory. A woman is, on the contrary, to be protected; a woman is the materialization of limited resources and vigor which have to be economized, and which are depleted in the reproduction for which the woman sacrifices herself for the life of the species.

For the Sambia, it is the woman's body that is the locus of excess, of excess blood that streams from her menstrual-blood organ, materialization of great health, unbridled sensuality, reproductive powers that are natural, uncontrolled, and threatening to the social order men create. Sambia men do not experience in the nocturnal emissions the insignificant or glorious discharge of an excess. For them male fluid is a scarce resource that they will not squander in masturbation. It is donation, and not gratuitous discharge, that focuses their surveillance and intensifies their voluptuousness.

When a child is born, there is no male presence. Genital copulation—polluting contact with the bloody womb from which the child came—is taboo for up to three years after the birth of a child, and a father will very often not so much as see his son for the first six months of his life. The boy lives entirely with his mother, her breasts always accessible to him, and the father has no role in the disciplining or education of his son until initiation. Physical contact with him is scrupulously avoided, since the child bears too much the smell and stains of vaginal blood. Fathers avoid sleeping near their sons, for since they share the same male fluid the spirit familiars that dwell therein may wish to migrate from the fathers' bodies into the more handsome bodies of the sons.

Psychoanalyst Robert Stoller speaks of the first months of an infant's life as a conflict-free phase, in which nonmental learning, conditioning or imprinting, biologic and biopsychic patterns are merged with behavior patterns imprinted by the mother. This complex forms a matrix of habitual, automatized core character, free of intrapsychic conflict, whose gratifying affective nature confirms it and implants it as a set of repetition compulsions. The primary fantasy-field is generated at this stage, "to modulate the impact of the outer world and inner stimuli, protecting us from—*giving us explanations for*—otherwise unmanageable forces that impinge from outside and from within."[30] The long duration of this primary maternal symbiosis among the Sambia—well beyond the year and a half or two years in which, according to Stoller[31] and Money and Ehrhardt,[32] core gender identity is formed, beyond the five or six years at which, according to these authors, it is almost irreversible—must mean that this maternal symbiosis remains an exceptionally cohesive stratum of the erotic subjectivity of Sambia throughout life. The dominant theme of breast-feeding in all their adult eroticism—orgasm (*chemonyi*) in males coming with fellatio with boys or wives, orgasm in women associated with breast-feeding their children rather than with vaginal intercourse—figures as the index of this primary eroticism.

At the first initiation, at the ages of seven to ten, boys, hitherto maintained in the most stern sexual ignorance, are forcibly separated from their mother's sphere, and initiated into homosexual fellatio. The boy will have to not only sleep in the communal men's house, but hide his face from all women, and avoid so much as walking on the women's paths in the hamlet, garden, and forest. The weaning of the boy from mother's breast to brother-in-law's penis is then a break of the most radical, and emotionally traumatic, sort, for both mothers and sons. These "late procedures of ritualized gender surgery must rattle the very gates of life and death."[33]

The extreme emotional tension and violence of this forced initiation is coded in secret male collective rituals, in which the most secret myths, culminating in the great myth of male parthenogenesis, are revealed. Nothing in Sambia culture is more invested with mystery and sacred awe than the wailing songs attributed to spirits and which are now revealed to issue from flutes offered to the boys for their first fellatio, sucking these songs into their bodies and male-fluid organs.

It is true that the initiation involves castration threats—if the boys will be found seeking sexual commerce with senior men's wives. But, unlike the Freudian Oedipal scenario, the severance from the mother is not here an initiative of paternal jealousy intended to create sexual anxiety and make the incest taboo sure, and inaugurate the long sexual latency period that will endure until puberty. Here the boys, far from being forced into self-castration and self-excoriation of the primary-process erotogenic surface of their sensuality, are weaned upon a relay of the paternal penis, and are offered a more powerful, virilizing breast milk. The initiates are indeed subjected to psychologically traumatic and physically painful ordeals, stretching, egestive, and ingestive rites, such that the homosexual fellatio is forced upon them in the midst of fear, worry, and anger. But the fear, worry, and anger are not contrived to implant a permanent castration anxiety before adolescent sexuality; they are intended to open the heart, to produce a heightened awareness of seeing, hearing, tasting, touching, and smelling, in which sexual excitement flares.[34]

A Sambia's homosexual partner is typically the husband of his sister. Layard[35] argued psychoanalytically that the junior partner realizes his repressed sexual desire for his sister through a homosexual relationship with a man eligible to be her husband. The symbiosis in which the daughter continues to live with her mother would motivate this erotic transference of the boy upon his sister, which in turn would motivate the transference upon her future husband. Then, in the kind of severance Sambia initiation effects, incest is not so much prohibited, as in the Oedipus scenario of Freudians, as it is displaced and then positively valued. It is the mother's brother who acts as ritual sponsor for the boy, conferring upon him his sister's future husband as the boy's maternally sanctioned sexual partner.

The initiates now enter years of avid craving for male fluid and dreamy romanticism over males, nowise drenched with shame but annealed with honor, with both their own sense of virile, self-virilizing pride, and their sense of the nobility of the males they seek out as sexual partners. The magic flutes, detachable penises, fetishized in both the psychoanalytic and the anthropological sense, script their public eroticism. Among boys the fellated's penis size is not accorded much importance, whereas the amount of flow, consistency, and savor is. Fellators are fascinated with the quantities, densities, textures, and tastes of male fluid, which they discuss interminably, Herdt reports, like wine tasters.[36] For boys become literally addicted to the drinking of male fluid, mystical participation in the primal myth of male parthenogenesis will script the erotic imagination of the homosexual infatuations.[37]

At the third initiation, youths must reverse positions in homosexual intercourse; an older male must never again serve as fellator for a younger. The youth experiences the male identity of being male fluid donor and the pleasure of that identity.

At the fourth initiation, the youths are given access, in addition to boy fellators, to the fellating mouths of the wives with which they have been betrothed since infancy. The social and erotic access to sexual contacts with both males and females must determine the individual's sense of erotic impulses in himself. "The social acceptance of same- and opposite-sex contacts introduces the experiential element of subjective comparison—the feelings and consequences of homosexual versus heterosexual contacts—in organizing sexuality, which is alien to most Westerners' experience," Herdt writes. "This dual sexual regime makes homosexual and heterosexual relationships far more open to self/other evaluations."[38] It makes gender identity relational and multiple. It must make the erotic feeling multiple and relational.

At the fifth initiation, the male becomes functional in heterosexual genital intercourse. For us, the extreme sexual polarity—of economic roles, political status, and social esteem—maintained by the secrecy of the Sambia male ideology, which has as its effect that the real lives, thoughts, and experiences of women are inaccessible to males, makes it astonishing that the same overwhelming majority of males in this society become preferentially heterosexual as in any other society, the percentage of adult males preferentially homosexual in their practices about the same—perhaps 10 percent—as in our societies. Anthropologists since Mead, Read, Burton and Whiting have expatiated on the "sexual antagonism" characteristic of Papuan cultures. Herdt also speaks of the visible awkwardness of the bridegroom before his bride, delaying intercourse with her sometimes as long as a year or even beyond after they begin cohabitation. But in the end he appeals to Stoller's recent psychoanalytic theories of sexual excitement. "Homosexual experiences, distance, and dehumanization of woman are often needed to create *enough* hostility to allow the sexual excitement necessary for culturally appropriate heterosexuality and the 'reproduction' of society. Men need this sexual polarity and hostility to maintain their personal boundaries in love, marriage, and sex.... In place of dry typologies of ritual, we urgently need a theory of sexual excitement."[39]

With the sixth-stage initiation, upon the birth of the first child, the male acquires the social personhood of one responsible for the reproduction of the clan. He must give, with his male fluid, maleness to his wife's real or classificatory younger brothers. We are confounded over how a married man, enjoying exclusive conjugal rights over his wife and with licit and enjoined access to her mouth for fellatio, can be libidinally satisfied by being fellated by a seven-year-old boy. But his erection—the only part of a man that never lies, Cocteau said[40]—proves that he is.

Male-fluid flow that is orgasmic is categorized as play (*chemonyi*). Orgasmic play is asymmetrical, episodic, and nonappropriative. In Sambia culture the husband/wife dyad is the most symmetrical relationship; two males considerably separated by age introduce asymmetry. Thus a male fluid recipient is perceived as having "more heat" and being more exciting the younger he is. Exclusive access to a fellating mouth is inversely related to play; a man's wife, as his sexual property, is less exciting than a boy or woman taken at first (as a virgin) or once only, on the sly.

Regular, constant, frequent seminal transmissions, such as those which are necessary to keep the womb full of a mix of female blood and male fluid in order that the infant can coagulate, are categorized as work (*wumdu*). The male's fluids are a limited resource; the donor male is being depleted. Work is expenditure at a loss.

Voluptuous symbiosis with the mother, incestuous relationship with the sister's husband, voluptuous fellatio, voluptuous male-fluid donation in homosexual and heterosexual fellatio, voluptuous vaginal male-fluid donation to a woman positioned at a distance of ritual antagonism and excitement, reciprocal blood-letting in battle—how do these radically disjunctive formations of eroticism fit together in the unity of one individual?

The codes of our culture have as their aim to make isomorphic primary core gender identity, determined by genetic psychobiochemical factors and by the character of the biopsychic imprinting of the first months of life, the gender identity attributed to us by others and that we attribute subjectively to ourselves, and the optative gender identity we desire or envy.[41] For the Sambia, there is no innate core gender identity, and attributed gender identity, subjective gender identity, and optative gender identity come together and come apart in different ways at different stages of life. Clifford Geertz instructs us that "the Western conception of the person as a bounded, unique, more or less integrated motivational and cognitive universe, a dynamic center of awareness, emotion, judgment, and action organized into a distinctive whole and set contrastively both against other such wholes and against a social and natural background is, however incorrigible it may seem to us, a rather peculiar idea in the context of the world's cultures."[42]

The unparalleled secrecy that rules in the sphere of male culture in Sambia does not only function to maintain male solidarity, to sanctify ritual knowledge, to support the economic division of labor, and to serve the perceived need for power and control over women. In addition, secrecy maintains the social space for one's own compound of fragments of knowledge, ritual behavior, and fantasy that is one's personal identity. The Sambia sensuality is an erotic field of episodic, asymmetrical, nonreciprocally appropriating foci of erotic subjectivity. Intrapsychic walls of secrecy maintain the psychic space for them.

A Fluid Self

We conceive of our person as a subsistent constant, perceivable in the stable shapes and contours of our bodies, the recurrent verbal and behavioral patterns of our initiatives, and the recurrent diagrams of our emotions, attitudes, and posturings. It would be perceivable too in the consistent ways in which we clothe and adorn our bodies and in the stable social roles and functions in which we insert ourselves. We were not especially confounded by the psychoanalytic thesis that our identities are phallic, that they find in the hard erection of the concealed organ of our gender difference their corporeal materialization. We relegate the body fluids to the status of transitory properties of this subsistence; their passing does not undermine it as it does not enter into its specific identity. The fluids in our substance but transport refurbishments to this substance, and lubricate its morphologically fixed operations. Their seeping into and evaporation or discharge from it does not enter into the discourse in which our identities are coded. Our biology differentiates sexes by their distinctively functioning organs, and differentiates and relates species—dinosaurs and birds—by skeletal morphology; fossils reveal species and gender differences. We have fossil identities.

For the Sambia, gender identity determines economic and political tasks and roles, social attitudes, behaviors, emotions, and the very sense of selfhood. To be incomplete or immature sexually is to be not yet a person and not yet a self. But gender identity is not determined by the innate morphology of the substantive body. The bodies of men as of women, and their distinctive organs, *tingu* and *kereku-kereku*, are receptacles, depositories, and conduits for fluids. Power, strength, growth, and spirituality are possessed only in giving or receiving their material, fluid, substance. The specificity of fluids, and of their courses, determine gender; male and female gender identity, and identity *tout court*, are predicates of fluids that pass through these conduits. Agnatic blood, male fluid, menstrual blood, and milk form the basic elements from which the essential nature of the self is formed. It is the flow of blood that defines femaleness, the donation of male fluid that defines maleness. One's sense of selfhood is an essentially erotic, an orgasmic adhesion to this donation, this outpouring into another.

While female nature is in potency innate, and unfolds into girlhood naturally as the blood stored prenatally is released, it matures into womanhood
only upon being coupled orally and vaginally upon the penis from which it
draws the male fluids that make it reproductive and nutritive. Sterile women
are not complete persons; reproductive and nutritive functioning defines integral femaleness.

Hermaphroditism is known to the Sambia, is perhaps even more prevalent
among them than the statistical average in the human species,[43] and Sambia
acknowledge change from maleness to femaleness or from femaleness to maleness even at an adult age. They know a dozen such cases in their own small
population.

Maleness and femaleness exist only within the transactional field, which
circles across nature and society and spirals down generations. Maleness and
femaleness are episodic, fluid, formations, perceived in an intensive sense of
one's own inner fluid substance, identities forming and passing in the course of
fluids through one's body. The individuality of an individual male or female is
a fluid individuality, forming episodically as strategies become possible for
manipulating the productive force of time, for creating a supplement of value
for one's resources in the transactional circuits by manipulating the delay of
the obligatory return.

Sambia identify very strongly with the spectacular birds-of-paradise whose
glittering and phosphorescent plumes they incorporate into their headdresses. As among themselves, gender identity among the birds is volatile and
episodic: chicks are recognized as all female; fully plumed adult birds with
shimmering colors are recognized to be all male; the dull-colored birds that
lay eggs are taken to be older birds, which become female again.[44]

Fluid History

The introduction of colonialism and neo-colonialism has altered male power
in Melanesia. Young men in ever greater numbers leave their hamlets for years
to work on plantations, factories, and tourist resorts. When they return they
see that their wives, betrothed to them in infancy, have matured to menarche
without their male-fluid infusions. They return with European goods, which,
unlike shells, feathers, and tusks, are not incorporated into their bodies to
become parts of their bodies, but remain external representatives of their
power. They have had access to women far from the adjacent villages with
which their clan had long established political and economic reciprocity. Do
not these new conditions—far more than the contemptuous moralities of mis-

sionaries and the Pax Australiana which puts an end to the traditional male destiny to be warriors—doom institutionalized homosexual male-fluid transactions? Will it not also put an end to the specific erotics which simmers over, intensifies, shapes their bodies as conduits of male fluid, blood, and milk, and makes their subjective identity a culturally shaped property of, rather than the subject of, these flows? In another decade or two will we not be describing their erotics, no longer with the hydraulic model we have here elaborated, but with the machinic model Deleuze and Guattari have elaborated[45] to describe the libidinal experience of sexually individuated couplings in the Western disciplinary archipelago? It is not only the informed transcultural observer, like Robert Keesing, who recognizes that "it is an unfortunate fact of contemporary Papua New Guinea that the alternatives to traditional cultures are marginal participation in world capitalist economy, with the frequent consequence of pauperization and exploitation, and an alien and anachronistic religious ideology of sin, fire, and brimstone;"[46] the Papuans themselves know this with their own daily perceptions and in their bodies. In still another decade or two, will we not be describing their erotics with the electromagnetic model Freud and Lyotard have elaborated[47] to describe the fields of freely mobile and unbound excitations of our sensuality in a universe we know through our physics and whose energy is controlled by our electronic and thermonuclear technology?

The answer, we think, is not yet decided. The demise of all "primitive" cultures in the face of modern communication systems and post-colonial systems of politico-economic exploitation, a common theme of the last fifty years of anthropology, to be regretted or accepted with resignation, is not as complete as has been predicted. Many zones have shown obstinate cultural conservatism and even resurgent traditionalism. It is not certain that imposed obligatory schooling, the evidences of scientific anatomy, physiology, and biology, will convince them that the terms with which they code their bodies as conduits for fluids, and their identities as transitory predicates of those fluids, are but those of a fraudulent ideology. Cultural history today can no longer hold to the simple Durkheimian view that the ideology of a culture expresses in an integral manner the ecological, economic, and political structures that condition the survival and productivity of a people.

The Sambia coding of their own natures, bodies, identities, is an affirmation of their distinctness. "Different cultures within a region appear to be commenting on one another," Lindenbaum wrote, "quiet chamber music performances, with each group attuned to the sounds of their neighbors."[48] Each improvisation elaborates its own difference, "statements of their own distinctiveness, expressions of their identity," Keesing says.[49] One possible response to the current European invasion, alien influences, and cultural destruction and subversion is to use these symbols of ethnic distinctiveness to express commitment to continuing survival as a people, to a culturally expressed identity.

It is known that the Sambia, in particular, had immigrated between two hundred and a hundred and fifty years ago from the Great Papuan Plateau, and that their culture is a collage of elements brought with them, elements answering to their new ecological, demographic, political, and economic situation, and elements borrowed from their neighbors. What they will now borrow from the neo-colonial implantation may also figure in the collage.

We must recognize a specific force to erotics. The perception of their bodies as conduits for fluids, for those scarce resources which are male fluid, blood, and milk, is not simply the by-product of a social organization that structures its political economy in terms of a strict division between women's gardening and men's hunting and warfare, sister and niece exchange between potentially enemy hamlets, and the absence of material wealth that would be equivalent to human bodies themselves. The eroticization of body-fluid hydraulics functions as a force fixing this perception. As, in Freud, the primary-process sensuality of infancy persists, timeless and compulsive, beneath the Oedipal, phallic, and genital stages that succeed it, so, among the Sambia, the intensive eroticization of their own body fluids has a force that is not simply reducible to the structural force of a coded economy where people transact predominantly with portions of self rather than with representatives of self.

If, as the ecological, demographic, political, and economic conditions for the survival and productivity of a people change, their specific erotics, outlining their bodies as conduits of fluids, could persist, what about us? Will the machinic model of our erotics prevail among us as long as the ecological, demographic, political, and economic conditions of our existence are those of disciplinary biopolitics? Will an electromagnetic model of our erotics prevail in our advancing post-industrial revolution, driven with electrical and nuclear energy, under electronic, self-regulating surveillance, programmed cybernetically? Might our own erotics elaborate something like a perception of our orgasmic bodies as conduits of fluids? Might, as the Sambia borrowed their agriculture and their hunting from their new neighbors in the Eastern Highlands, some of us borrow our erotics from them, and thus formulate the distinctiveness of our identities and that of our pleasures?

Strange Lusts That Are Our Own

The libidinal and phallic character of our identity is exhibited in psychoanalysis, which supplies its genetic analysis. But psychoanalysis itself is the outcome of a history, which Michel Foucault has delineated.[1]

In nineteenth-century industrial Europe, the family was no longer the basic unit of production, knowledge, and authority. The sons leaving the family to work in factories and in colonial enterprises were coming to have more knowledge, authority, and productivity than their fathers. The state, having overthrown its monarchs, ceased to be the image-writ-large of the patriarchal family.

Pinel in France and Tuke and the Quakers in England established insane asylums for citizens whom the economic and administrative institutions of the disciplinary archipelago had failed to socialize. In the disciplinary archipelago, the asylums figured as zones on the margin of history. In them the family was reconstituted as a locus of authority, without knowledge or productivity. Civil and criminal law assigned the mad the status of minors. The asylum director was selected less for his medical science—a science of bleedings, drugs, baths, heat and cold treatments, and enforced rest—than for his authority, sobriety, judiciousness, and equilibrated character.[2] The obsessions, traumas, anxieties, and lusts of the confined were elaborated no longer across nature, the economic sphere, the political order, and the cosmic and sacred spaces, but in the confined space of confrontation with the director. Action was reduced to furious speech. The director calmed the ravings of the interned not so much by the rationality of his judgments as by his paternal demeanor and tone.

Freud abandoned completely all the pharmacology and hydrotherapeutics, the thermic and mechanical methods, and soon even hypnosis, still used by psychiatrists on the "mentally ill" outside of asylums, to confine the patient in a tête-à-tête with the doctor as father-substitute in that one-room asylum which is the psychoanalytic consultation room. For psychoanalysis, every madness that makes one malfunctional in nature, in society, in the cosmic and sacred order, owes its origin to a malfunctioning of the Oedipal family. The ravings of delusional discourse reveal speech not subject to law, to the paternal word; the symptoms of neurotics—from Anna O.'s psychosomatically paralyzed arm to Schreber's bestial violences—are so many blows struck against the father. The regressions toward infantilism are inscribed not, as in what Deleuze and Guattari call the epoch of nomadism, on the body of Earth, nor, as in the epoch of imperialism, on the body of the despot, nor, as in what they identify as the epoch of capitalism, on the abstract body of capital,[3] but on the body of the mother. The identity of the child, extracted by the castrating law of the father from symbiotic contact gratification, is formulated as a sign addressed to the mother and her substitutes. The therapy takes hold only when transference occurs, and the doctor as father-substitute leads the patient back through the Oedipal triangle. When the patient has passed this time definitively through the primary-process fixations into reproductive genitality, has taken on phallic identity, and has become capable of founding an Oedipal family in his turn, he will be recognized as cured.

Psychoanalysis does reveal the genesis and history of the passage into discourse of the libido of Western *man* at a certain period of Western institutional history. Perhaps, like the owl of Minerva, it takes flight as dusk falls over this history. If the hospitals, childcare centers, schools, factories, offices, barracks, hospitals, asylums, and retirement colonies in which we today in the West lead our lives are not superstructures built on the nuclear family, they can, after the execution of the divine-right kings and the death of God, only resort to the family as the locus where authority subsists and is reproduced. The normative discourse the disciplinary archipelago elaborates is only statistical. It requires individuals whose identity is vocative and imperative and whose individuality is a value. The institutional and social structure of late capitalism in the West is such that it is the individuals with phallic identity that it enlists.

But human history is a history of discontinuous inventions of material and social technology, and of the specific resistance of matter and of subjected individuals. Our own culture is a collage of elements retained from the past or evolving more slowly, elements answering to our present ecological, demographic, political, and economic situation, and elements borrowed from other cultures. Our economy is a patchwork in which there is also in North America an "informal sector"—and not only in the production and distribution of illegal substances—nineteenth-century laissez-faire capitalism, multinational corporations essentially dependent on government financing, trade and protectionist legislation, and sectors of Third-World economy, for example, migrant laborers without education facilities or social security coverage.

The cross-section of that history in progress which is our time reveals multiple foci of eroticism and multiple inventions of social technology bracketed upon our erotic relations with one another. Those elaborated in earlier periods subsist: the libertinage of the eighteenth century, the romanticism of the troubadours, the extended family, the family as alliance, the theologized Christian family, the Greco-Roman ethics of pleasure and of self-mastery. Those elaborated in anticipation of a coming ecological, demographic, political, and economic situation are already there: an eroticism dogged by the specter of planetary overpopulation, a reproductive practice freed from the patriotic imperatives to produce soldiers, freed from concerns about resources and care for one's old age. Those elaborated in other cultures are there: macho culture, the harem, Mormon polygamy, the erotic arts of India, Persia, China, Tibet, the eroticism of Rio de Janeiro and Jamaica—and perhaps one day soon, that of the Sambia. Modern erotic culture too is a motley cow.[4]

The ever-growing world communications systems, and the ever-more abundant opportunities for erotic contacts in the resorts of industrialized tourism make it predictable that our erotic figure will be ever more a motley cow. Different semiotics of identity in contact with adjacent regions and with regions across the planet comment on one another. Each improvisation elaborates its own difference, a statement of one's distinctiveness, a formulation of one's identity. The social field does not simply show so many instantiations of the dominant phallic—medically, pedagogically, sociologically, and psychiatrically sexually-individuated—or biopolitical semiotics.

In the phallic, sexually individualizing, biopolitical semiotics and social technology of today there is another history to be recounted, not simply a reflection, a mirror image of the male history, advancing at a different rate. This history is not that of female semiotics and feminine culture, but of a field of multiple, disjoint female semiotics and feminine cultures, a collage including elements from past epochs, elements of contemporary inventions, elements of cultural regions across the planet, and anticipatory or prophetic elements, improvisations—not simply resisting, evading, mocking male culture, but elaborating their own identities and distinctness. Men like Herdt, Freud, Lacan, and this author could not integrate them into their discourse to produce a unified understanding of our male and female identity, our behaviors, the totality of our bodies.

More elided still from the dominant semiotics are all those whose personal culture is not shaped according to the masculine-feminine dyad. Both Freud and Jung recognized not only a physiological, but also a cultural bisexuality in the individual semiotics or myth of concrete individuals. Herdt discovered hermaphrodites and transgenderists among the Sambia, without having been able to enter into the place Sambia culture reserves for them nor into the semiotics with which they enter into exchanges with one another and with the others. Most likely every culture has elaborated nonmasculine nonfeminine zones. The Plains Indians of North America, the Mayas, the Javanese, medieval Japan—and our culture too—have elaborated semiotics with which the virile and the feminine enter into exchanges with hermaphrodites, transgenderists, Siamese twins, those lacking functional reproductive organs, the chaste, the retarded, eunuchs (infants, the chronically or terminally ill, and the aged are functionally and culturally eunuchs; in our culture, too, maleness and femaleness are phases most, but not all, individuals go through).[5] Is there not in the semiotics of individuals a whole array of evasions, resistances, ruses, and mockeries with which nonmale-nonfemale body parts exchange with one another and with the nonmale-nonfemale body parts of others?

There is a specific force to the erotic exploration of one's own body and those of others, a specific force to the erotic quality of one's life, a specific force to one's inner erotic states. We have not yet spoken of this force when we have diagrammed the psychogenesis of identity and the entry into discourse that is always also a discourse about objectives of desire. We have not yet spoken of it when we have brought to light the economically and politically coded forms of association and transactions with portions, parts, or representatives of the self. The libido is a field not only of significations that coalesce, contextualize, and segment into disjoint fragments; it is also a field of body parts, portions, and pleasures. There is craving, pleasure, and orgasmic release in the couplings of hermaphrodite, transgendered, Siamese-twinned body fluids, body parts, and representations. Those who can speak of the specific force of the erotic exploration of their own distinctive bodies and of others are those who have the experience.

part four

Imperative Bodies

Imperative Surfaces

We define death in terms of the arrest of the vital organs buried in the depth of the organism. We encounter the work of death in a corpse—torso and limbs immobilized in their weight, an encumbrance in the field of the activities of the living, a burden to bear for those who cared and who loved. But it is peculiarly on faces that death is visible. To look upon faces is to look upon expressions, moods, attitudes, solicitations. When this vibrancy and volatility is effaced by death, the face is vacant and desolate, as the surfaces of things cannot be. To look upon faces is always to sense this death that is latent, visible in the frail freshness of youth, the wrinkles of age.

As we advance surveying the surfaces of things we order our progress, organize the surfaces into planes, paths, destinations, and reorient the forces they contain. As we advance among the faces of others in the streets, in the parks, in the corridors of buildings, and in the night, our moves are being ordered by them. A face turned to us is an appeal made to us, a demand put on us. Among the surfaces we survey and manipulate according to our own intentions and caprice, there lies the force of an imperative that touches us, caught sight of wherever we see a face turned to us.

Since David Hume, the ought has been divorced from the is; the things that surface about us are exposed to our power and our caprice. The sense of being ordered and obligated would come from the weight of a sphere of principles and ideals. But the subsistence of such a sphere has been judged dubious, and the weight of an imperative relocated within consciousness or conscience itself. The weight of the imperative would be the weight of our own representations. Yet we encounter the force of an imperative outside, in the naked eye turned to us in the passing flux of the city, a bare hand glimpsed suddenly in the debris of the back alley of a slum, and the exposed thigh of a child in the wreckage of a bus in a mined road—on the vulnerability and susceptibility of faces.

One can turn away from faces as one can turn away from the surfaces of things; one can push them aside, strike them, crush them, as one can manipulate and mutilate the surfaces of things. The torturer lashes away at the victim's face and proves to him that what he believed in are lies, that his demands are those of a terrorist and his appeals those of a coward. The instruments and techniques of torture have the power to render a body incompetent and impotent and brutish, tearing away at its integrity, proving it is craven, and reducing it to carrion and filth.

The faces of the tortured in Peru, in El Salvador, in Cambodia, the skulls smashed, the intricate circuitry of the brain turned into gore and covered with flies, encumber the world in which we order our steps and our initiatives. From the black hole of death there issues something still that can no longer give expression to itself, but that imperatively afflicts us; we do not shake loose its grip wherever we flee. Death summons us in the faces of the living; an imperative is addressed to us in the faces of death.

The Surface That Faces

The face of another can be perceived as the exposed surface of a depth-structure. The contours and the tightness or looseness of the skin can show the observing eye the thickness of flesh and the shapes of the bones beneath. The movements that agitate the surface and the secretions that glisten in the eyes and on the skin can make visible the frettings of the facial muscles and can anchor on palpable reality the divining of glands embedded in the flesh and of nerve fibers extending back into the cerebral mass and down the torso and limbs. Here the seeing is penetrating, a depth perception; it envisions the contours and movements of that face as surface effects of processes in the organism behind the surface and of impulses coming from the depth of the physical world behind that body.

We can also look at a face for signs—signs indicating the positions and shapes of surfaces in the environment that the other faces and signs informing us about our own surfaces. Here the perception does not penetrate toward patterns of agitation in the substance behind the face; it is held on the surface, it attends only to perceiving the patterns forming there clearly and distinctly. I see the eyebrows move, not as surface effects of nervous spasms in the muscles, but in frowns, suspicion, or surprise. I see the eyes turning to diagram doubt, indifference, annoyance, invitation, or summons. I see the lips tensing and shaping to issue vocalizations, which lead me not back to the throat and lungs in the depth-structure behind them, but to the patterns in the landscape that they make surface about me. For it is just by talking, just by vibrating the air between us, when I face another, that the field of patterns that surface about me gets extended with the paths and landscapes of the field that has surfaced about the other, and with the other fields of those with whom he or she has spoken. In facing others the world takes form about me.

Here the face of another extends before me as a surface forming itself minute by minute into so many signifiers. A face is a sign, a sensible signifier continually articulating itself, the original locus of signification. For it is before the face of another that I first entered speech, and my own surfaces first became significant.

The informative forms of the other's spontaneous intentions and the indicative movements of his or her attitudes materialize on the surface patterns and contours, on dry or moist skin, on coarse or light complexion, on thin or vibrant tones of the voice. The eyebrows that with their momentary shiftings signal the dubiousness or aberrancy of what is before them modify a contour of a material anatomy. Heavy, overhanging brows, dull eyes, huge bright-colored eyes, thick, carnal lips, dull complexion materialize before me an attitude with which the face of another confronts the world and confronts me. The other can, through the reflection of his or her own countenance in a mirror or in the mirroring attitudes of others, become aware of the glum, closed, resentful, or vibrant, beguiling countenance his or her surface involuntarily turns to the world and to others. He can learn to maneuver this surface of inert signs as an instrument of his will; he can turn his face with a pose and in a light he knows will be intimidating to the visitor, he can choose to station his bulk in a group in a way he knows will be discomfiting to them, as he can deck out his trunk with apparel and his eyes with glasses that he knows will look authoritative. She can position her face at a degree of proximity and at an angle and purse her lips in ways she knows will be disarming and suggestive. As the years pass, the anxiety and fatigue of the day sink more heavily into the materiality of a face and the repose of the night is less able to efface their weight. The face that greets the morning loses the natural brightness of youth; one learns, Mishima wrote, to mold over it the inert optimism of a mask.

I can perceive the shape of the skull as I perceive the shape of molded clay, and perceive the grain and hue of the complexion as I perceive the matter of carved wood only when, absorbed elsewhere, distracted, asleep or dead, the other is not facing me. When the other faces me I cannot apprehend the color and shape of his or her eyes; the look, Sartre wrote, hides the eyes. It is not that then the materiality of the eyes, of the moving contours of eyebrows, lips, and jaws becomes imperceptible; it is not that then my brain ceases to circumscribe and shape sensory patterns and now sees—beyond them, or hovering before them, or suspended in its own inner space of comprehension—purely ideal configurations, the invisible forms of information, the purely intelligible shapes of concepts. It is that the carnal density of eyes, lips, and skin does not hold my gaze; this carnality is the place where, with a movement it originates toward a signified form in the world before it—inducing in me a movement that follows in the direction it signals—there originates a movement addressed to me, summoning me, calling upon me and demanding that I face it. Looking at a face I see it looks at me, appealing to me and demanding my attention. By its contours and its shifting patterns of movement the face that turns to me surfaces as an indicative and informative movement; by its carnal materiality it surfaces as a vocative and imperative advance unto me.[1]

We thus can distinguish between a "depth perception" of the surface of a body, a "surface perception" of the face as surface of inscription of intentional signs and involuntary indexes, and a "surface contact" with the importunate carnal opacity of the face.

Emmanuel Levinas has elucidated the contact with the surfaces of the other that appeal to me and order me through an analysis of touch.[2] The hands are the organs of a comprehensive touch that handles a detachable form and apprehends the system of its sides. The hands that pass over the surface can divine, through the grain, texture, surface cohesion, and contours of a material surface, the inner consistency and structure of the independently existing thing. The hands that touch the surface lightly can read off the patterns engraved or embossed on it, images or conventionalized diagrams of things or of landscapes far from it. The hands that caress the surface of alien flesh lose their initiative, penetrate into no organization, and capture no messages; they profane the zone of the clandestine without discovering a secret.[3] They are sense-organs that have ceased to be sentient and have become surfaces of sensitivity, sensuality, susceptibility. Their aimless advance, which no longer probes and draws back to contemplate its prey, bares the surface of what does not resist but does not display its organization and its messages; it uncovers a nudity without discovering anything, uncovering skin wrinkled with its own mortality, flesh tormented with its own vulnerability, complacent in its languor. The hands that caress do not move with their own goals in view; they are moved, troubled by the touch of the other with which they make contact, afflicted with the pleasure and the torment of the other. They make contact with a vulnerability that summons them, a susceptibility that puts demands on them.

The perception that reads off the signs forming there also *touches* the carnal opaqueness of the face, a zone of materiality not given but appealing and demanding. This touch that does not penetrate and is not being refracted off to the referents of signs discerned on the surface, is moved to tact and tenderness. The eyes touch the imperative and vocative force that faces when the gaze finds its intentions troubled, its self-assurance decomposed, its agility held in the gaze of another. The voice touches the imperative and vocative force of another when it finds its intentions faltering, its order and direction contested, when it finds itself moved by the vulnerability and the pain in the voice of the other.

The Trace of an Imperative

Facing me, the other exposes to me the defenselessness of his or her eyes. I saw the other's look, agile and penetrating, measuring the distances, surveying the obstacles, disengaging the objectives—the dominant and wary eyes of someone protecting, supplying himself or herself. But when they turn to me, their direction wavers and their objectives disappear. They turn to me a liquid pool waiting for unforeseeable disturbances. They are more naked than the flesh without pelt or hide, without clothing, divested even of their initiative and position. They are more naked than things can be, than walls bared of their adornments and revolvers stripped of their camouflage; they bare a substance susceptible and vulnerable.[4] The eyes turned to me are denuded even of any information they had picked up and which could be scrutinized, of any form I could manipulate. Their nudity exposes them to whatever message I may want to impose, whatever offense I can contrive. Exposing to me what is most naked, most vulnerable—the liquid disquiet of the eyes—the other faces with indigence and mortality, exposing his or her wants to me.

In facing me, the other addresses me with his or her word. Passwords and words of order, information and instructions circulate anonymously and program the movements of people turned to their tasks and their preoccupations. The other, in facing to speak, interrupts the circulation of information and directives. He or she identifies himself or herself as one who has something to say on his or her own, he or she takes something formulated in the common discourse and undertakes to answer for it. But in the same move he or she presents his or her information and judgments to me—as though they are not solid for having been based on what his or her eyes have seen and hands touched, and for having found reasons for themselves in the established dis-course. The other's identity is in question with the statements with which he or she has identified himself or herself. In facing me, the other divests himself or herself of his or her idealized identity, his or her value, submitting himself or herself to my contestation and my judgment. To be sure, the other can clothe his or her words, as he or she can mask his or her eyes—in contrived intonations, affected timber, in the polite and polished forms which are the commonplaces and uniforms of authority. But this garb is diaphanous and only reveals the tenuousness of the words. The words the other briefly makes his or her own and addresses to me pass without leaving a trace. His words or hers are not arms or instruments; I can resist them without doing anything, by just doing whatever it was I was doing. Confiding his or her presence to a breath that hardly stirs the air, the other comes disarmed and disarming. I perceive this vulnerability in the momentary timbre and vanishing breath of the alien voice.

In facing me, the other signals to me with a gesture of his or her hand. Hands are prehensile organs, implements; with them I see the other's compe-tence and discipline take hold of being. They are also sense organs; when they make contact with the solid but refrain from taking hold, I see what they explore and perceive. When hands take hold of nothing and draw nothing to themselves, when they are opened and turned to me, taking form and deform-ing themselves, forming nothing, I see them speak. To speak is to approach empty-handed. The hands that speak put aside their competence, grope for information and instructions, but first appeal to me, for my assent and my assistance.

The eyes and the hands and the voice of another appeal imperatively; their movements facing me can address an appeal to me because they summon me, putting me in question. The eyes of the other slide across my paths and axes of organization; they are not simply ignorant of them, they disturb this order, question it, put demands on it. The hands of the other turned open to me no longer maneuver things into another arrangement in a sector of the terrain I have left unguarded; they intercept my orders, contest my management. To respond to another's voice, to answer his or her greeting, is already to recog-nize the other's right to question me. What I say and do I address to the other for his or her judgment. I can, to be sure, debate what he or she says, set myself up as the judge of my judge, question his or her right to question me, deny him or her rights over me. But these stratagems arise because his or her approach puts me in question. The cunning that takes stands and employs signs to produce effects on the other, the rhetoric, seduction, propaganda, human engineering that there is in all speech, are possible as ruses, betraying a situation in which I find all that I am put into question by the exactions and exigencies of the other. In the face of another, the question of truth is put on each proposition of which my discourse is made, the question of justice put on each move and gesture of my exposed life.

The Other

I do not perceive what I take to be sounds made by the wind or by machines in the same way that I hear utterances whose meaning I understand. I do not perceive what I take to be marks inscribed on the rocks by the rain and the freezing in the same way that I perceive what I take to be inscriptions left by the priests of a culture and a people that have disappeared. The expressive utterances, looks, and gestures I perceive on the surfaces of phenomenal nature about me are the primary evidence I have that I am not the only mind on the planet.

In the perception of visible or audible patterns as signs, Edmund Husserl distinguished[5] between significant signs, which refer to meanings which are generic or ideal, and indexes, where the perceivable reality of the sign is associated with another reality particularized in a here and now. Expressions have both references. In every expressive sign I perceive, I take the signifier uttered or inscribed to refer to a real or unreal referent via a meaning which is ideal. I attend to its perceived form and the distinguishing features relevant in an established vocabulary and grammar. I simultaneously take the tone, emphasis, and tempo of the utterance, the style of that inscription, as an index, that is, a material reality associated with the here and now reality of the intention and attitude of the one that spoke or wrote. Because I find the signs meaningful, I find them to indicate a signifying intention in the speaker or writer. Because they indicate for me the reality of someone's intention and attitude, I take them to be meaningful.

Husserl explains: In the perceptual coupling by which I perceive the surfaces of another body diagramming signs whose meanings are variants of those of signs I make, and its moves diagramming attitudes that are variants of my own, there is induced in that body the sense of an expressive intent and an attitude that are variants of my own.[6] As I have learned to associate a specific tone of voice, stress, and rhythm, with the affirmative, dubious, skeptical, or sarcastic intention with which I issue my own utterances and to associate the tropes, periodicities, and inversions with the peremptory, polemical, insinuating, or seductive intentions with which I make my inscriptions, so I take the tone, rhythms, and recurrences I perceive in the utterances and inscriptions made by another as indexes of the reality of his or her intentions and moods.

From this double association, in the space of memory, what results is a hypostatization of another mind as a variant of my own, an alter ego.

But in what is the other *other*?

The other issues expressions whose meaning can conflict with how I understand their referents. The conflict can be understood and would have to be resolved by integrating the conflicting expressions into the consistency and coherence of a universal and impersonal discourse, which would articulate the depth-structures of an interpersonal or objective universe. I and the other, as speakers of expressions that refer variously to the objects of the common universe, would differ as bodies formulating signifiers from two different positions in the common world, and as voices that utter two different segments of the common discourse.

But the other is not simply different from me—an alter ego in a different place I could occupy in the common field laid out about us, occupying that place at a different time from when I do or could. His or her otherness is not simply the distance of places and the deferring of times in which an ego-structure occupies sites in the common field and formulates expressions of the common discourse. The other is other, not in exchanging places in the common world with me, but in putting demands from his or her own place on my occupancy of a place. He or she is other, not in formulating different words from the common discourse, but in contesting what I say. We are not different instances of a universal ego-structure in a field I can survey from above; the field in which we exist is the space opened by our confrontation.

The vocative and imperative voice of the other interrupts the order of what I formulate and contests the world I integrate about my perceptual field with the words I make my own. The vocative and imperative words the other makes his or her own contest the world articulated in the common discourse.

The indicative and informative words of the other articulate the world open to all, but the vocative and imperative force of his or her words judge the course of the world. The tears, the blood, the outcries of its victims contest the course of world history, which, Hegel wrote, is the imminent tribunal which judges all things in the world. These outcries separate from the course of the world; the otherness of the other—other than me, other than the world—is an appeal made to the world, a contestation put on the world.

The other rises in his or her alterity before me in appealing to me and in contesting me. The other is the one before whom I find myself held to answer for the course of world history.

The other reveals his or her otherness in facing, in addressing me. By the meaning of his or her words he or she designates the world open to me too. By the tone, emphasis, and tempo of his or her utterance, the style of his or her inscription, his or her expression indicates the reality of his or her attitude and intention, a variant of my own. By the imperative and vocative force of his or her words and gestures, he or she reveals his or her otherness. This vocative and imperative force is in the very move by which the other *faces*; to face me is to appeal to me and put demands on me. Levinas says that the face is not the significant sign nor the index, but the *trace* of his or her absence, his or her otherness.[7]

When I see traces of footsteps on the sand, I am put in touch with some-one who has passed without having presented himself. I can see them as index-es of the intention of a child to inscribe his presence on the beach among the tracks of the sea birds and the crabs. The intruder who enters into my home as a thief or a spy comes to interrupt and intercept the order I impose on my environment and my enterprises. His presence leaves traces on the surfaces of things. Upon leaving he takes pains to efface his traces, to depart absolutely. But his movements to efface the traces of his departure themselves leave traces; the order is disturbed irrevocably. The detective discovering them does not find in them the mark of the identity of the intruder nor of the order the departed one wished to impose. The traces left by his movements to efface his traces only mark an alien initiative to disturb the order of my environment. It is this sense of trace that Levinas isolates, differentiates from significant signs and indexes, and reserves for the move of facing with which the other con-tests and appeals to me, the move in which not his or her identity but his or her alterity is revealed to me.[8] For in facing me, calling upon me, summoning me, the other presents himself or herself, not as something identifiable but as other. It is true that as we speak, I progressively identify him or her and his or her intentions and attitudes. I interpret what he or she says and how he or she stands and moves with my own codes and my own categories. And I pre-sent to the other the representation of him or her that I form. But in facing me, contesting or confirming that identity I have assigned to him or her, the other arises apart, beyond the representation—other. His or her move in fac-ing puts the trace of this removal in the visible.

Through the meaning of a sign, I am put in the presence of its signification, an abiding and ideal presence. Through the meaning of the signifier "4" I am put in touch with what is signified by that figure, something not here and now, but recurring, representable anywhere, anytime. Through the perceived reality of the tone, emphasis, and tempo of an utterance, I am referred to the reality of an attitude and an intention in a speaker now present but only indi-rectly perceived as such, through association with the perceived reality of the utterance. In the vocative and imperative force with which another faces, I am put in touch with someone who is not identifiable as a variant of my own presence, someone whom I cannot capture in a representation, someone there as other. On the carnal materiality of his or her face—disarmed, denuded, and vulnerable—I perceive the trace of the passing of alterity.

It is the vulnerability, the susceptibility, the mortality with which the other faces that makes his or her signs have not only informative and indicative form—expressive of meanings that designate referents in the world, indicative of intentions and attitudes like my own in the depth-structure behind that face—but also vocative and imperative force. The force to contest what I take him or her to mean does not lie in the pure form of his or her signifiers, which can signify meanings inconsistent with or contradictory to what I affirm and verify to be consistent with the discourse of universal reason. It lies in their coming to me on a carnal surface exposed to me and afflicting me. These signifiers are perhaps inconsistent, perhaps barely articulated, reduced to a cry or an expletive, perhaps covered over with the scars the winds and the debris of the world have left on that surface, but they trouble me as the traces of an anxiety, a susceptibility, an importunate mortality.

The look turned to me, and whose expressive intention I detach from it in the measure that I make the path it indicates to a referent my own movement, whose indicative force I detach from it in the measure that I take it to issue from a specific intent and attitude I divine as a variant of my own, nonetheless remains on the face of the other. It remains there, inaccessible to me; it materializes in the liquidity, the nakedness, the vulnerability of his or her eyes, which I do indeed have the physical power to take hold of, to torment or to blind, but which foresee and forbid that power. The voice advancing unto me, and whose expressive intention and indicative force I detach from it in the measure that I comprehend its meaning and the attitude in it, nonetheless remains on the face of the other. Issuing from a reserve withdrawn from the hubbub of the coded world, from a silence that maintains itself and returns to itself, it abides in the face that faces; remote, intractable, it materializes on the insubstantiality of this carnal presence, disarmed and disarming. The hands that open to me and speak, and whose expressive intention and indicative force I detach from them in the measure that I perceive them as parallel to the moves with which I handle the impersonal manipulanda of the practicable field about us, variants of the postural diagram with which I handle them, nonetheless remain alien surfaces. They remain hands of the other, out of reach; their moves materialize on the sensitivity, the susceptibility of his or her flesh, which interdicts my manipulations, is wounded and violated by my manipulations. From the face of another I detach the meaning and intent of his or her signs; there remains a surface of vulnerability, of susceptibility, in which the otherness of the other is exposed. The skin of the other extends before me not as the membrane that contains his or her substance in a depth structure exposed to my comprehensive hold nor as the sheath that holds him or her at a distance from me, leaving me master in my own space; it extends before me its anxiety and its pain. The other is backed up against himself or herself in his or her own skin, constricted in anxiety—*angustia*.[9] I do not envision the carnal surfaces with which the otherness exposes itself to me; in that carnality I make contact with an importunate force with which he or she designates objects and indicates his or her attitude and intention, with which his or her information puts demands on me and his or her indications appeal to me.

The tears and outcries afflict us before they are interpreted or put in perspective. The naked eye turned to us in the passing flux of the city, a bare hand glimpsed suddenly in the debris of the back alley of a slum, the exposed thigh of a child in the wreckage of a bus in a mined road are there in an obsessive immediacy before we sink them back into the course of the world by entrenching ourselves in our own projects.

The gaze that stops on the skin and the touch that caresses make contact with the organic dead ends of birthmarks, with the languor of eyes that close, and with the insubstantiality of another's voice that passes. They are, in the contact, afflicted by the susceptibility of another youth, the frailty of the aging by which the other passes in another trajectory of time from that in which I maintain myself present. Our gaze that meets the naked eyes of the other, the order of our voice that is troubled by the voice of the other, and our manipulating hands that meet the empty hands of another are touched by the vulnerability, the susceptibility of what is separated from the world—what is other. In the other that faces, we see the traces of this departure. This departure concerns us, orders us.

The Imperative Death

The force of an imperative weighs in our lives—in our thought, which organizes our experience, and in our action, which orders the layout of our environment. The imperative is not a program we elaborate for ourselves; it weighs on us with the force of exteriority. It is in our mortality that we know the force of the imperative; in the exteriority of the imperative the absolute exteriority of death summons us. The figure of our fellow human, whose face is somehow more exterior to us than the surfaces of the exterior world, exterior as death, turns to us as the concrete phenomenon of the imperative.

Immanuel Kant, Martin Heidegger, and Emmanuel Levinas have understood that the imperative, death, and the other reveal one another. But the imperative materialized on the figure of the other and the mortality revealed there are differently understood by these thinkers.

Ancient philosophy recognized in the cosmic order an ordinance that commands our thought and our action. The cosmic order is known in the ordered representation we construct by empirical and technological reason. Thought formulates what is universal and necessary in the array of appearances and forces as empirical laws and practical principles.

The empirical and technological principles that represent the cosmic order are formulated in conformity with an exigency for coherence and consistency. In every representation of the order of surfaces and forces, thought recognizes an ordinance put on its own spontaneous movements. The coherence and consistency of our concepts and of the principles that organize them commands the progress of our spontaneous thought, as the coherence of our concepts and the consistency of our principles that represent the practicable layout of resources and implements regulate the initiatives we conceive.

In formulating the principles of coherent and consistent thought and the maxims of effective action, thought programs itself—obeys laws, as Kant put it, that it itself formulates—and commands its practical will.

If our thought is to maintain itself, it must subject itself to the laws of thought; if our action is to be effective, it must subject itself to technical principles. But we do have to think, and we have to act. The imperative to think and to act thoughtfully is imposed unconditionally. The imperative to order precedes any reason we can formulate for having to think and having to act, which reason could only be formulated by a thought already subject to the imperative for coherence and consistency. It is immediately, in our own faculty of thought, Kant argued, that the force of the imperative to order is recognized, in what he identified as the sentiment of respect.

The formulation of the imperative as an imperative for law—for the universal and the necessary—is a product of thought. The formulation is a program that thought itself legislates, a representation that thought maintains present within itself. But the force of the imperative precedes the formulation; it is as subject to and obedient to the imperative that a thought which formulates consistent representations becomes possible. In subjecting itself to the order of the exterior world, thought subjects itself to the exteriority of the imperative that weighs immediately within it. Though found immediately within, the force of the imperative weighs on thought with the weight of an a priori exteriority.

Thought, which finds itself subject to the imperative for order, must command the sensory faculties to collect data in such a way that they can be understood with coherent and consistent concepts and correlated with empirical laws; it must command the motor powers that they meet and measure the forces of reality in such a way that those forces can be understood with practical principles. The imperative that commands the mind to order the sensory reality appearing about itself, to represent that exteriority as nature, also commands the mind to promulgate universal and necessary laws throughout its own composite nature. It must subordinate its own episodic and reactive sensory will to the imperative for order.

Sensory patterns, generating and corrupting—living—are, in the instant of their plenary present, not identifiable. A concept that identifies them requires an interval across which to view the form; the identification is always ex post facto. A life in its moment of living presence is unconceptualizable; it is the life passed that is identified. What is conceived is always the death of the animal. To fix the flux of sensory patterns with coherent and consistent terms within universal and necessary laws, the mind is imperatively ordered to detach itself from the generation and corruption—the life—of sensible things.

The generation and corruption of sensory patterns is first recorded by the sensibility as the approach and the departure of lures of pleasure and threats of pain. These affect the core vital force and its reactive sensory will.[10] To fix them with consistent concepts, to represent the sensory patterns as natures, that is, as wholes organized by intrinsic laws, the sensory receptivity must cease to sense sensory patterns as lures of pleasure and loci of pain. The subject that exists to promulgate universal and necessary laws must cease sensing sensory patterns as values, confirmations of or subverters of its own core vital force; it must cease to will with the sensory will in its core vital force. It makes itself, in Kant's terms, indifferent to its own core vital appetite—apathetic; it must mortify its core vital will. It then finds that what commands in the imperative for law is death. In the imperative for law it is the universality and necessity of death that must be obeyed.

Respect for the other, Kant says, is respect for the law that rules in the other.[11] Kant separates the perception of another as a psychophysical organism in nature from the perception of another as another rational agent. The perception of another as a psychophysical organism is what we have named the depth perception of the other. It is the perception of the surfaces with which the other's psychophysical being is phenomenally exposed to me as comprehendable in terms of the psychophysiological laws that produce this surface effect, and these, in turn, as comprehendable in terms of the physico-chemical, electromagnetic, and dynamic laws that make the phenomenal field in which the other surfaces the extension in depth of nature. The perception of another as another rational agent is what we have named a surface perception of the other—the perception of the figure and movements I perceive on the other as governed by representations of what is imperative, which his own mind puts to his will. It is by commanding his positions and movements by these representations that the other is a nature on his own, autonomous, *other*.

I do not perceive causality generally; I do not perceive the causality of the representations his mind formulates on the nervous circuitry and musculature of his body; I do not perceive the representations he formulates within his thought. But I sense there the force of the imperative. This sense of the imperative at work in him is immediate; it is because I sense the force of the imperative in him that I perceive his positions and movements not as so many spasmodic reactions to the forces about him, but as postures and operations programmed by his thought.[12] I sense in him the force of the imperative for law that commands me also.

What makes me perceive the surfaces of the other as the phenomenal evidence of an *other*, of a law that the other himself represents to his will—rather than as evidence of the psychophysiological laws that regulate his nature and the physico-chemical, electromagnetic, and dynamic laws that regulate universal nature—is the evidence of pain on those surfaces.[13] It is in perceiving the surfaces of the other as pained by the array of objects into which he advances, a pain the other produces within himself by his willful advance, that I sense in him another law than those that regulate the reciprocal adjustment of objects in physico-chemical nature. Through this pain I sense in him the apathy, the indifference to the sensory will of his own core vital force, the assent to the death inwardly afflicting that will. In the pain I sense the death at work in him that commands my respect. The respect for the imperative for law in him is a respect for the mortification it commands in his core vital force—the selfsame respect that the imperative for law that I know within my own understanding commands in me.

The sense of the imperative for law is felt positively—in me as in the other—in the intellectual sentiment of respect, and it is felt negatively in the willed apathy to the sensuous will of my own core vital force and in the willed apathy of the core vital force I sense in another. The exteriority of the force of the imperative that weighs on the thought that produces the formulations with which it programs its will is also the absolute exteriority of death to which it must subject its core vital force.

I find the imperative for order immediately incumbent on my own understanding. This inward respect, constitutive of my thought, only yields a formal principle. My thought, subject to the force of the imperative, formulates it as an imperative for the universal and the necessary in all my representations and practical maxims. The figure of the other diagrams for me what this respect is in the concreteness of a perceptible situation in the world. It diagrams for me an advance representation of rational activity, sensuous mortification, and tasks to be performed. The imperative that weighs on my own understanding commands a mortal solidarity with others.

Heidegger too has understood that our being that ex-ists through casting its forces unto the exteriority of the environment does so under the force of an imperative laid on it. This imperative is more exterior still than the environment it comprehends and whose resources it appropriates. Heidegger has understood this exteriority to be the exteriority utterly exterior to our being: the nothingness of death. But he explains how this imperative mortality does not order me to divest myself of all particularity; instead, it singularizes me.

Our environment extends about us as a field of possibilities—resources, instrumentalities, resistances, paths, and obstacles. Possibilities are apprehended and comprehended by powers.[14] The perceptual and motor powers in us are self-mobilizing movements that direct themselves down paths with implements toward ends. Our environment is a field where every entity is a means because it leads to an end, and is itself an end enclosed in its own frontiers, its *fines*.[15] Our forces are powers inasmuch as they determine and direct themselves. Our powers can determine series of means that lead to ends because our existing can terminate its own movement. The power to determine, to terminate, is the power to extend a movement that ends, that proceeds to its own end.

The powers with which we envision ends and which proceed to their own termination advance toward the eventuality of their definitive impotence. The real possibilities of the world are not simply alternative arrangements that we elaborate by our own thought and represent before ourselves. The contingent realities that we reach out for with our powers are really possible because they are possibly impossible.[16] In reaching for them our powers may prove impotent. In envisioning possibilities we extend our gaze toward its possible impotence; in groping for things we extend our skills toward their possible incompetence. With every step into the world we advance toward impasses and traps.

The world to which we devote all our powers harbors the eventuality of our total and irreversible impotence. We sense this in advance; we sense that the world of possibilities is suspended in the imminence of nothingness. There come times when the substantial and sustaining forms of the world lose their significance and show themselves indifferent to us, when the paths their possibilities trace out lose their urgencies and become equivalent and interchangeable. In this insignificance and insubstantiality of things that have lost the force of their presence, nothingness gapes open about us.[17] Anxiety is the sense of finding oneself adrift, nothing to hold on to, nothing sustaining one's initiatives, nothing answering to one's gropings. The future, which the possibilities in things had suspended before our powers, now shows the possible impossibility with which those possibilities were made and presses upon us as the imminence of our own reduction to definitive and irreversible impotence.

Anxiety understands that in the world that solicits our forces, it is the nothingness of death that summons us. The irreversible summons of death makes us apprehend the irreversible order by which ends command means, and makes us able to envision ends this side of death.

Anxiety is the shrinking back in the face of imminent nothingness. Adrift in the emptiness, sustained by nothing, one is thrown back upon oneself; anxiety is the force and heat of a being still existing that clings to itself. What it cleaves to is not its being—which is given and is without needing to be supported—but its ex-isting, that is, a nexus of singular powers it senses in itself, which have not yet been realized and which long to be.[18]

The power to sense the powers that are singularly one's own, and to sense the possibilities of the world for which they are destined, Heidegger identifies as *conscience*.[19] The anxiety which senses that death is imminent clings to these singular powers, which it senses to be imperative. To realize these powers, to pursue the possibilities of the world for which they are destined, is to discharge one's forces in a dying that is one's own.

Thus for Heidegger it is not first the universal form of one's thoughts and one's undertakings that is imperative, but their singular force. Prior to the imperative that thoughts have a universal and necessary form is the imperative that one, oneself, think. But to know the singularity of one's own powers is to discern the environment or predicament singularly one's own. By understanding, inhabiting, and acting upon the situation that is one's own, one becomes a thinker who can then find himself or herself required to formulate his or her insights in universal and necessary formulations. In the inexorable approach of this death singling one out, the singular possibilities of the world answering to one's own powers are first visible and imperative.

The one that has not felt the singularity of his or her own powers discharges his or her forces in the possibilities open to him or her as to anyone. Death befalls him or her as an eventuality and a fatality. The anticipation of a death coming singularly for oneself throws one back upon oneself, upon the singular powers one senses in oneself which are not yet realized and which will to be. In resolute conscience one knows that to live out one's own life is to locate the possibilities open singularly to one's own powers and to discharge one's singular forces in a dying one's own. In the anxious resolve of conscience, one senses the imminence of death as the weight of an imperative; one converts death from a fatality into a singular destination.

The obedience to the imperative of death then takes on the form, not of a sensuous mortification, but of a resoluteness in thought, feeling, and action. This resoluteness consists in discerning ends open to one's own powers alone, and in actualizing the powers of understanding, feeling, and action which terminate in the accomplishment of or in impotence before just those ends.

But Heidegger also has understood that the palpable evidence of a line of tasks destined for my singular powers cannot surface in the abysses of nothingness that anxiety senses about me. I can find my own tasks only in a field already articulated by the signs that the paths of others have traced out there. The possibilities open to anyone have been marked out by the diagrams of action each one picks up from others and passes on to others, and by the anonymous discourse that is passed on from one to another. It is in the figure of the singular ones, those that have come to know the forces with which they have been singularly invested and have resolutely pursued to the end the singular tasks that answer to them, that, Heidegger says, I find the diagram of my own tasks and my own destiny.[20] Each one that undertakes resolutely to live out the powers that were born in him, inevitably, tragically, also consigns to nonrealization other powers that were also born in him, and which he leaves for others. The one who finds himself born with the singular power to be an artist finds he leaves aside, consigns to death, the dancer, thinker, lover he was also singularly born to be. Being born means not being able to be the basis of one's own powers, for had one been able to give oneself one's own powers one would also have given oneself the power to realize them. The one that resolutely sets out to exist with his own powers discovers the fatality, the dying, of having been born; he finds himself, with every figure of power he makes live, consigning to nothingness other figures of power he was also destined to make live. His existence, in pursuing the path to which his singular powers had destined him, delineates in the world other paths he leaves for others. Among these I find traced on the world the path of a destiny my own.

For Kant the rational agent finds the imperative laid inwardly on his own faculty of understanding; for Heidegger the practical agent reduced to himself in the withdrawal of the world's support finds an imperative laid on all his own sensory, affective, comprehensive, and practical powers. For Kant to perceive the other is to respect in him the imperative for law that rules in him and that commands me also. It is to perceive in the diagram of his position and actions an advance representation of actions incumbent on me too, on anyone. For Heidegger the anxious care for my own singular powers menaced imminently by death can become the advance project of tasks to be accomplished only when I find those tasks traced out for me by the paths others have taken in the resolute and deathbound pursuit of their own tasks. In the figure of the other, Kant sees a mortification exemplary for me, a concrete instantiation of the universal and necessary law. In the singular figure of the other, Heidegger sees a resolute discharge of all his or her vital forces—including his or her powers to comprehend possibilities rationally, but in a situation singularly his or her own. In taking hold of the possibilities singularly his or her own, the other also delineates other singular possibilities he or she leaves for me. In sensing my own mortality, I advance upon those possibilities, in the measure that they answer to my own singular powers. The others, in pursuing their singular destinies, deliver over to me the possibilities of a task and a destiny singularly my own.

What is this *care for the other* to which my own imperative destines me? The mortality the Kantian subject sees as exemplary for himself in the other is the continual mortification of his sensory appetites for the lures of pleasure in the world, a mortification that is simultaneously the affirmation of a will for the universal and the necessary which wills itself always. The respect that cares for the other in Kantism is a will for a self-maintaining figure of the universal rational agent that rises over the pain of his sensory mortification. Then my care for the other is an interest that I have to maintain stable, in the world before me, the other as a purely rational agent, that is, a will that wills the universal and the necessary in all circumstances and always, a will that thus in every situation maintains itself present. My interest in the other amounts to my practical need to maintain before myself a model, a "type,"[21] of the rational agent that supplies an advance representation of what I have to do.

For Heidegger, the authentic care, that which envisions the other in the distance of his own place and of his own time, is a vision of the other as one who resolutely set out on his or her own path, and a will that the other advance to a death that will be his or her own. It is in pursuing his own mortal destiny that the other traces out the singular possibilities and tasks his deathbound forces did not actualize. The care for that other, inasmuch as I can find in his itinerary the paths he left for others—for me, maintains his figure by re-presenting the path through which his life passed. It does not go to accompany the other in his or her own dying; for Heidegger the best thing I can do for another, if I care about him or her, is to pursue resolutely the tasks I make my own.

But the other whose stands and whose pain can be exemplary for me, the other whose resolute advance in the anxiety that anticipates his or her dying can diagram for me the path of destiny before me, also afflicts me with his or her carnal materiality. The other faces me. Kant and Heidegger have not studied the face-to-face encounter, and the imperative it reveals. Levinas has brought us to see the surfaces of the other as the locus where vulnerability, susceptibility, mortality are materialized, exposed to me, and afflict me with the obsessive urgency of an imperative. This vision makes it possible to understand positively our mortal solidarity.

We greet the other as a depth structure of forces, and recognize community with him or her, in the handshake that seals a pact—a community that is realized in the collaboration in which each has his or her own tasks. We perceive the other as a surface on which informative and indicative signs are continually formed, and recognize community with him or her in the assent of the head that marks an agreement—a community that is elaborated in the discourse by which my own field of perception is extended and integrated with the fields others have perceived and formulated, and in which the conflict between what I have seen and say and what they have seen and said is resolved into the consistency and coherence of universal reason. But beneath or prior to this, we make contact and establish community with the other in the touch that caresses his or her carnal surfaces and that is afflicted with, obsessed by, their vulnerability, susceptibility, mortality—the touch that has no power to and does not seek to heal,[22] but has to go accompany the other in his or her own dying.

The hand and the gaze that touch mortal flesh do not apprehend a message or uncover a secret and do not learn what lies in or beyond the abyss of nothingness. The hand that caresses mortal flesh seeks without knowing what it seeks, and does not draw from its gropings the resources for a power to postpone or turn aside the death that advances upon it. The touch of compassion extended unto the surfaces of the dying one is there so that the other not be alone in his or her dying, that he or she be able to die. For this power our faces, which are turned to exteriority, to the surfaces of things beyond in the transcendent spaces of the world, are exposed to one another.

Elemental Bodies

Robinson Crusoe is twenty-two years old, has a wife and two children. He has been libidinally "triangulated," Gilles Deleuze says; he has achieved the telos of reproductive sexuality that the Oedipus structuration is the instrument for. Now he enlists as a seaman on the *Virginia*; he sets out to go far—far from the objectives of his English world, libidinally far beyond paternal and reproductive sexuality. Michel Tournier, in his novel *Friday*,[1] tells of this voyage to a remote, exotic, ultimate sexuality, which is not a return to infancy or to aboriginal humanity and which will take Robinson beyond what carnal desire can long for. This voyage begins on a deserted island, where terra firma is doubled by the objects situated on it and objectives sought on it, and doubled by the free elements—by light that does not elucidate or clarify, wind-intoned musicality without a text, sun that fecundates an inhuman progeny. The book charts a voyage *sur place* across the ontological region of doubles, and discovers the destiny of the metamorphoses of the libidinal body.

Of whom is this the adventures? Tournier's book comprises both autobiography—pages from a logbook—and an interpretation of Daniel Defoe's book. Defoe's narrative of an individual reduced to solitude on a deserted island contains its own interpretation in terms of the master-narrative of Victorian imperialism; Tournier's book interprets pages of a logbook with a new interpretation of the twentieth-century master-narrative of libido. Deleuze has said[2] that Tournier's novel recounts not the adventures of the one identified as the Robinson of Defoe's book, but the adventures of the deserted island. The adventures of the island begin with writing; after the abandonment of the project of escape—after the abandonment of the unlaunchable skiff *Escape* Robinson had built—Robinson's first act of cultivating—making intelligible— the island is the "sacred act of writing"[3] with which Robinson begins his logbook. The act is sacred in general, but here sacred too because Holy Scripture, his sole book, progressively interpreted by the island, will dictate his writing.

It is not the genre of the novel—a fictional recasting in libidinal terms of the fictive adventures which Daniel Defoe cast in terms of the master-narrative of Victorian imperialism—that first makes the I, which, on the deserted island, subsists only as the *subject of the text*, equivocal; the book discovers the vanishing, metamorphosing movement that makes the I. The I is in the adventures of the island Speranza. If its life is libido, the I is in a libidinous absorption in Speranza—an I that "is conscious of [itself] only in the stir of myrtle leaves with the sun's rays breaking through...knows [itself] only in the white crest of a wave running up the yellow sand."[4] The I that separates itself draws out of the stir of the myrtle leaves and the white crest of the wave their phosphorescence, makes that phosphorescence its own light and takes itself as a candle that moves among things. This separation is not the effect of its own power. The myrtle leaves and the waves and the sand refract from themselves their surface patterns and the will-o'-the-wisp of the I that will glow over them. The separate I is produced as a reject. But the writing itself also works this separation. The autobiographical writing consigns to pages an I with characteristics and adventures. The I that writes and thus separates an I from the island to consign it to the autobiography, and the island itself that rejects into the I the light that stirred in its substance, are one and the same agency of separation.

> For some time indeed I have been performing an act of surgery on myself which consists of stripping away in turn all my attributes—I say *all*—like peeling an onion. And at the same time I am constructing, separate from myself, a man called Crusoe, Christian name Robinson, six feet tall, etc.... and I watch him live and grow on this island, without participating in his good fortune or suffering from his bad luck. What "I" is this? The question is far from an idle one, nor is it even unanswerable. Because if it is not *him* then it must be *Speranza*. There is a fluttering "I" which comes to rest now on the man and now on the island, making of me one and the other by turns.[5]

The pages we read are the logbook pages and narrative of a fluttering *I*, which is sometimes that of a Robinson Crusoe as far from the writer of those pages as from their reader, sometimes that of Speranza—the island also deserted of the I of the writer—and sometimes that of the reader. For the book works to bring the reader too to the deserted island, and to conduct him or her through the libidinal metamorphoses by which he or she too will find himself or herself on the Island of Desolation, and then on Speranza, and then on the *other island*.

The Currency of Metaphors

Existence on a deserted island reveals how the presence of the other works. Robinson discovers that the others are not a contingent multitude of factual substances whose approaches and departures are contingent events; they surround one as a system of *possibles*. When I look at the face and the position of another, I see him or her stand there where I might be standing; his or her body is stationed there as a possible variant of, a signifier for, a metaphor for, my body—which I do not look at, whose actual substance I do not see. In addition, the other's body is a signifier for what is possible in what he or she faces: his or her color and contours do not hold my look on themselves; they refer me to the frightening or alluring configuration of something it is possible that I shall see. The possible configurations which extend the margins of my narrow zone of perception are maintained there by the visible, audible, and tangible figures of the others.

> Each of these men was a *possible* world having its own coherence, its
> values, its sources of attraction and repulsion, its center of gravity....
> And each of these possible worlds naïvely proclaimed itself the reality.
> That was what other people were: the possible obstinately passing for
> the real.[6]

This obstinacy is posited in language which designates things by metaphor, designating a deep well as a quality of thought and an emotion. For language signals sensory patterns as loci for multiple figures of the possible and signals them to the others as materialized indexes of systems of possibility.

The others as a constellation of possibles cushion the impact of reality. When the others are no longer there and language fades out, darkness closes in on the radius of Robinson's visual field, where any reality turns up abruptly like an assault on him.

Robinson finds nakedness a torment—things coming in contact with his surfaces with blows struck without warning. He takes pains to dress as befits his status in civilized society, as though seemly clothing could hold still on his body the eyes of others to cocoon his surfaces from the malevolence of bare reality.

What the others, that system of possibles, make one take as obstinately actual are strands of *objects-objectives* strung over the malevolent quicksands of bare reality. An object is a sensory pattern in which the marginal presence of the others has affixed some possibilities. The object subsists upright and holds upright the powers with which one takes hold of it. The one who exists in a land populated with others is a "framework of habits, responses, reflexes, preoccupations, dreams, associations"—a stabilized and erect figure of power.

Without the others, objects relapse into transient sensory patterns, and the upright posture wavers, lurches, and collapses. Robinson "knew now that man resembles a person injured in a street riot, who can only stay upright while the crowd packed densely around him continues to prop him up."[7]

One day Robinson sees himself, in a mirror salvaged from the wreckage of the *Virginia*:

> Although there was no marked alteration in his features, he scarcely recognized himself. A single word occurred to him—disfigured. "I am disfigured," he said aloud, while despair clutched his heart. Vainly he searched, in the tightness of the mouth, the lackluster eyes, the characterlessness of the forehead—faults with which he had always been familiar—for something to account for the shadowy distortion of the mask that gazed back at him through the damp-stains in the mirror. The cause lay in something wider and deeper, a kind of hardness, a hint of death such as he had once seen in the face of a prisoner set free after years of captivity in a lightless dungeon. It was as though a winter of pitiless severity had passed over that familiar countenance, ridding it of all light and shade, congealing its mobility, simplifying its expression to the point of coarseness.... "An expressionless face. A degree of extinction such as perhaps no human being has ever before undergone." Robinson spoke these words too aloud, but his face as he did so betrayed no more emotion than if his voice had issued from some brass instrument.[8]

It is the others too that constitute one as a light-source that circulates among objects. Without them there is not first a theater of objects into which one watches oneself enter; there is only a moving zone of patterns glowing with their own phosphorescence. Alone, Robinson "is conscious of himself only in the stir of myrtle leaves with the sun's rays breaking through, he knows himself only in the white crest of a wave running up the yellow sand."[9] On these glowing patterns the others fix possibilities, turning them into objects that are exposed to outside beams of light the others turn on them and to the hands with which they reach for them. In the absence of these other lights, the phosphorescence that was in the shifting sensory waves and troughs can come out of them and get shut up in itself as that separate entity, one's subjectivity, a candle with which one seeks out objects. The subject maintains itself by noting qualities glowing in itself that had come from the objects. But it finds that what has been deposited in itself has been taken away from the objects.

> The light becomes the eye and as such no longer exists: it is simply the stimulation of the retina. The smell becomes the nostril—and the world declares itself odorless. The song of the wind in the trees is disavowed: it was nothing but a quivering of the timpani....
>
> The subject is the disqualified object. My eye is the corpse of light and color. My nose is all that remains of odors when their unreality has been demonstrated. My hand refutes the thing it holds.[10]

This disqualification of the objects, which the subject maintaining itself without the lights of others suffers, is, Tournier affirms, the obscure will of the *other island*, the elemental island, which emerges, rejecting out of itself the objects and the separated subject. "A knot of contradiction, a center of discord, it has been eliminated from the body of the island, rejected, repudiated.... The world seeks its own reason and in doing so casts off that irrelevance, the subject."[11] The subject is not a torrent of voracity that would have in itself the momentum to drive itself; the momentum in the subject is the repulsive force of the elemental.

The voracious subject, devouring the qualities taken from objects, is stricken with desire. Desire, craving for the unseen, the untouched, the unapprehended, arises in a sensibility that is turned to the others, those carnal lures that circulate as stand-ins for the possible, for the future. To desire is to desire what the other desires, and to desire the other. What I desire are made into objectives by the others; exchangeable, they are *currency*. Conversely, the desire that turns to the others is a desire for wealth. Robinson sets out to subject the disqualified expanse of the island about him to measure, and make it into wealth. It is the sole way the desire for the other can be maintained.

The luxuriant life of the Island of Desolation had sustained Robinson's life as well: for days, for weeks, for months, he had eaten of its abundance on hand without thought or initiative. There was no utilitarian motive to subject it to cultivation. Robinson sets out to remake the Island of Desolation, this island of abundance, into Speranza—hope for the civilization he had lost, desire for the currency of others.

For Freud, the basic acquisitions of civilization—the building of shelters, the taming of fire, the fashioning of tools—did not, could not, originate out of utilitarian pressures. It is true that the human mutant is a particularly vulnerable species of animal, but this species became naked and muscularly weak as a result of living indoors, warmed by fire, his implements freeing his own muscles to atrophy. For Freud, it was our unseasonable libido and not our utilitarian needs that contrived shelters of branches and moss as a substitute for the womb with which our nostalgic sensuality retains a bond, that invented tools which prolong and enhance our orifices and our couplings, and that domesticated the fire that heats and excites the men that gather about it in homosexual competition with one another and with nature.

What motivated Robinson's project for civilization on a deserted island was the libidinal desire for the desire of others. "All those who knew me, all without exception, believe me dead.... No matter what I do, I cannot prevent that picture of Robinson's dead body from existing in all their minds."[12] His own belief in his existence is not enough to maintain upright the subjective posture the others no longer sustain. He then conceives the project of maintaining a vortex of subjectivity while working all its energies back into the substance of the island.

> This prickly formula gives me a somber satisfaction. It shows me the rough and narrow road to salvation, at least to a kind of salvation—that of a fruitful and harmonious island, flawlessly cultivated and administered, strong in the harmony of all its attributes, steadily pursuing its course without me, because it is so close to me that even to look at it is to make it too much myself, so that I must shrink to become that intimate phosphorescence which causes each thing to be known while no one is the knower, each to be aware while no one has awareness.... Oh, subtle and pure equilibrium, so fragile and so precious![13]

The prickly formula for this self-conscious syncope, the laborious swoon into the fecund substance of Speranza, begins and culminates in contradiction. In fact, Robinson does not evolve his cultivating presence in the substance on Speranza out of the fragile and precious equilibrium he caught sight of and its exigencies; he hauled up everything he could find from the wreckage of the *Virginia*, which had been stocked with foodstuffs and tools to sustain a whole community of men at sea, and with luxuries destined for commerce. Robinson builds on Speranza a shelter in which he will never sleep, cook, or wash himself, a "museum of civilization." He puts into his armory and his warehouses all the weapons and tools taken from the *Virginia* which he will never use—he has no need of guns to kill the animals on Speranza, for its boldest bucks can be slaughtered with a blow with any branch, and he will till and harvest with his hands and with shells, sticks, and flails. The fire he tends will not serve for warmth; he maintains it in order, one day, to be able to signal from afar to others.

The subtle and pure equilibrium Robinson now pursues on the island will be commanded by the clepsydra he devises. It commands the flow of life, making it a movement where another present jostles on the heels of each present. In the absence of the others, it maintains the pure form of their presence—the form of a present always crowded by another, by the form of a possible. It maintains the time in which an imperative is put on, an objective assigned to, each present.

> Henceforth, whether I am waking or sleeping, writing, or cooking a meal, my time is marked by this regular ticking, positive, unanswerable, measurable, and precise.... I demand, I insist, that everything around me shall henceforth be measured, tested, certified, mathematical, and rational. One of my tasks must be to make a full survey of the island, its distances and its contours, and incorporate all these details in an accurate surveyor's map. I would like every plant to be labeled, every bird to be ringed, every animal to be branded. I shall not be content until this opaque and impenetrable place, filled with secret ferments and malignant stirrings, has been transformed into a rational structure, visible and intelligible to its very depths![14]

This intelligible structure is in space what the clepsydra is in time: the pure form without the materiality of the presence of others. The deep intelligibility Robinson pursues is not a total transparency of the bare reality that leaps up through the tube of his vision from the impenetrable night outside; it is the lateral intelligibility other views bring when they situate one's actual view in a system of possible views. The impersonal table of the contents of the surveyed island will chart the stirrings of every plant, bird, and animal in a system of possible places; the labeling, ringing, and branding will fix the possibilities on the things themselves. The things will then be perceived from the start as currency.

Robinson's efforts are devoted entirely to undoing the effects of solitude on the format of things. He is engaged in, not a husbandry that has as its purpose to ensure his own physical survival, but a metallurgy laboring to smelt the opaque ferments of the island into currency. His driven labor, which has as its side effect to make him completely self-sufficient on his island and in need of no one, functions to make his existence entirely venal, that is, wholly one of love of the others.

> Money spiritualizes all that it touches by endowing it with a quality that is both rational (measurable) and universal, since property reckoned in terms of money is accessible to all men…. The venal man suppresses his murderous and anti-social instincts—honor, self-pride, patriotism, political ambition, religious fanaticism, racism—in favor of his need to cooperate with others, his love of fruitful exchanges, his sense of human solidarity.[15]

In the absence of collaborators, Robinson himself builds a venal society of one regulated by the clepsydra, amassing an enormous fortune that could extravagantly return any gesture of human solidarity vouchsafed to him. The transition, Burridge explained,[16] from a society based on the exchange of goods and services, a society governed by the rigorous obligation incumbent on the receiver to give goods of equivalent use-value in return, into a society where the giving of goods and services can be repaid immediately with the useless substance of gold coins, is a transition to a society in which nonreciprocity, love—that is, unreciprocated service—becomes for the first time possible.

The Elemental

Robinson's libidinous commitment to Speranza, to working all his energies into the fecundity and harmony of the island, is not reciprocated. It is not only that there are in the island secret ferments and malignant stirrings of resistance to his labor; there is the emergence of an element that repudiates all labor as irrelevance—an *other island* than that which Robinson embraced, and which was rising to embrace him, or to embrace another Robinson. To admit such a teleology one would have to bypass the ontology that posits an underlying substance, which is formed by the work of our perception into phenomena that reveal it as it is, and to conceive an ontology in which the elemental of its own movement produces a double of itself in phantasmal free elements. This would be an ontology not only of forms that contain and articulate the substance, but of free elements which issue out of the elemental depth and which catch up our predatory substance in their ascent. The movement that leads Robinson to the zone of the free elements engenders a phantasmal double of his libidinal body.

From the first the bounteous Island of Desolation, which offers its nourishment to Robinson's hand without effort or concern on his part, invites him. For days, for weeks, for months, he is immobilized in passive contemplation of the "vast gently heaving expanse of the ocean, green-tinged and glittering." A great cedar, tutelary genius of the island, brings him up to the air, the skies, and the light.

Then the mire, the zone of indistinction of waters and earth—two elements of death—draws him voluptuously. The plenum of the mire is not the zone of infantile escapism after the practical failure of his adult project of building the bark *Escape*; it is not the zone of the inability to endure failure, abandon, discord, and the master-opposition of life and death, which Nietzsche denounced in the ecstasy-into-mildness of Jesus and of every redeemer type. It is the place of a present in which everything he had escaped from is rediscovered and possessed "more observantly, more intelligently, and more sensually than was possible in the turmoil of the present."[17]

The mire, incestuous promiscuity of seas and earth, reunites Robinson with his sister. The other, come to him on a phantom ship, does not disembark as another figure of the possible. Lucy appears to him in the free elements "suspended in the blue gaps between the motionless foliage," signaling to Robinson only as the sign of the definitive departure of every possible.

Robinson, unnerved by the notion that the zone from which the others, the possibles, have departed is a zone where the things have been undermined not only in their meaning but in the very roots of their being—a region of hallucination and madness—plunges then into his enterprise of transforming the island into a rational structure, where the things will be made into objects visible and intelligible to their very depths—that *other madness*. He sets out to replace this apparition of a past brotherhood that floated in the mire with his own labor, making himself a venal society of one, of unreciprocated service. He has not understood that the bond of fraternity with the other is discontinuous with association in an enterprise, and that it is revealed only by death and departure. The bond with the other that consists of being his or her brother is opaque to the understanding which understands the possible, and can understand the other only as a possible within a common field of projects and enterprises. Later Robinson will become the brother of Friday, but as Friday departs on the *Whitebird* become as phantomal as Lucy, Robinson will be as agitated and uncomprehending.

Yet Lucy has appeared to him as a first *elemental sign*, and will return to guide him in the person of Friday. The sign, not understood, has nonetheless had its effect, and beneath the rationality Robinson will impose on the island he instinctually understands that the mire was the zone of *another telos*.

At the antipodes of the mire, the elemental will beckon to him further from the rock core of the island. He feels obscurely that he is seeking there that recess in sacred constructions, in cathedrals, where the least whispers in the transept, the reredos, or the nave can be heard. He follows the summons, down into the hollow core of the summit—not the vantage-point from which he surveys the map of the island, but the point where his own eyes are completely darkened and it is the island itself that is conscious in the stir of myrtle leaves with the sun's rays breaking through, that knows itself in the white crest of a wave running up the yellow sand. In this darkness, in which all the force of the sun on the horizon can only send in a beam that is indistinguishable from a momentary phosphorescence on his own eye, Robinson finds another transparency and visibility of the plants he had labeled, the birds he had ringed, the animals he had branded.

> Seated with his back to the rocky wall, his eyes wide open in the darkness, he saw the white unfolding of the sea on all the shores of the island, the benevolent sway of palm leaves stirred by the wind, the red flash of a hummingbird against a green sky. He smelled the moist freshness of the sand uncovered by the ebb, and watched a hermit crab as it took the air at the doorway of its shell. A black-headed gull slowed down suddenly in its flight to swoop down upon a small creature half-hidden in the red seaweed, gleaming brown in the drag of the undertow.[18]

From this nerve-center Robinson descends to the darkest recess, the womb. There his body learns that it is by a movement of systole and diastole to the core, the inner substance of earth, that the surface life proliferates. He discovers the maternal substance of terra firma, the flawless, dry tenderness, the unfailing, undemonstrative solicitude he had known in childhood in his mother—strong, high-souled, but deeply reserved and not given to a display of sentiment.

It would be quite wrong here to treat these words as metaphorical transfer—to begin now to make the novel an allegory, and the philosophical encounter with it a hermeneutical enterprise of translating its metaphors into the master-narrative of those Foucault and Deleuze identify as universal, university, intellectuals.[19] It is on the crust of objects laid over the elemental that the other is a figure of the possible obstinately passing for real, his objects currency, and his signs metaphors. On the island deserted of others, the fringe of variations and exchanges is blacked out and Robinson's perception cannot skew the immediate blows of the actual. The language he maintains in the museum of his logbook is stripped of metaphoricity; he can no longer understand a deep well as a profound thought or an intense emotion.

Beneath the crust of currency and metaphors, while the clepsydra is stopped, Robinson has descended to a sphere where experience is without the conditions of possibility for metaphor. Here his libido no longer leans in passing on terrestrial substances on the way to the womb of his human mother and of his own child—substances that would metaphorically transfer his energies toward that objective. Here there are no objectives, no objects, only the rock core of the island engendering and making luminous the white unfolding of the sea and the red flash of a hummingbird against a green sky. Robinson can have no idea of what he desires, no idea of objects to seek in this zone beyond light and darkness; his fetus libido, a driving force that is not dissipated for not having an objective, is not an Oedipal desire but a tellurian cause. "Previously…I sought to console myself with visions of a house, *the* house in which I would end my days, built out of massive blocks of granite resting on unshakable foundations. I no longer indulge in that dream. I no longer need it."[20]

A libido that is no longer shifted metaphorically from objective to objective beneath objective, that no longer finds the pole of its craving in the objective another's craving designates as possible, a libido that rests on its terrestrial causality, while being there so close to death that the least shift of attention is enough to make it slip over into death[21]—this libido nonetheless finds in its dark immobility a specific energy to extend itself in surfaces. With no objective of its own, it sends its tellurian causality into ever more dispersed objectives of the surfaces themselves.

> It seems to me that a feeling such as love is better measured, if it can be measured at all, by the extent of its surface than by its degree of depth. For I measure my love for a woman by the fact that I love indiscriminately her hands, her eyes, her carriage, the clothes she wears, the commonplace things she merely touches, the place where she dwells, the sea in which she bathes…. All this, it seems to me, is decidedly on the surface! Whereas a lesser love aims directly—in depth—at sex, and leaves all the rest in a shadowy background.[22]

Robinson's libido intensifies in becoming superficial, but it does so by disseminating on the surfaces the causality of the core. This causality is the transfer of life. "Robinson reflected that there might be trees on the island, which, like the orchids with the hymenoptera, might be disposed to make use of him for the transference of their pollen."[23] The surfaces are no longer profiles of objects-objectives, no longer cross-sections opening upon a depth, but themselves surface causes of his libido without objective. "He felt as never before that he was lying on Speranza as though on a living being, that the island's body was beneath him.... His sex burrowed like a plowshare into the earth, and overflowed in immense compassion for all created things."[24]

Robinson comes to understand that this surface discharge of the tellurian libidinal causality in him—that given by this descent into the elemental and not by the alluring figures of the possible the others present—is also a dying. He comes to understand this through the death the others have put in him.

> All those who knew me, all without exception, believe me dead. My own belief in my existence is opposed to that unanimous belief. No matter what I do, I cannot prevent that picture of Robinson's dead body from existing in all their minds.[25]

His death in their, and consequently in his own, mind reveals the dying in all libido. The transfer of life from the old to the new is evacuation and sacrifice, it is the "living presence, ominous and mortal, of the species in the essence of the individual."[26]

> Under the influence of darkness, warmth, and languor the enemy revives, unsheathes his sword, and diminishes the man, makes of him a lover, plunges him into a brief ecstasy, then closes his eyes—and the lover, couched on earth, lost in the rapture of forgetfulness and renunciation of self, sinks into that little death which is sleep....
>
> Earth irresistibly draws the enclasped lovers with joined lips, cradling them after their embrace in the happy slumber of sensual delight. But earth also harbors the dead, sucks their blood and devours their flesh, that these orphans be restored to the cosmos from which for the length of a lifetime they were parted. Love and death, two aspects of the defeat of the individual, turn with a common impulse to the earth. Both are of their nature earthly....
>
> Deprived of that fruitful byway which a woman's body affords, I must turn directly to the earth which will be my last resting place. What happened in the pink coomb? I dug my grave with my sex and died the transient death that we call pleasure.[27]

This sexuality is not a function of the personal structure we and the others erect in our lives; it is what the ancients called the vegetative system in our bodies—not organs by which our bodies are self-moving, animate, animal, but glands, sap, seed. Our sexuality, conceived as causality and not as objectifying desire, is terrestrial. It is that by which we belong to the vegetative abundance of earth. "He buried his face in the grass roots, breathing open-mouthed a long, hot breath. And the earth responded, filling his nostrils with the heavy scent of dead grass and the ripening of seed, and of sap rising in new shoots."[28]

Robinson lays out his vegetative body on the surface of the pink coomb, which gives birth to mandrakes, those plants whose thick white forked roots lead the mind by metaphorizing transfer to the body of a child. It is the sole magical incident in this otherwise rigorously naturalist novel. But we readers are also required to read this magical causality as naturalist and not allegorical.

For sexual reproduction, as Robinson remembers he had been taught by the old naturalist Samuel Gloaming, before we were taught by Deleuze,[29] is not the reinstatement of the same, but the repetition that engenders the different. The reproductive causality which is libido is not a mechanism for the re-presentation of the same individual in the form of an immortal genus. Reproductivity in the individual is the ominous and mortal force that sacrifices that individual to something that is not of the same kind—because the individual is not one of a kind. The reproductive libido is engendered by earth's need to produce that gratuity and superabundance which individuals are, and to produce unending mutations of vegetative life so that something would survive "were the earth to be frozen to a block of ice, or burned by the sun to a desert of stone."[30]

The pink coomb where Robinson's penis burrowed like a plowshare was then too a "fruitful byway," not where an individual emerges to refuse his mortality and pursue his own objectives, but where the tellurian causality of libido surfaces. Then, may not a woman's body too be, not a deviation for a tellurian libido, a possible obstinately passing for real, but a hollow on the substance of earth, where the love that surfaces there is still what Robinson came to call the *vegetative way*? And the male body too?—when it shall be as vines intertwined that Robinson and Friday make libidinous contact.

To reach this point Robinson will be in need of a guide, an incarnate sign of the elemental. The dying that is coextensive with a libido become elemental was revealed to him by the death to which and in which the others have consigned his mind. The force of this death is in the whole civilization he maintains in his person without them. It will be with the murderous force of this civilization that he confronts the others who, one day, arrive on the shores of the Bay of Salvation.

Perverse Brotherhood
– – – – – – – – – – – – – – – – – –

The Araucanians return—those people whose civilization is guided by the female seer who rules according to the law stated in the Gospel of St. Matthew: "If thy right hand offend thee, cut it out and cast it from thee." Her entranced finger points to a half-caste fifteen-year-old boy to be cast off. Robinson, deciding in accordance with his own imperative to save his patriarchal, Mosaic, civilization, aims his pistol at the fleeing victim, but the dog Tenn struggles in Robinson's grip; Robinson misses his aim, and kills one of the pursuers instead. Thus, unintentionally, he saves Friday's life.

Venal civilization—that which "suppresses murderous and antisocial instincts," that which exchanges goods not for goods of equivalent use-value, but for useless specie, and thus liberates love—had at last met the others, for whom that venal civilization is wholly the materialized desire—and had met them with "self-pride, patriotism, political ambition, religious fanaticism, racism." Robinson immediately inserts Friday into his metallurgical enterprise; he teaches him English, teaches him to plow and sow and reap, to thresh and winnow, grind and cook. He sets him to work milking the goats, making cheese, collecting turtles' eggs and soft-boiling them, digging ditches, tending the fish ponds, trapping vermin, caulking the canoe, mending his garments, and polishing his boots, forcing him to listen "devoutly to words such as *sin, salvation, hell-fire, damnation, Mammon, and apocalypse....* He paid Friday. He paid him a wage of a half-sovereign a month. Friday could spend the money on...trifles brought from the Virginia, or simply on buying himself a half-day's repose...which he spent in the hammock he had made for himself."[31]

Searching Friday's face, Robinson never finds the smile of complicity he had found on the dog Tenn—the smile that his own face, disfigured by solitude, had acquired from Tenn—never finds a mirror of the total intelligibility of the transparent island. One day he recognizes there is in the face turned to him only fear. This fear makes Friday's face turned to his own a mirror of the demented. The other he had awaited so long, and whose function he had maintained on the island by regulating all his moves with the imperatives of the clepsydra, had not come to situate and guarantee the intelligibility he had forged for himself.

That night Robinson goes to make love with Speranza in the coomb of the mandrakes, and in his absence the water of the clepsydra stops. Friday reverts to his nature, his libidinous, vegetative causality. Robinson finds him first in the magnolia trees, transformed into a vine, then in the mandrakes that extend Friday's reproductive libido across the surfaces of Speranza.

Friday will finally totally destroy the museum of civilization Robinson had built, destroy his granaries, all his irrigated rice fields, disperse all his domesticated animals—as inadvertently as Robinson had saved Friday's life from the matriarchal New-Testament civilization that had encroached on his island. But Friday's hand will save Robinson's life the night the great cedar—the tutelary genius of Robinson's island—turns its roots too in the air, like the willows Friday had planted. "He would never again let go the hand that reached down to save him on the night the tree fell."[32]

Friday will continue his destruction of civilization. The great buck Andoar recreates a social order of command and subordination among the goats after Robinson's pens and stockades are destroyed. Friday engages in combat with him, and Robinson sees them fall from the cliff in mortal embrace. Robinson rushes to the heights, which await him with mortal attraction, to recover Friday. Seized with vertigo on the rocky cliffs, Robinson sees that the vortex of death that draws him is also the locus in which he shall rise to become Friday's double.

> He realized that vertigo is nothing but terrestrial magnetism acting
> upon the spirit of man, who is a creature of earth. The soul yearns for
> that foothold of clay or granite, slate or silica, whose distance at once
> terrifies and attracts, since it harbors the peace of death. It is not the
> emptiness of space that induces vertigo, but the enticing fullness of the
> earthly depths. With his face now turned to the sky, Robinson felt that
> something stronger than the insidious appeal of those scattered grave-
> stones might be found in the summons to flight of two albatross,
> companionably soaring amid the pink-tinted clouds.[33]

It is because Friday casts himself into the death that waits under the figure of Andoar that, even engaged in mortal combat with him, he becomes his phantasmal brother, his double. And it is because Robinson rushes into the mortal attraction on the cliff where Friday and Andoar had fallen that he is reborn as the double, the phantasmal brother of Friday, and the sign Friday makes of Andoar doubles into a sign for Robinson.

Robinson and Friday form now, not a society—figures of the possible which stabilize the elemental patterns into objects-objectives, each for the other a desire for another desire of other objects, an association for the circulation of currency and love—but a brotherhood, their hands clasped like vines, an elemental association of two effects of vegetative sexuality.

Their fraternity is a bond that is formed by eros and not by pact, to be sure, but this eros deviates from the eros that engenders the structures of family and civilization. In normal sexuality, the individual makes himself or herself the locus of the reinstatement of the norms. In the normal family, the genus is re-presented, reduplicated, and functions normatively. The filiality it engenders makes being-a-brother an obligation. This filiality is continued in the civilization that is founded on the family, where the generic, the universal, is re-presented, and functions normatively—first in language, which formulates the normative and the universal, formulates imperatives for work that is common, and makes everything detachable from the earth into currency. Those who communicate in civilized language recognize a normalizing brotherhood. They recognize in the universal formulations of language the generic commonality of their bodies. In all civilized discourse a normal sexuality is being articulated.

It was not because Friday recognized in Robinson a duplicate of the genus in himself that his hand reached out to save him the night the tree fell. He had fled to the magnolia trees because he had come to see on Robinson only the appalling face of the demented. Robinson saw in him the one who destroyed all the intelligibility he had put on the island and whose touch now uprooted the trees to replant their roots in the sky. It was at the extreme point of recognizing the alien in one another that their hands clasped never to let go again. In their fraternal association Friday does not now begin to implant in Robinson his civilization.

The fraternity of these strangers eludes being made comprehensible in our language, whose norms rest corporeally on kinship, the community of individuals in the species; Robinson does not succeed in speaking of it in his logbook.

The two that arrive on the deserted island from remote extremities of humanity do not become each one the double of the other through natural or normal filiality; to the contrary, not only Robinson's but also Friday's civilization make the one the object, slave, or domestic animal of the other. The one becomes the double of the other when he puts himself wholly in the place of the death that gapes open for the other.

The fraternity which Robinson and Friday now form is the association contracted by a perverse libido. They do not form a homosexual couple. Homosexuality, where each seeks in the other a figure of sex the same as himself, is as normal, normalizing, as the heterosexuality where two individuals seek in reproduction a re-presentation of individuals of the same species as themselves. Pierre Klossowski had defined perversion as a sexuality in which the genus, the representation of the same, is destroyed in the individual.[34] The brotherhood that now binds Robinson and Friday is libidinal if Samuel Gloaming is right to say that sexuality is the sacrifice of the individual for another, for their association is based on the fact that each—at the extremity of their otherness from one another—has put himself in the place where death had gaped open to take the other. In doing so each had thrown into the place of death the force of representation of himself, of reproduction in himself. There has occurred in each a deviation with regard to the end: the earth that irresistibly draws enclasped lovers with joined lips and engenders unending mutations of vegetative life so that something would survive were the earth to be frozen to a block of ice, or burned by the sun to a desert of stone. Their libido is no longer terrestrial. Hands clasped, the one the mortal double of the other, they will become the more strangers—an albatross companionship, destined to depart from one another in the skies.

Robinson becomes now as naked, copper-colored, and beardless as Friday. Their phantasmal bodies are each for the other the more strange.

> Two days ago, he came up to me while I lay dozing on the beach. He stood for some moments gazing at me, a dark, slender figure outlined against the brilliant sky. Then he knelt down beside me and began to examine me with an extraordinary intentness. His fingers wandered over my face, patted my cheeks, followed the curve of my chin, tested the flexibility of my nose. He made me raise my arms above my head, and bending over my body he explored it inch by inch like an anatomist preparing to dissect a corpse. He seemed to have forgotten that I lived and breathed, that thoughts might enter my head, that I might grow impatient.[35]

Robinson in turn studies the utter strangeness of his fraternal double. "When a painter or engraver introduces human figures into a landscape or alongside a monument, they are not there merely as an accessory. Human figures *convey the scale*, and what is still more important, they represent attitudes, possible points of view, which enrich the picture for the outside observer by providing him with other, indispensable points of reference."[36] Now, in the wet mirror of the lagoon, Robinson sees Friday come to him, and the desert of sky and water is so vast about him that nothing supplies the scale any more. Friday's movements are not in a time each of whose present moments is a vacuum jostled by the moment to come. He is decked out in his nudity, bearing his flesh with a sovereign ostentation, carrying himself forward like a carnal monstrance.

> He skips lightly, bringing to play a ripple of muscles.... Seated near him, I note the part of his leg situated behind the knee, its pearly lightness and the pattern it forms, a capital H. It is like a throat, firm and

smooth when the leg is stretched, soft and hollow when it bends.

I put my hands on his knees, cupping them to fit the shape of the knee and feel its life. In its hardness and dryness, by contrast with the softness of the thigh, the knee is the key to the vault on which the earthly frame is borne, raising it aloft in a living equilibrium to the sky. There is no movement of the body, no tremor, no impulse of hesitation, that does not proceed from that warm, moving disc and return to it. During several seconds my hands learn that Friday's motionless stance is not that of a stone or tree stump, but the quivering outcome, constantly varied and readjusted, of a series of actions and reactions, the play of all his muscles.[37]

As Friday walks with his hands as readily as with his legs, each joint of his body is such a throat from which tremors and hesitations proceed and to which they return, such a key of the vault of his posture, such a pivot disc. In Friday's mobility Robinson learns a polyvalence of the limbs and members.

He learns too the solar splendor of organs that are not molds for the possible. After the death of Tenn, who had maintained on the island the smile of benevolence, of understanding, of reciprocal confirmation of the project of constituting objects-objectives, Robinson does not find and does not seek on Friday's face the smile of complicity. Instead, he discovers the strangeness of eyes without searching, desiring, demanding looks.

And it was now that he became aware of something pure and sensitive gleaming amid the unsightly, mishandled flesh. He noted Friday's eye, beneath its long, curved lashes, seeing how the wonderfully smooth and limpid ball was incessantly wiped clean and refreshed by the beating of the lid. He noted the constant widening and shrinking of the pupil, in response to the scarcely perceptible variations of light, as it regulated the message to be transmitted to the retina. Within the transparency of the iris was contained a tiny, intricate pattern like feathers of glass, a fitted rose-window, infinitely precious and delicate.[38]

Friday's knee and his joints were not figures of the possible but pivots about which all his muscles play. His is not the body that is a framework of habits, responses, reflexes, preoccupations, dreams, and associations held upright, as in a street riot, by the crowd densely packed about it; it is a body in a space without scale of the free elements, holding itself in equilibrium on any of its members. His eye—not a surveying instrument stopped down for searching, desiring, demanding looks—is a rose-window of feathers of glass set up to flame with the glories of inner and outer suns. In it Robinson sees another recess, like that of the cave, beyond light and darkness, where the plants he had labeled, the birds he had ringed, the animals he had branded, are seen with another visibility and transparency. Friday's ear is another recess, like that found in cathedrals, from which the least whispers in the abside, choir, sanctuary, or nave are heard. What is seen and heard there are the imperative signs of the elemental.

The Elemental Imperative

This imperative is not revealed in the intelligible structure of the objective world; for the objects themselves, their order, and their intelligibility have issued out of Robinson's legislative decrees. Nor is it Friday's will that makes the signs of the elemental imperative for Robinson. It is true that Friday makes signs. He shows, with the arrow finned with albatross quills, that the most perfect arrows are not made for hunting but for flying forever into the skies. He makes of Andoar an aeolian harp upon which the winds play an instantaneous symphony, a symphony played in the circular time of the gods where the present no longer exists as a recompense for a moment past and lost and a demand put on a moment to come. Friday makes signs because his nature is a sign of the elemental, imperative for Robinson. "Friday was not a rational being, performing deliberate, considered acts, but rather a force of nature from which actions proceeded, and their consequences resembled him, the way children resemble their mother."[39] His eye does not, through an interrogating, querulous look, bring a possible to things, making them into objectives; it captures the imperative signs of the elemental as sacred rose-window glory. His posture does not hold itself upright to erect objects-objectives on its planes; its everywhere polyvalent limbs and members materialize a polyvalent availability for the beckonings of the free elements.

It is in his libido, his vegetative nature, that Robinson recognizes an imperative put on him. For if sexuality is accomplished in the vegetative reproduction of the different, the mandrakes, it is also agitated with an imperative beyond the finality Samuel Gloaming had understood. In obscure obedience to this imperative Robinson climbs the araucaria tree, tree of Friday's birthplace, and it is there that his libido understands an imperative laid on it from the beyond.

> He continued to climb, doing so without difficulty and with a growing sense of being the prisoner, and in some sort a part, of a vast and infinitely ramified structure flowing upward through the trunk with its

reddish bark and spreading in countless large and lesser branches, twigs, and shoots to reach the nerve ends of leaves, triangular, pointed, scaly, and rolled in spirals around the twigs. He was taking part in the tree's most unique accomplishment, which is to embrace the air with its thousand branches, to caress it with its million fingers. As he went higher he became conscious of the swaying of the giant architectural complex through which the wind blew with the sound of an organ....

The laboring of that living mast, with its great burden of branches carding the wind, was like a deep hum broken every now and then by a long moaning sound. He listened to this soothing music for a long time, and by degrees his terror left him.... The tree became a great ship anchored to the earth and struggling under full sail to break away from its mooring.... "The leaf is the lung of the tree which is itself a lung, and the wind is its breathing," Robinson thought. He pictured his own lungs growing outside himself like a blossoming of purple-tinted flesh, living polyparies of coral with pink membranes, sponges of human tissue.... He would flaunt that intricate efflorescence, that bouquet of fleshy flowers in the wide air, while a tide of purple ecstasy flowed into his body on a stream of crimson blood....[40]

Robinson's vegetative system has now passed beyond the tellurian stage of propagation without objective, to become uranian. It espouses the longing that is in the vegetation of the earth, that rises in the highest trees, the longing of life in them—to sail in the free elements, without returning, like the albatross quill finned arrow Friday had sent into the skies. Here the aspiration of the *spiritus* that moves across the waters does not imperatively demand that the carnal eros be subjugated to the domination of a mind. The spirit is the movement of free elements in us, making our organs, no longer voracious, assimilating, but forms of exposedness. The spiritualization of the body is not the domination over, but the *exteriorization* of even our libidinal, vegetative bodies. The solar force that engendered living polyparies in the deep had beckoned terrestrial bodies forth onto islands, and now summons Robinson's body, that vesicle that contains within its coral ribs the vegetative organisms of the deep, irrigated with its blood the chemical and saline composition of seawater. This body now hears an order, articulated by the wind as chant, to ascend to the uranian element, to expose all the life it contains, its inner polyparies, gorgorgonians, and sponges, to the free elements.

Friday makes for Robinson a sign of this spiritualized eros: the satyr become aeolian harp. It is also a sign that the imperative opens up before the eros of Robinson not a future but the time of the other, the double without the possible, the time without future.

It was not a melody to pluck at the heart with its form and rhythm, but a single note, infinite in its harmonies, which took possession of the soul, a chord composed of countless elements in whose sustained power there was something fateful that held the listener spellbound....

The aeolian harp is not merely an elemental instrumental drawing song from the winds: it is also the only instrument whose music does not need time for its development but exists entirely in the moment. You may increase the number of its strings and tune them to whatever notes you will, but still you are composing an *instant symphony* whose first and last chord sounds whenever the wind touches the harp.[41]

Robinson's sensuality, invaded by the uranian elements, his body laid out, like the body of the island under the skies, in a total submission, now resounds with such an instantaneous symphony. The aeolian harp replaces the clepsydra to mark the form of time in which the imperative is heard.

What has most changed in my life is the passing of time, its speed and even its direction. Formerly every day, hour, and minute leaned in a sense toward the day, hour, and minute that was to follow, and all were drawn into the pattern of the moment, whose transience created a kind of vacuum. So time passed rapidly and usefully, the more quickly because it was usefully employed, leaving behind it an accumulation of achievement and wastage which was my history. Perhaps the sweep of time of which I was a part, after winding through millennia, would have "coiled" and returned to its beginning. But the circularity of time remained the secret of the gods, and my own short life was no more than a segment, a straight line between two points aimed absurdly toward infinity, like a path in a hedged garden that tells us nothing of the curve of the earth....

For me the cycle had now shrunk until it is merged in the moment. The circular movement has become so swift that it cannot be distinguished from immobility. And it is as though, in consequence, my days had rearranged themselves. No longer do they jostle on each other's heels. Each stands separate and upright, proudly affirming its own worth. And since they are no longer to be distinguished as the stages of a plan in process of execution, they so resemble each other as to be superimposed in my memory, so that I seem to be ceaselessly reliving the same day.... Are we not now living in eternity, Friday and I?[42]

The Imperative Departure

In Tournier's novel, a fictional recasting in libidinal terms of the fictive adventures of Daniel Defoe's hero of Victorian imperialism, the *Whitebird* sails on, toward its further imperialist adventures, with Friday, who sees in it a white bird taking flight on the seas, on board. Robinson remains. Or rather, he pursues ever further his departure. He finds a new companion and brother, whom he names Sunday. Sunday is ourselves, the readers, stowaways from the *Whitebird*. The reader is himself or herself led far from the objects-objectives he has arrayed about himself, to the *other island*. Enticed, seduced, transported—by what? Tournier's fiction, Robinson's adventures, far from aleatory fabrications issuing from a free imagination seated in Robinson, or in the author, or in us, reveal an elemental imperative.

The objects we know, the means and the ends we pursue, the others with whom we interact, are not laid out in empty space, the infinitely empty theoretical space extended by geometrical dimensions along the infinite linear axis of time in which thought situates its representations of them. They are found in the light, along the ground, in the air—in the elemental.

As soon as we open our eyes, without any seeking, any intentionality, our eyes are flooded with light. As soon as we stir, we make contact with the earth, which extends as an indefinite reservoir of support maintaining us and all things in their places, itself supported by nothing. As soon as we awaken, the element of sonority resounds about us in indefinite depth.

This elemental exteriority weighs on us as an imperative. The first imperative, priori to the a priori forms of thought, is not formal; Kant obscurely recognized this when he recognized that the imperative for thought to think content precedes and makes possible the imperative that it conceive content with coherent and consistent forms. Prior to the imperative that thought command the sensory-motor faculties of the psychophysical composite to gather sensory patterns in ways that could be identified with consistent concepts and organized with coherent laws, to expose oneself to forces that could be understood with practical maxims, to expose oneself to the relations of command and obedience in economic, political, and cultural society, there is the imperative that our sensibility expose itself to the *element* in which sensory patterns and forces could take form: the earth, the flux, the air, the light.

It is in obedience to this elemental imperative that our thought can order and be ordered by objects, that our action can organize means and be organized by ends, that our approach to others can order and be ordered by them. By holding ourselves upright, by taking a stand, we are enabled to grasp things held in position, objectives. There is an imperative obeyed in this stabilizing of ourselves on terra firma: we are bound to perceive things, face on, in a normal position with regard to us, with real or normal properties, at the optimal distance—that which is fixed by the imperative to take as real the profile that answers to the twofold exigency for amplitude and for detail. In the contact with the support of the earth, we answer to an imperative to ground, to fix, to stabilize. In following the light, we are enjoined to elucidate the reliefs and the contours of things. In the contact with the sonorous medium, the vibrancy of silence, we find ourselves bound to let the things resound, to utter their orientations in the signifying sounds of discourse.

On terra firma, in the light, in the sonorous medium we stabilize the means and the ends, we survey the contours and the pathways, we label the things. The weights and the measures of things and the map of their layout address us as the form of an imperative. In the possibilities things sustain in a practicable field, in the substance of the earth trodden by feet other than one's own, the others address us in the form of a social imperative.

The imperative behind the imperative force of the mapped, labeled, ringed, branded world is an imperative to elucidate, to ground, to express, which is the way the elemental is addressed to us. The elemental imperative precedes and makes possible the perception of consistent and coherent things and a consistent and coherent world. It precedes and makes possible the imperative form of the map of nature, the practicable layout, the constellation of others.

Tournier's book shows that the elemental imperative also repudiates the world of things, of objects-objectives. The surveying, ordering subject, which shuts up the phosphorescence of the shifting sensory waves and troughs in itself, which encloses their qualities in its own organs, and affixes to objects possibilities in their stead, is repudiated in turn as a knot of contradiction, a center of discord, by the free elements. The other island summons and casts off that irrelevance, the subject. The economy Robinson had made of its plants, birds, animals, contours, and hollows is revealed, when the depths rise up and the tutelary cedar turns its roots to the skies, as a surface madness by the depths Robinson now recognizes as imperative. The fraternal imperative Robinson discovers in the elemental figure of Friday repudiates the social imperative that the *Whitebird* brings to him, even as it, an elemental figure of the albatross, brings to Friday himself the imperative to depart. The summons of the elemental reveals the adventures of Robinson Crusoe to be adventitious only in the understanding of a rationality that is *the other madness*. It reveals that the itinerary of his sensuality—become tellurian, solar, and uranian—obeys a destiny.

The imperative that now commands destines the subject to be reborn as the locus in which the free elements are glorified. It is an imperative received in the receptivity of our bodies, in the rose-windows set up in our eyes, in our lungs made to card the wind, in our muscles made to make ostentatious and splendid the repose of the earth and the mobility of the winds, in our voices made to intone the aeolian instant symphony when the clepsydra has stopped.

Foreign Bodies

What makes commands mandatory may be the superior force of the speaker to sanction the one ordered. But we also recognize as imperative the words of the sick and the dying. What makes directives obligatory may be some structure of the culture of which the speaker is the mouthpiece: the Japanese who invites the foreign visitor to take off his shoes before entering the house, the priest who orders in the name of divine law, or the ethical theorist who works out what is reasonable. But we also recognize as imperative words of foreigners and of those without scientific culture, and the nonsense of children, the laughter of adults, and the nonwisdom of the aged.

The imperative is not the coherence and cohesion of a common discourse, the universality and necessity of reason that commands the grammar and rhetoric in which we must fit the insights that flash in the carnal density of our separate organisms; the stumbling voice, the outcries and the sighs of a voice muted by strange dreams and torments interdict the pronouncements of that representative of reasonable speech we put ourselves forth to be. The imperative is not the transpersonal monumentality of the projects of civilization; the outstretched hand of the outcast with whom we have sealed no collaboration with a handshake binds us. The imperative is that bond between strangers with whom we have no kinship, no language, religion, land, age in common, with whom no practicable field and no common enterprise is possible.

Appeals and orders are formulated in the vocative and imperative forms of grammar. Jean-Luc Nancy says that the imperative belongs to language, is possible only in language.[1] The very word was invented by Kant. But this thesis is impossible. Language is a second-order conventionalization of the expressive body. It can no more condense in its formulations all that appeals and demands in that body than it can tell all that one sees, touches, and feels as one walks in the forest. Emmanuel Levinas contrasts sight with hearing, and locates the vocative and the imperative entirely in the face with which the other speaks. The eyes do not shine, they appeal, he writes. The face and surfaces of another are simultaneously signifiers for indicative and informative significations and traces of the signifying hollow, which is emptied out in vocative and imperative moves. Just as the substance of the paper dematerializes for the reader and figures only as an abstract extension in which the signifiers are suspended, a face, Levinas says, is the invisible that summons from the distance of alterity. But the production of a discourse in the terms of a common language, a body of statements reciprocally affirmed, is not the telos of the face-to-face encounter, any more than self-consciousness is of life. Speech only supplements the physical and ethical experience of the face in its immediate phenomenality, its materiality.

As one listens, the light molds the shifting contours of the cheeks, the teeth flash. The handsome face of a man casts a seductiveness in advance upon all the words that issue from his mouth; his cleft lip shadows all his glamorous words with vulnerability. The mouth is an organ that segregates the regulated phonation of speech from intakes of air, panting, hoarseness, coughs, sneezes, hiccups, laughter, outcries, sobs. It is a low-tech organ, unlike today's digital reproducing systems, which eliminate all noise from the equipment to fill the listening space with the music itself. The voice issues from a throat parched with the dust or tightened with fear. The individual geography of the corrugated roof of the mouth and the gums overtone and reverberate the voice as it issues forth its conventionalized phrases and exhalations. They are shaped by the tongue wet with saliva released by food and spices; the words pass through the spray of carbonated mineral water or champagne. The voice pushes over a desert made of hunger and fever. The breath whistles through the teeth, the edges of phonemes are muffled across the mouth toothless with disease or age. The tones are rasped by unseen scars and sores in the tissues of the mouth. The face speaks with lips wide and carnal or thin and wrinkled or blistered. The voice speaks with lips puckered and languid, its stream of words pulsating with a yearning to kiss, to draw in the tongue of another, to swallow erections and discharges.

Levinas's later work recovers the phenomenality and immediacy of the imperative experience when he writes about contact with the surfaces of the other. He distinguishes, in *Totality and Infinity*, erotic contact from the informative closeness of the Heideggerian *Entfernung*. It is the exposed surfaces upon which the expressions take form and are engulfed in the evidence of impressionability and vulnerability, the skin which is not observed but which afflicts and troubles me, that make the imperative not a hypothesis I represent but a given, a fact, a phenomenon. Levinas will separate all eroticism out of the contact with the other who orders and appeals. It is with the skin weighed down with wrinkles and wounds that the alterity of the other, which is made of susceptibility and need, touches me and makes my existence *Zum-Tode-Sein*, a care for the absolute alterity of dying, the dying of the other.

Thus the central paradox found in Heidegger—an ex-istence that is simultaneously a transcendence toward the being of the world and toward the nothingness of death, a world that is simultaneously the array of possibility and the imminence of impossibility—is found again in Levinas: the absence from the world and the mortality that constitutes alterity make the ex-istence ordered by it transmundane and metaphysical.

The face and surfaces of others afflict me, cleave to me, sear me. They solicit me, press their needs on me; they direct me, order me. The face of a stranger in the crowd turned to me is an imposition. The face of a Somalian looking at me from the newspaper page intrudes into my zone of implantation; I am relieved that the opaqueness of the paper screens me from him. In the corridors of my projects, my goals, and my reasons, the tormented laughter of the visionary and of the one lost in orgasmic abysses arrests my advance.

The impact of the imperative is incontrovertible in the step heard in the corridor while I was peering through a keyhole, the glance suddenly turned to me of the one I had been contemplating seated across from me in the bus, the touch of the beggar child felt when I am seated in the café in the night. The force of an appeal and demand comes in the isolation and denuding of carnality.

We associate with those of our own kind, and go to meet them clothed and uniformed—career woman, hip teen-ager, professional, seductress. While a conversation made of information and indications, and requests and importunities extends between us, the alterity of the other denudes before my eyes, suddenly again and again divested of their lines of sighting. I see you fatigued by the heat of the day and from too much conversation, your bare arm, divested of its gestures, resting on the table. I see you bent to wash, the labored curve of your spine buzzing with undecipherable messages that your organism communicates within itself, the back of your thighs, the blind eye of your navel exposed to my eyes, denuded of their images of you. In the weariness of courting and of the choreography of seductive games, lust surges; the forces of abandon badger and demand and strip the pride and the fantasies of conquest from my eyes.

The otherness of the other is seen with the naked eyes. It is the naked eyes that penetrate the authority, myth or legend, or the fantasy of himself or herself through which the other approaches to make contact. My eyes that look to you undress you to touch you. Your bare hands, your exposed face beneath makeup and conventionalized expression strip away, like so many veils, the categories, the tabulated memories, the interpretative codes with which I turn my practiced eyes to others. Contact with the bare hands and naked face of the other unveils my eyes and leaves them naked.

The naked eyes record the flash or the dulling of your eyes and the tremor or tightening of your lip that signal how a message being formulated in the available phrases is to be taken. My eyes shift like buoys in the liquid of their sockets, but they are connected to networks of throbbing fibers everywhere in my body. These tremble at minute changes in the skin temperature of the hand or thigh mine touches, sensing the skin tightening there, the blood vessels swelling, and the pores expanding. The smells of your hair, mouth, armpits, loins enter me with every breath.

This nudity is made of the darkness showing through the mandalas of your eyes, the stumblings and the avid discomfited silences that break through the conventional garb and rhetorical adornment of your sentences, the weight and torpor of flesh that needs support to rise and orient itself.

In the commerce with others, the appeal and demand with which they face me disturbs the array of my practicable field and the carpentry of the world. To see the other as another sentient agent is to see his postures and movements directed to a layout of implements and obstacles about him. To see the other is to see her place as a place I could occupy, the things about him as harboring possibilities that are open to my skills and initiatives. It is to see the other as another one like I am, equivalent to and interchangeable with me. It is the sense of the death awaiting me that circumscribes the range of possibilities ahead of me that are possible for me. To see the other as one who has his or her own tasks and potentialities is to sense another death delimiting the field of possibilities ahead of him or her.

But the other turns to me, empty-handed, from across that wall of death. You appeal to the skills and resources of my hands. Heidegger calls inauthentic, inauthentifying, the solicitude with which I substitute my skills for another's, take over his tasks for him. What you ask for is not this disburdening, this displacement from your concerns. You ask of my hands the diagram of the operations your hands are trying to perform, and ask the assistance of my forces lest yours be wanting. But you ask first for terrestrial support. The fatigue, the vertigo, the homelessness in your body appeal for support from my earthbound body, which has the sense of this terrain to give. If, while extending my skills to your tasks, I do not offer this support, I will see you prefer to work out the ways and the operations on your own by trial and error.

The hand of the other extended to mine seeks not only the skills in my hand, an instrument among others available for his or her tasks; in the clasped handshake with which we greet one another and set out each to his or her own tasks, each one seeks the warmth that the fingers and palm of another's hand extends.

The other—whom I see as a focus of vision open to surfaces and contours of the landscape that is open to me too, a different vision that surveys a range of possibilities whose relief the black wall of his or her own death circumscribes about him or her—looks at me with the nakedness and vulnerability of his or her eyes. Your look appeals to the vision in my eyes. But not only for the foresight and hindsight that can chart your way for you; you appeal first for light. Your look requires my eyes to keep the light luminous beyond the narrow radius of what is actually visible to you.

Sometimes, to be sure, the other looks to me to receive from me the image of what my eyes have seen; the other I meet on the Himalayan trek asks of me if I have seen the path to the grand visions that eyes are made to see. Yet the other's look does not look to my eyes to see there the relief of the landscape upon which I hold my look. It first seeks the vivacity and delight of the light in my eyes and the shadows and darkness my eyes harbor with care. If it does not find them, if it finds only the look of a surveyor recording the topography, it will prefer to look on its own for the radiance and the twilights of the world.

The other facing me addresses me. His or her words, which I understand because they are the words of my own tongue, ask for information and indications. They ask for a response that will be responsible, will give reasons for its reasons, that will be a commitment to answer for what it answers. But they first greet me, appealing for responsiveness. Your words seek out a voice voluble and spiritual, a voice whose orders and coherence and direction are interrupted of itself, by hesitations, redundancies, and silences—questioning you by questioning itself. In the very explanation and instruction you seek, you seek your own voice in my silences and my questions. If my voice is not

responsive to this quest, you will seek in manuals the answers to your per-
plexities.

What the face of the other asks is not the inauthentic and inauthentifying
solicitude with which I substitute my skills for his, take over her tasks for her,
survey the forms and the landscape for him, formulate the answers to the
questions in her stead. He or she does not seek his or her contentment in the
content that will satisfy his or her needs and wants, which I can supply from
my place and my resources and with my skills—the contentment which, when
he or she has been displaced by me and disburdened of his or her tasks, will
leave him or her only the weight and death of the inorganic. In your face and
surfaces upon which the axes and directions of your posture and the intentions of your movements are exposed to me, upon which the forms of your
comprehension are expressed to me, I see another dark light that solicits the
light in my eyes, I hear a resonance held back, which seeks its voice in my
silences and questions, I feel bare hands that order the warmth and stability of
my stand on the earth. Your face is a surface of the elemental, the place where
the elemental appeals and requires the involution in enjoyment which makes
my eyes luminous, my hands warm, my posture supportive, my voice voluble
and spiritual, my face ardent.

Those of grace and strong heart, without masks, unmanipulative—for
whom the problem is not to relate with fellow humans but with the powerful
and the frail animals and birds, with the sea and the mountains, and with the
omens of destiny and the unknown powers and the sacred and death—turn to
me, to give. They turn to give the radiance of their eyes, the strength of their
hands, the torments and courage of their heart. It is an imperative gift; to
refuse to receive is desertion from my post. There is culpability in the one
who has been visited by angels and who has preferred his own path, servile,
but his own. Each time one's hands retreat before the kisses of a child, one's
eyes turn away from the shining eyes of a reveler, one's throat becomes the
grave of a song cast one's way, one degrades one's existence into "a series of
defeats without combat followed by impotent retreat."[2] To walk down the way
with someone whose sensitivity illuminates secret splendors and desolations,
demands that one open one's heart to him. The thumbs-up that the Brazilian
street kid—his mouth too voraciously gobbling your leftover spaghetti to smile
or say *obrigado*—gives is a gift given you that you have less right to refuse
than the honors of academia or the medals of heads of state.

A face is a layout of cavities. It is by puncturing a sphere, a pumpkin, an arc
drawn with a careless stroke, or a pool of light on the movie screen with dark
holes that one makes a face. The skull with its thirteen bones is not a helmet

strapped over a life where another world is being made and identified according to its own codes and grammar. The contact with your cheeks touches porous tissue and warmth that welcome like a shelter. Your skull, thinly covered with skin and hair, touches mine, rolling toward hollows and orifices. Your ears, too close for receiving my voice, press against my lips and tongue. Sometimes your teeth bite, leaving shallow wounds in my neck or shoulders.

The eyes that open upon my eyes empty them out, leaving them cavities in my skull full of chaotically arcing electrons. My mouth empties of its words by the mute invasion of yours, my ears empty of their channels by yours pressed against them. My skin and muscles, whose texture and pulp I do not feel, are agitated by the squalls of pleasure across your skin and in your muscles. My orifices emptied of their dense darkness are filled by your longings and cravings. The dull pumping of my heart sequestered behind my ribs feels your heartbeat quickening. In my entrails and bones so deeply interred from my view and insulated from my feelings, I feel the reproaches and insistence of your bones and entrails.

It is said that to strip the meaning off someone, to divest him or her of role and purpose in the map of industry and society, not to recognize those categories of "person," "thinking subject," "will of his or her own," "woman" or "man," and the categorical frameworks in which they figure, is to reduce the other to a "body," an "object," a "thing." The person loved is overdetermined with roles in the conversation and activity of society, the theater of femininity and masculinity, one's future and past family, the songs, chronicles, and epics of the social and civic order. Love, more than sex, would be this exorbitant attention directed to a nexus of a categorical network. Love is a spiritual devotion to the carnal; when one loves someone it is an ideal one is captivated by or pursues.

But one finds oneself drawn to divested and denuded bodies as to animals of grace and courage: human bodies whose charged nerves and enchanted musculature belong in the carnival of the powerful and the frail animals and birds and contend with the tides and the storms, whose gracious sensibility and strong heart capture the omens of nature and advance in the corridors of the occult powers and death.

There is a specific enthrallment with the animal splendor of a female body opulent and exposing a sensuality without body armor, of a male body turning compact and fluid power in all directions, of the inadmissible combinations of an androgenous body welcoming itself with invented gestures and rhythms, in the shy tenderness and effortless youth of a naked adolescent. In our obsessed senses and our thought subjugated to the tides of our instincts, the superbly bared body of another becomes a perfection, an idol. It mesmerizes the imagination and engenders private myths and pagan religions.

In such a body or in an unexceptional or imperfect body, one is drawn down the predestined paths to someone whose nervous circuitry is connected to the signs and surfaces of one's own practicable field, whose dreams navigate about the contours of one's own private landscapes, whose steps move with the rhythms of the ballads one has in one's heart, whose wit and nonsense ricochets off one's own. One teams up for picaresque escapades in the halls and desks of office buildings, for adventures into the nights of the foreign cities—our talk an idiolect of clandestine allusions, private jokes, whimsical taxonomies, perverse explanations. The teeth, small and set askew, the cleft chin, and the twiggy breasts of one's interlocutor and intimate become charmed signs—a calligraphy read simultaneously in Chinese and Japanese or a palimpsest where multiple arcane texts are instantly understood among initiates. One comes to love the owlish eyes, the pouting lips, the thin bony fingers of one's pal and coconspirator more than the body idolized in one's religion of the human species. There come moments when this buzzing network of escapades and adventures, idiolect and legend between us is troubled with the temptations of carnal contact. These lips, which bring wry nonsense into the sobriety of our workplace and narrate as soap-opera melodrama the trivial events of my kitchen—I find myself wanting to press my lips against them, push my tongue through them. These limbs which pitch in sync with my own prowling the alleys of cities and hiking mountains—I find myself one day or night yearning to cover them with the heat and weight of my body. This torso—I find myself longing to sever it, dismembered and soaked in commingled body fluids.

Caressing hands not gathering information or uncovering secrets, belly and flanks and thighs in a contact that apprehends and holds on to nothing, listing in the blind passion of the other—the erotic craving is the most extreme transcendence, Levinas wrote, a projection out of oneself onto the substance of the other. One can feel all the status one has from the social organization and hierarchy, the talent and industrious achievements that adorn one, the seductive femininity or fashionable masculinity one parades, as so many garde-fous against trust and craving and pleasure. It happens that in the night and the long loneliness of an alien city the torments of one's flesh move one to respond to a chance encounter. One exchanges only first names, and if the other finds my foreign name difficult to pronounce, I change it. The incomprehended and destitute stranger before me offers her or his body, abyss of unmarked wounds and dark exhilarations, in an imperative assignation. I denude myself and give myself over to the strange passions of a stranger; we part without compensation or exaction.

In eroticism, in its extreme fascination with the exoticism of another, the alterity of the other is not difference. Whether abandoning myself to one of my idols or a stranger, to one of the other sex or the same, of the same age or another, so much of what I am and what the other is shows no difference. Hands that do not know what they are doing or why, touch hands; the ridges of the spine fit the fingers that push into them; sex organs penetrate orifices made for them. In this nondifference and this interpenetration and confluence of cravings that prove anonymous, there is the searing of what is most strange, most alien, more impenetrable than mineral substances and incomprehendible than invisible gases can be for me, the body of one of my own kind.

On the surfaces the sensitivity of another is visible and tangible as a susceptibility, his or her spontaneous motility a vulnerability. In the contact murmurs a feeling which is care, made of fear and amazement, and a vertiginous abandon. Levinas says that alterity is the region where the other, susceptible and vulnerable, abides in mortality. The mortality from which he comes he can turn contagiously or murderously to me. The response to the other braves and overcomes that fear. This death that summons is not the abstraction of the Heideggerian nothingness; it is the materiality of all that is seductive and passing. Your contours are made of light and shadows, your tissues are made of carbon compounds absorbing and flaking away, your eyes glisten and move with the moistness of the decaying blanket of earth over the rock of the planet, your voice is made of air and warmth exhaled and lost. My flesh is drawn to your cavities and hollows open to death and worms. It makes contact with your surface of dead cells, your parched throat, the lurchings of your heart in the paroxysms of orgasm. My kisses and caresses are a consolation made of protection and accompaniment.

The posture that held her or him in identifiable tasks and hopes dissolved, the limbs dismembered in the night, the muscles gelatinizing, the astute and wary eyes now membranes exposed to my tongue, breath turning into fog and odors, glands hardening and abruptly liquefying: the body of another transubstantiates in a bog of musks, excretions, discharges. It is like an ancient city in the jungle disintegrating under the gnawing threads of lichens, the voracity of underbrush, the harsh sun, and the rains, its gods departed, its memories clouded in vapors, sinking into an irrecoverable past. With tormented laughter I cover the body of a stranger with kisses and caresses, sweat and secretions, as the body of another not different from my own sinks into the inapprehendable, the unimaginable, the irrecuperable.

It happens in the high noon of days, and in the comings and goings of one's practicable field extended by tasks and goals, that the susceptibility of flesh under one's vested identity recoils at a chance encounter. With briefcase and cellular phone in my hand, stepping out of the Intercontinental Hotel to go to a conference, I halt before the sight of an immigrant seated against the building wall repairing a predigital watch, like someone who did not die when the Visigoths sacked Rome. Late already for the theater, I stop to have my shoes shined by a kid who probably was there in front of the hotel all along; I look down upon the lean strong muscles of his bare back and think that he is probably twenty-one, the age that I got accepted to law school on another continent. My eyes touch and are moved by an old woman carrying paper bags full of unwearable pieces of discarded clothing and old legends, from lands effaced by the furies of history, in her head. In an outdoor café I notice a transvestite prostitute seated at a table with a group of tourists, turning again and again to contemplate with pleasure a couple of street kids eating from a plate of spaghetti left on the adjacent table. I travel for weeks in the high Andes, and, save for asking directions, have nothing to say to the people. I end up taking photographs, concentrating on studying the shadows and the angles, knowing that it is only the plastic forms of these people that could hold the eyes of anyone back home I talk to. Knowing too that these images are still more screens from what my deep body craves and what is imperative: to make contact, to touch them. Tact itself interdicts it. I suffer, from not embracing them.

In pubic places we encounter those of our own kind, and stop for a conversation made of information and indications, requests and importunities, wit and seduction. The word of mouth, an obsolete organ of communication, mixing in its own noise and a noise that is not its own. With the intakes of air, panting, hoarseness, coughs, sneezes, hiccups, laughter, outcries, sobs come the voices of a nocturnal world cemented over and made invisible by the white-out of cities full of florescent human affairs. In the cries and babble of children, murmur and badger of beings not seen or heard by adults. In the wrinkles of the skin yellowed with aging, in the veins exposed, innumerable and nameless ephemeral beings appeal for care. The bones, dry and brittle with age, echo with the complaints of the trees on the sidewalks and the flickering voices of lost asteroids. In the dirt-caked legs of Indians, the besieged grandeur of the high Andes summons compassion. In the luminous darkness of one's eyes emptied by contact with another's eyes, the light and the night call from outer spaces. The fervor and nonsense of orgasm responds to the ardent voices of night birds and insects without concepts or grammar. The flakes of dead skin that silently drift off our bodies settle into the humus of exquisite micro-worlds. In the secretions and toxins, invisible beings seek one another and embrace. In the warmth of one's hands lost in the hollows and orifices of bodies so exclusionarily devoted to one another, vibrates the imperative that is in the sun giving its warmth to teeming life on the cinder of this planet without asking anything in return, the imperative that the life that captures that warmth give in return. In the terrestrial materiality of bodies in interpenetration, care, made of fear and amazement, and a vertiginous abandon, responds to the imperative of the earth.

Notes

Chapter 1 / The Competent Body

1. Maurice Merleau-Ponty, *The Structure of Behavior*, trans. Alden L. Fisher (Boston: Beacon, 1963); *Phenomenology of Perception*, trans. Colin Smith (London: Routledge & Kegan Paul and New Jersey: Humanities, 1986); *Signs*, trans. Richard C. McCleary (Evanston: Northwestern University Press, 1964); *Eye and Mind*, trans. Carleton Dallery in James M. Edie, ed., *The Primacy of Perception* (Evanston: Northwestern University Press, 1964); *The Visible and the Invisible*, trans. Alphonso Lingis (Evanston: Northwestern University Press, 1968).
2. Merleau-Ponty, *Phenomenology of Perception*, p. 4.
3. Ibid., pp. 319-21.
4. Ibid., p. 327.
5. Merleau-Ponty, *The Visible and the Invisible*, pp. 131-33.
6. Merleau-Ponty, *Eye and Mind* in James Edie, ed., *The Primacy of Perception*, pp. 178-88.
7. Merleau-Ponty, *The Visible and the Invisible*, p. 133.
8. Merleau-Ponty, *Phenomenology of Perception*, p. 317.
9. Goldstein and Rosenthal, *Zur Problem des Wirkung der Farben auf den Organismus*, Schweizer Archiv für Neurologie und Psychiatrie, 1930.
10. Kurt Goldstein, *The Organism* (Boston: Beacon, 1963), pp. 222-23.
11. Merleau-Ponty, *The Visible and the Invisible*, p. 139.
12. Marcel Proust, *Swann's Way*, trans. C. K. Moncrieff and Terence Kilmartin (New York: Random House, 1981), pp. 6-7.
13. The artist is not a visionary but an explorer; *Eye and Mind* promotes the Heideggerian thesis that art is the graphic statement of the truth, the truth of the real world. The argument of *Eye and Mind* is that it is the hand of the artist that knows how, with a few strokes of color, a few lines, to materialize things. He then is not materializing visions; the artist is not an Apollonian eye that makes dreams visible in full daylight; he is an eye and a hand, a body that moves in the real world where to see things is to know

how to approach them, where the space of visions is inscribed in the paths of movement.

14. Merleau-Ponty, *The Visible and the Invisible*, p. 8.

Chapter 2 / Orchids and Muscles

1. André Leroi-Gourhan, *Le geste et la parole, Technique et langage* (Paris: A. Michel, 1964), parts I and II.
2. Franz Kafka, "Josephine the Singer, or the Mouse Folk," in *The Complete Stories*, trans. Nahum N. Glatzer (New York: Schocken, 1976).
3. Michel Foucault, *Discipline and Punish*, trans. Alan Sheridan (New York: Viking, 1979), pp. 135ff.
4. Tamotsu Yato, *Young Samurai, Bodybuilders of Japan*, introduction by Yukio Mishima, trans. M. Weatherby and Paul T. Konya (New York: Grove Press, 1967).
5. Ernest Hemingway, *Death in the Afternoon* (New York: Scribner, 1932).
6. Leroi-Gourhan, *Le geste et la parole*, chap. 11.
7. Adolf Portman, *Animal Forms and Patterns*, trans. Hella Czech (New York: Schocken, 1967).
8. Yukio Mishima, *Sun & Steel*, trans. John Bester (Tokyo and Palo Alto: Kondasha International, 1970), p. 23.

Chapter 3 / Bodies Our Own

1. Martin Heidegger, *Being and Time*, trans. John Macquarrie and Edward Robinson (New York: Harper & Row, 1962), pp. 196-97; *On the Way to Language*, trans. Peter D. Hertz (New York: Harper & Row, 1971), pp. 121-25; Maurice Merleau-Ponty, *Phenomenology of Perception*, trans. Colin Smith (London: Routledge & Kegan Paul, 1986), pp. 174-99; *The Visible and the Invisible*, trans. Alphonso Lingis (Evanston: Northwestern University Press, 1968), pp. 118-19, 125-27.
2. George Lakoff, *Women, Fire, and Dangerous Things* (Chicago: University of Chicago Press, 1987), chaps. 4-7.
3. Clifford Geertz, *Local Knowledge* (New York: Basic Books, 1983), "From the Native's Point of View': On the Nature of Anthropological Understanding," pp. 55-70; Paul Feyerabend, *Against Method* (London: Verso, 1975), pp. 280-82.

Chapter 4 / The Subjectification of the Body

1. Michel Foucault, *Madness and Civilization*, trans. Richard Howard (New York: Vintage, 1973); *The Birth of the Clinic, An Archaeology of Medical Perception*, trans. A. M. Sheridan Smith (New York: Pantheon, 1973); *Discipline and Punish*, trans. Alan Sheridan (New York: Vintage, 1979); *History of Sexuality, Vol 1*, trans. Robert Hurley (New York: Pantheon, 1980); *Power/Knowledge: Selected Interviews and Other Writings*, trans. Colin Gordon (New York: Pantheon, 1980); *I, Pierre Riviere, Having Slaughtered My Mother and My Brother...*, trans. Frank Jellinek (New York: Pantheon, 1975).
2. Gilles Deleuze, "Ecrivain non: un nouveau cartographe," *Critique*, 369 (décembre 1975): pp. 1207-1227. Gilles Deleuze: *Foucault* (Paris: Editions de Minuit, 1986).
3. Ernst Kantorowicz, *The King's Two Bodies* (Princeton: Princeton University Press, 1957).
4. Not all crimes come under the royal order: guilds, chartered cities, feudal lords, town councils, and the Church all had spheres of jurisdiction.
5. Michel Foucault, *Discipline and Punish*, trans. Alan Sheridan (New York: Vintage, 1979), pp. 40-47.
6. Ibid., pp. 160-61.
7. Ibid., p. 138.
8. Ibid., p. 199.
9. The value of a student, as measured by examinations, identifies him by the percentile of other students who have performed a set of exercises established as normal for that group. His individuality is neither that of an individual essence nor that of the index of a transcendent referent. He is identified neither by a singular sensibility and individual genius, an autonomous mind, nor by identifying the transcendent

figure of the sage or the intellectual in him.

Similarly, compare the soldier with the knight or the guerrilla, the worker with the craftsman, the student with the apprentice, the sufferer with the patient, the one marked with a singular destiny—zealot, shaman, or possessed—with the mentally ill, the entertainer with the visionary, etc. See John Berger, *Pig Earth* (New York: Pantheon, 1979), pp. 195-213.

10. The published reports on the Rasphuis of Amsterdam, the Maison de force at Ghent, and the Walnut Street Prison were the models used throughout a Europe that, twenty years after the Constituent Assembly adopted a penal code elaborated by the theorists of penology, would be covered with prisons.

11. Report by G. de Rouchefoucauld during the parliamentary debate on the penal code, 1831. Foucault, *Discipline and Punish*, p. 265.

12. Norman Mailer, introduction to Jack Abbott, *In the Belly of the Beast* (New York: Random House, 1982), pp. xii-xiv.

13. Ibid., p. xii.

14. See the social pact with drug users in Holland; drug addiction has been decriminalized; free needles and methadone treatment are supplied.

15. Proposals are made to shut down immigration and deport illegal aliens, perceived as an undisciplined sector responsible for most crimes.

16. "If you can conceive of a society (it is very difficult these days) that is more concerned with the creative potential of violent young men than with the threat they pose to the suburbs, then a few solutions for future prisons may be there. Somewhere between the French Foreign Legion and some prodigious extension of Outward Bound may lie the answer, at least for all those juvenile delinquents who are drawn to crime as a positive experience." Norman Mailer, *In the Belly of the Beast*, p. xii.

17. In the United States capital punishment is being reintroduced in more and more states and for more and more offenses. Capital punishment has now been decreed for juveniles and the mentally retarded.

18. "Half Irish, half Chinese, Jack Abbott was born January 21, 1944, in Oscoda, Michigan. He spent his childhood in foster homes throughout the Midwest. At the age of twelve he was committed to a juvenile penal institution—the Utah State Industrial School for Boys—for 'failure to adjust to foster homes,' and was released five years later. At eighteen he was convicted of 'issuing a check against insufficient funds,' and was incarcerated in the Utah State Penitentiary on a sentence of up to five years. By the age of twenty-nine Abbott had killed an inmate and wounded another in a fight behind bars, had escaped from maximum security, had committed bank robbery as a fugitive, and had served time in such federal penitentiaries as Leavenworth, Atlanta, and Marion. Since the age of twelve Jack Abbott has been free a total of only nine and a half months. He has served a total of more than fourteen years in solitary confinement." (Biographical notice on the jacket of the book of Jack Abbott, *In the Belly of the Beast*.)

19. And with delinquents themselves. Prisons, whose entrances lie beyond the corridors of detectives with the instincts of hunters, campaigning prosecuting attorneys, politically ambitious judges, sadistic and cowardly guards, are hardly places where impartial and dispassionate justice is inculcated. Prison populations divide into the "normal"—who accept all the structures of policed and mercantile society and judge themselves framed, betrayed, or stupid—and the "creeps"—sexual offenders, immigrant minorities, and the mentally retarded or disturbed, whose punishment decreed by the courts is daily supplemented by torments inflicted by the "normal" prisoners. Four convicts a day are executed in the penitentiaries of the United States, with the complicity of the guards, who often lock in the same cell prisoners they expect will batter or kill one another. Prisoners do not leave prison revolutionaries for a new social order, but bandits.

20. Michel Foucault, *History of Sexuality*, trans. Robert Hurley (New York: Vintage, 1990), vol. I. , pp. 103-5.

21. Demetrius Zambaco, "Onanism and Nervous Disorders in Two Little Girls," *Semiotext(e)*, IV, no. 1 (1981), *Polysexuality*, pp. 22-36.

22. Foucault, *The History of Sexuality*, Vol. I, pp. 38ff.

23. Pierre Klossowski, *Sade My Neighbor*, trans. Alphonso Lingis (Evanston: Northwestern University Press, 1991), pp. 28-33.

24. Foucault, *The History of Sexuality*, Vol. I, pp. 108-9.

25. Ibid., pp. 124, 147.
26. Ibid., pp. 18ff.
27. Ibid., p. 154.
28. Michel Foucault, *Power/Knowledge: Selected Interviews and Other Writings*, trans. Colin Gordon (New York: Pantheon Books, 1980), p. 56.
29. Hubert Dreyfus and Paul Rabinow, *Michel Foucault: Beyond Structuralism and Hermeneutics*, (University of Chicago Press, 1982), p. 236.

Chapter 5 / The Insistence on Correspondence

1. Yukio Mishima, *Sun & Steel*, trans. John Bester (Tokyo and Palo Alto: Kodansha International, 1970), pp. 19-20.
2. He published his first novel at the age of thirteen.
3. Ibid., p. 69.
4. Ibid.
5. Ibid, p. 8.
6. Ibid., p. 9.
7. Ibid., p. 64.
8. Ibid., p. 23.
9. Friedrich Nietzsche, *The Gay Science*, trans. Walter Kaufmann (New York: Random House, 1974), sec. 354.
10. Mishima, *Sun & Steel*, p. 7.
11. Friedrich Nietzsche, *The Gay Science*, sec. 354.
12. Yukio Mishima, *Confessions of a Mask*, trans. Meredith Weatherby (New York: New Directions, 1958). Published when Mishima was twenty-four.
13. Ibid., p. 13.
14. Ibid., p. 14.
15. Ibid., p. 101.
16. Ibid., p. 25.
17. Ibid., p. 32.
18. E. M. Cioran, *Précis de décomposition* (Paris: Gallimard, 1949), pp. 125-28.
19. Mishima, *Sun & Steel*, p. 35.
20. Ibid., pp. 28-29.
21. Ibid., pp. 32-33.
22. Ibid., pp. 22-23.
23. Ibid., p. 34.
24. Ibid., p. 40.
25. Ibid., pp. 40-41.
26. Ibid., p. 46.
27. Ibid., p. 44.
28. Ibid., p. 42.
29. Ibid., p. 92.
30. Ibid., p. 42.
31. Ibid., p. 92. Socrates claimed for himself none of the intellectual virtues; the sole virtue he claimed for himself, citing the proofs at the trial, is courage. In the *Phaedo* he argues not only that courage is the specific virtue of the philosopher, but that only philosophers are utterly fearless, for warriors show no fear of death and are courageous only because they fear something else more—dishonor or the enslavement of their comrades and kin. For Socrates the philosopher overcomes fear through the construction of a chain of ideas whose connection is clear. But, Mishima wrote, "however much the closeted philosopher mulls over the idea of death, so long as he remains divorced from the physical courage that is a prerequisite for an awareness of it, he will remain unable even to begin to grasp it." Ibid., p. 44.
32. Ibid., p. 99.

33. Ibid., p. 100.
34. Ibid., p. 101.
35. Ibid., pp. 101-3.
36. Ibid., p. 69.
37. Ibid., p. 77.
38. "People will probably say that he hardened those muscles for his death that day; those muscles, however opposed his death." Nagisa Oshima, *Cinema, Censorship, and the State: The Writings of Nagisa Oshima, 1956-1978*, trans. Dawn Lawson (Cambridge: MIT Press, 1992), p. 228.
39. Yukio Mishima, *Yukio Mishima on Hagakure* (New York: Penguin Books, 1979), p. 93.
40. Marguerite Yourcenar, *Mishima, The Vision of the Void*, trans. Alberto Manuel (New York: Farrar, Straus & Giroux, 1986), pp.151-2.

Chapter 6 / These Alien Feelings That Are Our Own

1. Phenomenological psychology still thinks of pain according to the distinction between the activity of comprehension and the passivity of feeling. See Sartre's analysis of pain, in *Being and Nothingness*, trans. Hazel E. Barnes (New York: Washington Square Books, 1956), pp. 435-45, and Heidegger's distinction among comprehension, conceived as power grasping on to possibilities; project, the trajectory of the future; and affectivity, conceived as *Befindlichkeit*, disposition—the weight of the past. The violence of feeling is not elucidated.
2. Friedrich Nietzsche, *Thus Spoke Zarathustra*, trans. Walter Kaufmann, in *The Portable Nietzsche* (New York: Viking, 1954), p. 252.
3. When the mind seeks to disengage itself from the pleasurable or painful adherence of the sensibility to the sensations themselves, in order to apprehend them comprehensively, to relate them to one another and to the outside agencies that produce them, it will most often have to collate both pleasurable and painful impressions. The roses come with the thorns. To know something veridically, the mind will have to collate both affectively positive and affectively negative sensations as cognitively significant. The theory of mind of the ancients held that thought, due to its very nature as an activity that rises over the immediate adhesion to the sensations, is dispassionate. But Spinoza saw rather the dispassionate character of the mind, requisite for its veridicality, as something achieved. It is by collating both pleasurable sensations and painful sensations left by the encounter with the rose, with one's neighbor, that the conflicting affects neutralize one another and one achieves dispassionate comprehension. Understanding then is not only logically second, in that it presupposes and depends on data left on the senses, which it inspects and interprets, but it is also chronologically second, resulting from the exhaustion of conflicting affects. It would record the pact or compromise left by their conflict. Friedrich Nietzsche, *The Gay Science*, trans. Walter Kaufmann (New York: Vintage: 1974), sec. 333.
4. Ibid.

Chapter 7 / Hard Currency

1. Jaako Hintikka, *The Intention of Intentionality and Other Models for Modalities* (New York: Kluwer Academic, 1975), pp. 205-8.
2. Edmund Husserl, *Ideas for a Pure Phenomenology and a Phenomenological Philosophy*, trans. F. Kersten (The Hague: Martinus Nijhoff, 1982), pp. 8-11.
3. The Freudian account is charted on the history of the son. The history of the daughter will be diagrammed after the history of the son.
4. Piera Aulangier, "Remarques sur la structure psychotique," *La Psychanalyse* 8 (1964): 47-67.
5. Gilles Deleuze and Félix Guattari, *Anti-Oedipus*, trans. M. Seem, R. Hurley, and H. R. Lane (New York: Viking, 1977), pp. 9-15.
6. Vincent Descombes, *L'inconscient malgré lui* (Paris: Minuit, 1977), pp. 10-15.
7. Sigmund Freud, *Beyond the Pleasure Principle*, trans. James Strachey, *The Standard Edition of the Complete Psychological Works of Sigmund Freud*, vol. 18 (London: Hogarth Press, 1955).

8. Ibid., pp. 14–17.

9. Ibid., p. 16.

10. Ibid, p. 20.

11. Gilles Deleuze, *Différence et répétition* (Paris: Presses Universitaires de France, 1968), pp. 138–40.

12. Freud's famous conception of sexual pleasure—the supreme pleasure we can know, and the model for all pleasure—as the release of a surplus tension and a return to the quiescence of the inert has as its physiological model genital orgasm. But the death drive internal to this pleasure cannot serve as the theme for the primary death drive of the id.

13. Gilles Deleuze and Félix Guattari, *Anti-Oedipus*, p. 329.

14. Ibid., p. 9.

15. Jean-François Lyotard, *L'économie libidinale* (Paris: Minuit, 1974), pp. 70–77 and passim.

16. Sigmund Freud, *Three Essays on the Theory of Sexuality*, trans. James Strachey, *The Standard Edition of the Complete Psychological Works of Sigmund Freud*, vol. 7 (London: Hogarth Press, 1953), p. 210.

17. Jacques Lacan, *Ecrits*, trans. Alan Sheridan (New York: W.W. Norton, 1977), pp. 255, 285–86.

18. A distinction that reflects Alexandre Kojève's distinction between need and desire in Hegel.

19. Lacan, *Ecrits*, p. 57.

20. Ibid., pp. 1–7; and Maurice Merleau-Ponty, "The Child's Relations with Others," trans. William Cobb, in James Edie, ed., *The Primacy of Perception* (Evanston: Northwestern University Press, 1964), pp. 125–41.

21. Freud, *Beyond the Pleasure Principle*, pp. 14–17.

22. Leo Bersani, *The Freudian Body* (New York: Columbia University Press, 1986), pp. 37–38, 59–61; and Robert J. Stoller, *Sexual Excitement* (New York: Pantheon, 1979), pp. 3–35.

23. Freud, *Three Essays on the Theory of Sexuality*, p. 203.

24. Freud, *Beyond the Pleasure Principle*, p. 20.

25. Bersani, *The Freudian Body*, p. 38–39.

26. Ibid., p. 40.

27. Jean-Paul Sartre, *Being and Nothingness*, trans. Hazel Barnes (New York: Washington Square Press, 1966), p. 3.

28. Ibid., pp. 416–31. See also Maurice Merleau-Ponty, *Phenomenology of Perception*, trans. Colin Smith (London: Routledge & Kegan Paul and New Jersey: Humanities Press, 1962), pp. 70–72.

29. In Husserl's thesis of the primacy of objective cognition, in Merleau-Ponty's thesis of the primacy of perception, as in Heidegger's thesis of the primacy of instrumental behavior, psychoanalysis sees an abstract and intellectualized version of the phallic subject constituted as the sign of prohibition, castration, renunciation of immediate gratification. Transcendental philosophy fixes as nature what genetic analysis shows to be a denouement.

30. "*Le nom du père, le non du père.*" Jacques Lacan, *Ecrits*, pp. 199, 217.

31. Sigmund Freud, *Civilization and Its Discontents*, trans. James Strachey, *The Standard Edition of the Complete Psychological Works of Sigmund Freud*, vol. 21 (London: Hogarth Press, 1961), pp. 96–97.

32. Hayden White, *Metahistory: The Historical Imagination in Nineteenth-Century Europe* (Baltimore: Johns Hopkins University Press, 1973), p. 295.

33. Gilles Deleuze and Félix Guattari, *Anti-Oedipus*, pp. 234–39.

34. Pierre Klossowski and Pierre Zucca, *La monnaie vivante* (Paris: Eric Losfeld, 1971).

Chapter 8 / Fluid Economy

1. Shirley Lindenbaum, "Variations on a Sociosexual Theme in Melanesia," in *Ritualized Homosexuality in Melanesia*, pp. 337–61.

2. Ibid., p. 344.

3. Ibid., p. 349.

4. Gilbert H. Herdt, *Guardians of the Flutes: Idioms of Masculinity* (New York: McGraw-Hill, 1981); Gilbert H. Herdt, ed., *Rituals of Manhood* (Berkeley: University of California Press, 1982); Gilbert H. Herdt, ed., *Ritualized Homosexuality in Melanesia* (Berkeley: University of California Press, 1984).

5. Herdt, "Fetish and Fantasy in Sambia Initiation" in *Rituals of Manhood*, pp. 17-27, 52-53.

6. Herdt uses the term "transformation," "that is, changing semen into something else, as medieval alchemists were thought to change lead into gold." "Semen Transactions in Sambia Culture," p. 175.

7. *Guardians of the Flutes*, pp. 188, 289.

8. Ibid., p. 165 n. 10. They also do not practice anal intercourse. Ibid., p. 3 n. 2.

9. Ibid., p. 143.

10. Ibid., p. 191.

11. Ibid., pp. 182, 190-94.

12. Ibid., p. 46.

13. Herdt, "Semen Transactions in Sambia Culture," p. 193.

14. Ibid., p. 210 n. 7.

15. Ibid., pp. 184-85.

16. Ibid., pp. 203-4.

17. Ibid., pp. 207-8.

18. Michel Foucault, *The History of Sexuality*, trans. Robert Hurley (New York: Vintage, 1990), p. 86.

19. Herdt, "Editor's Preface," in *Ritualized Homosexuality in Melanesia*, p. xv.

20. Herdt, *Guardians of the Flutes*, pp. 65, 262-63, 273, 275, 277-78, 284-85, 333.

21. Roger M. Keesing, "Introduction," in *Rituals of Manhood*, pp. 36-37.

22. Ibid., p. 27.

23. Terence E. Hays and Patricia H. Hays, "Opposition and Complementarity of the Sexes in Ndumba Initiation," in *Rituals of Manhood*, pp. 236, 237.

24. Bruno Bettleheim, *Symbolic Wounds* (Glencoe, Ill.: Free Press, 1954).

25. Robert J. Stoller, *Sexual Excitement* (New York: Pantheon, 1979), pp. 236-37.

26. Herdt, *Guardians of the Flutes*, pp. 303, 18.

27. Kenneth E. Read, "The Nama Cult Recalled," in *Ritualized Homosexuality in Melanesia*, p. 233.

28. Herdt, *Guardians of the Flutes*, pp. 18, 48, 52, 321.

29. Georges Bataille, *L'Histoire de l'érotisme*. *Oeuvres complètes*, vol. VIII (Paris: Gallimard, 1976). Translated by Mary Dalwood, *Death and Sensuality* (San Francisco: City Lights, 1986).

30. Stoller, *Sexual Excitement*, pp. 236-37.

31. Robert J. Stoller, *Sex and Gender: On the Development of Masculinity and Femininity* (New York: Science House, 1968), p. 232.

32. John Money and Anke A. Ehrhardt, *Man & Woman Boy & Girl* (Baltimore: Johns Hopkins University Press, 1972), pp. 176-79.

33. Herdt, *Guardians of the Flutes*, p. 305.

34. Fitz John Porter Poole, "The Ritual Forging of Identity," in *Rituals of Manhood*, p. 139.

35. J. Layard, "Homoeroticism in a Primitive Society as a Function of the Self," *Journal of Analytical Psychology* (1959) 4: 101-15.

36. Herdt, "Semen Transactions in Sambia Culture," p. 210 n.7.

37. Herdt, "Fetish and Fantasy in Sambia Initiation," pp. 74-76, 84-90; *Guardians of the Flutes*, pp. 283-84, 255-94.

38. Herdt, "Editor's Preface," in *Ritualized Homosexuality in Melanesia*, p. xii.

39. Herdt, *Guardians of the Flutes*, p. 325.

40. Jean Cocteau, *Le livre blanc* (Paris: Editions de Messine, 1983), translated as *The White Paper* (New York: Macaulay, 1958).

41. R. V. Burton and J. W. M. Whiting, "The Absent Father and Cross-Sex Identity," *Merrill-Palmer Quarterly of Behavior and Development*, vol. 7 (1961): 87.

42. Clifford Geertz, *Local Knowledge* (New York: Basic Books, 1983), p. 59.

43. Herdt, *Guardians of the Flutes*, p. 208 n. 7.

44. Ibid., p. 92.

45. Gilles Deleuze and Félix Guattari, *Anti-Oedipus*, trans. Robert Hurley, Mark Seem, and Helen R. Lane (New York: Viking, 1977).

46. Keesing, "Introduction," in *Rituals of Manhood*, p. 37.

47. Jean-François Lyotard, *Economie libidinale* (Paris: Minuit, 1974).
48. Lindenbaum, "Variations," in *Ritualized Homosexuality in Melanesia*, p. 340.
49. Keesing, "Introduction," in *Rituals of Manhood*, p. 16.

Chapter 9 / Strange Lusts That Are Our Own

1. Michel Foucault, *Histoire de la folie à l'âge classique* (Paris: Plon, 1961). Partial translation by Richard Howard, *Madness and Civilization* (New York: Vintage, 1965).
2. Foucault, *Madness and Civilization*, chap. 9.
3. Gilles Deleuze and Félix Guattari, *Anti-Oedipus*, trans. M. Seem, R. Hurley, and H. R. Lane (New York: Viking, 1977), part 3.
4. Friedrich Nietzsche, *Thus Spoke Zarathustra*, trans. Walter Kaufmann, in *The Portable Nietzsche* (New York: Viking, 1954), Part II, sec. 14.
5. The grammatical and rhetorical reforms that the feminist movement today advances function to marginalize further and to silence the semantics with which all these individuals, who do not recognize themselves under the male-female masculine-feminine dyad, exchange with one another and with others.

Chapter 10 / Imperative Surfaces

1. Emmanuel Levinas, *Otherwise than Being or Beyond Essence*, trans. Alphonso Lingis (The Hague: Martinus Nijhoff, 1981), pp. 45-50, 85-94; *Totality and Infinity*, trans. Alphonso Lingis (The Hague: Martinus Nijhoff, 1979, New York: The Humanities Press, 1979), pp. 197-201; *Collected Philosophical Papers of Emmanuel Levinas*, trans. Alphonso Lingis (The Hague: Martinus Nijhoff, 1987), pp. 102-7
2. Emmanuel Levinas, *Otherwise than Being*, pp. 89-93.
3. Emmanuel Levinas, *Totality and Infinity*, pp. 257-59.
4. Ibid., pp. 74-75.
5. Edmund Husserl, *Logical Investigations*, trans. J. N. Findlay (London: Routledge and Kegan Paul, 1970), vol. 1, pp. 271-73.
6. Edmund Husserl, *Cartesian Meditations*, trans. Dorion Cairns (The Hague: Martinus Nijhoff, 1960), pp. 108-20.
7. *Collected Philosophical Papers of Emmanuel Levinas*, pp. 102-7.
8. Ibid., pp. 104-5.
9. Levinas, *Otherwise than Being or Beyond Essence*, pp. 108, 194-95 n. 10.
10. Immanuel Kant, *Critique of Practical Reason*, trans. Lewis White Beck (Indianapolis: Bobbs-Merrill, 1956), pp. 21-23.
11. Ibid., pp. 79-80.
12. Ibid., pp. 79-81.
13. Ibid., pp. 80-81.
14. Martin Heidegger, *Being and Time*, trans. John Macquarrie and Edward Robinson (New York: Harper & Row, 1962), pp. 183-84.
15. Martin Heidegger, *Poetry, Language, Thought*, trans. Albert Hofstadter (New York: Harper & Row, 1971), pp. 33-34.
16. The really possible are not simply variants of the real which we can extend before ourself in representations.
17. Martin Heidegger, "What Is Metaphysics?" trans. David Farrell Krell, in *Martin Heidegger, Basic Writings*, ed. David Farrell Krell (New York: Harper & Row, 1977), pp. 102-3.
18. Martin Heidegger, *Being and Time*, p. 307.
19. Ibid., p. 343.
20. Ibid., pp. 434-35.
21. Kant calls "types" the advance representation that the practical agent forms, by imagination, of himself as an agent in the world subjected to the imperative. The other "types" are one's own nature, represented as a totality governed by laws, after the model of empirical nature, and one's faculties represent-

ed as a field of means at the service of an end, after the model of the practicable field about one. *Critique of Practical Reason*, pp. 70ff.

22. Emmanuel Levinas, *Existence and Existents*, trans. Alphonso Lingis (The Hague: Martinus Nijhoff, 1978), pp. 91-2.

Chapter 11 / Elemental Bodies

1. Michel Tournier, *Friday*, trans. Norman Denny (New York: Pantheon, 1985).
2. Gilles Deleuze, "Michel Tournier and the World without Others," in *Logique du sens* (Paris: Minuit, 1971). Translated by Mark Lester and Charles Stivale, *The Logic of Sense* (New York: Columbia University Press, 1990), p. 302.
3. Michel Tournier, *Friday*, p. 46.
4. Ibid., p. 93.
5. Ibid., p. 85.
6. Ibid., p. 220.
7. Ibid., p. 40.
8. Ibid., p. 86-87.
9. Ibid., p. 93.
10. Ibid., pp. 93-94, 95.
11. Ibid., p. 94.
12. Ibid., p. 123.
13. Ibid., p. 95.
14. Ibid., p. 66.
15. Ibid., p. 61.
16. Kenneth Burridge, *Someone, No One: An Essay on Individuality* (Princeton: Princeton University Press, 1979), p. 96.
17. Tournier, *Friday*, p. 41.
18. Ibid., p. 99.
19. Michel Foucault and Gilles Deleuze, "Intellectuals and Power," in Michel Foucault, *Language, Counter-Memory, Practice*, ed. Donald F. Bouchard, trans. Donald F. Bouchard and Sherry Simon (Ithaca: Cornell University Press, 1977), pp. 205-17; Michel Foucault, *Power/Knowledge*, trans. Colin Gordon, Leo Marshall, John Mepham, and Kate Soper (New York: Pantheon, 1972), pp. 126-33.
20. Ibid., p. 107.
21. Ibid., p. 105.
22. Ibid., p. 67.
23. Ibid., p. 115.
24. Ibid., pp. 119, 120.
25. Ibid., p. 123.
26. Ibid., p. 124.
27. Ibid., p. 125.
28. Ibid., p. 120.
29. Gilles Deleuze, *Différence et répétition* (Paris: Minuit, 1968).
30. Tournier, *Friday*, p. 123.
31. Ibid., p. 141.
32. Ibid., p. 181.
33. Ibid., p. 189.
34. Pierre Klossowski, *Sade My Neighbor*, trans. Alphonso Lingis (Evanston: Northwestern University Press, 1990).
35. Tournier, *Friday*, pp. 208-9.
36. Ibid., p. 54.
37. Ibid., pp. 206-207.
38. Ibid., p. 172.

39. Ibid., p. 179.
40. Ibid., pp. 192-4.
41. Ibid., pp. 198, 210.
42. Ibid., pp. 203-4.

Chapter 12 / Foreign Bodies

1. Jean-Luc Nancy, *L'impératif catégorique* (Paris: Flammarion, 1983).
2. George Bataille, *Inner Experience*, trans. Leslie Anne Boldt (Albany: State University of New York Press, 1988), p. 39.

Index

Abbott, Jack, 62
alterity, 114, 115, 120, 174-177, 205, 216, 217-218, 223
anxiety, 152, 169, 176, 177, 181-184
ars erotica, 68, 72, 73
Artaud, Antonin, 111
Aulangier, Piera, 111

Bataille, Georges, 150
Berger, John, 60 n.8.
Bersani, Leo, 120
biopolitics, 68, 72, 158
body in the first person, 47
body in the third person, 47
body-image, 15-17, 47
brotherhood, 197, 202-204
Burridge, Kenneth, 196
Burton, R.V., 153, 154 n.39

capitalism, xi, 128-130, 162, 163
causality, 70, 180, 199-202

Cioran, E. M., 83
circular time, 207
Cocteau, Jean, 154
confession, 55, 69, 70
currency, 125, 129, 140, 191, 193-196, 198, 199, 203, 204

death, x, xiii, 22, 33, 34-37, 41, 67, 78, 83, 84, 86, 89, 90-98, 103, 112-114, 123-124, 137, 138, 145, 147-149, 151, 162, 167-168, 177, 179, 180-185, 192, 197, 199-201, 203-206, 217-221, 223
death drive, 112-114, 147-149
Deleuze, Gilles, 57 n.1, 111, 112, 113, 124, 128 n.33, 157, 162, 189, 198, 201
delinquent, 54, 60, 61-63, 71, 98
depth perception, 168, 170, 179
Descombes, Vincent, 111 n.6

Ehrhardt, Anke, 151 n.30

erotic excitement, 120, 152-154
exchange-value, 125-128, 142, 144, 145

"Fort-Da," 112, 116
Foucault, Michel, ix, x, xi, 32, 53-73 passim, 145, 161, 198
Freud, Sigmund, x, 31, 37-40, 111-114, 116, 119, 120, 125, 150, 152, 157, 158, 162-164, 194

Geertz, Clifford, 49 n.3, 154
generic individual, 83
Goldstein, Kurt, 8, 13

Hays, Terence and Patricia, 147
Hegel, G. W. F., 114 n.18, 118, 174
Heidegger, Martin, xiii, 7, 21 n.13, 24, 47 n.1, 99 n.1, 123 n.29, 177, 181-184, 217-218, 223
Hemingway, Ernest, 35
Herdt, Gilbert H., xi, 133-158 passim, 163, 164
Hume, David, 167
Husserl, Edmund, 7, 10, 108, 123 n.29, 173

id, 111
identity, xi, xiii, 41, 43, 57, 59, 69, 70, 72, 100, 123, 124, 127, 138, 139, 148, 151, 153, 154-155, 156-158, 161-164, 172, 175, 224
imperative, x, xii, 20-25, 70, 117-121, 123, 162, 167-168, 170-171, 174-185, 195, 202, 204, 207-212, 215-217, 220, 222, 224, 225
inauthenticity, 220
individuality, 43, 58-60, 65, 69-70, 85, 95, 145, 148, 153, 154-156, 162, 163, 164, 200-201, 204

Jung, Carl, 164

Kafka, Franz, 32
Kant, Immanuel, xi, xiii, 19, 177-179, 183-184, 211, 216
Kantorowicz, Ernst, 55 n.3
Klossowski, Pierre, 66 n.23, 129, 204
Kristeva, Julia, 37
Lacan, Jacques, x, 114, 115 n.19, 118, 124 n.30, 163

Lakoff, George, 48 n.2
Layard, J., 152 n.33
Leroi-Gourhan, André, 30, 32, 38
levels 7, 9-10, 12, 13, 14, 16, 19-25, 47, 48, 101
Levinas, Emmanuel, xi, 167-185 passim, 216, 217, 222, 223
Lindenbaum, Shirley, 133, 157
linear time 58
Lyotard, Jean François, 113 n.15, 157

Mailer, Norman, 61, 62 n.15, 63
Marx, Karl, 125, 126, 128, 146
Merleau-Ponty, Maurice, viii, 3-25 passim, 47 n.1, 48, 83, 115 n.20, 122, 123 n.29
metaphor, 125, 191, 199
mirror, 15-16, 79, 115-117, 169
Mishima, Yukio, x, 33, 41, 77-98 passim, 169
money, 127-129, 136, 196

Nancy, Jean-Luc, 216
Nietzsche, Friedrich, vii, 32, 38, 44, 80, 100 n.2, 100 n.3, 101, 163 n.4, 197
nondifference, 223
norm, 4, 9, 12, 17, 60, 69, 95, 100, 204, 211

pain, 30, 35, 36, 37, 43, 54-56, 64, 68, 88-89, 92, 99-102, 112, 113, 146, 148, 152, 171, 177, 179,

180, 184

perversion, 66, 69, 71, 72, 96, 204

phallus, viii, x, xi, 34, 36, 37, 90, 92, 110, 119-121, 123, 124, 126-128, 155, 158, 161-163

plague, 59

Poole, Fitz John Porter, 152 n.34

Portman, Adolph, 39

postural schema, 13-17, 21, 47, 124

prostitution, 62, 66, 224

Proust, Marcel, 15

Read, Kenneth, 149, 153

repetition compulsion, 112

representatives of the self, 136, 164

resentment, 33, 34, 36, 40, 99, 100

respect, xi, 178-180, 183, 184

Sade, Marquis de, 66, 129

Sartre, Jean-Paul, 99 n.1, 121, 170

self-consciousness, 78, 79, 80, 88, 216

sensible essence, 5, 8, 11, 14, 47

sensuality, viii, ix, x, xiii, 71, 100, 101, 113-114, 120, 129, 150, 152, 155, 157, 158, 170, 194, 209, 212, 221

signs, x, xii, 1, 7, 54, 56-57, 65, 68, 69, 79, 100, 107-110, 115-118, 120-121, 124, 125, 168-173, 175-176, 183, 185, 191, 198, 201, 207, 222

skin, xii, 30, 41-43, 84-86, 168-170, 177, 217, 224-225

Socrates, 36, 89 n.31

sodomy, 66

speech acts, 47, 122

Spinoza, Baruch, 100 n.3

Stoller, Robert J., 120 n.22, 147, 151, 153

Stratton, G. M., 9

style, 5, 11, 14, 18, 66, 83, 85, 173, 174

subject of the text, 190

surface perception, 170, 179

surface self, 84, 86

surveillance, 30-31, 44, 59-63, 65, 71, 158

tellurian cause, 199

Tournier, Michel, xii, 189-213 passim

trace, 175-176, 177, 216

type (Kant), 184

value, x, 60, 67-69, 100, 109-110, 124-130, 142, 144-146, 156, 162, 172, 196, 202

vegetative body, 201

victory, 86-89, 96, 98

White, Hayden, 126, 127

Whiting, J. W. M., 153, 154

world-imperative, 20, 21

Yourcenar, Marguerite, 94

Zambaco, Demetrius, 65 n.21